Legal and Rhetorical Foundations of Economic Globalization

This book examines the subtle ways in which rhetorics of sacrifice have been re-appropriated into the workings of the global political economy in the 21st century. It presents an in-depth analysis of the ways in which ritual practices are deployed, under a diverse set of political and legal contexts, as legitimation devices in rendering exploitative structures of the prevailing political-economic system to appear inescapable, or even palatable. To this end, this work explores the deeper rhetorical and legal basis of late-capitalist governmentality by critically interrogating its mythical and ritual dimensions. The analysis gives due consideration to the contemporary incarnations of ritual sacrifice in the transnational neoliberal discourse: from those exploitative yet inescapable contractual obligations, to calendrical multi-billion dollar 'offerings' to the insatiable needs of 'too-big-to-fail' corporations.

The first part of the book provides a working interpretative framework for understanding the politics of ritual sacrifice – one that not only accommodates multi-disciplinary, interdisciplinary knowledge of ritual practices, but that can also be employed in the integrated analysis of sacrificial rituals as political rhetoric under divergent historical and societal contexts. The second conducts a series of case studies that cut across the wide variability of ritual public takings in late-capitalism. The book concludes by highlighting several key common doctrines of public ritual sacrifice which have been broadly observed in its case studies. These common doctrines tend to reflect the rhetorical and legal foundations for public takings under hegemonic market-driven governance. They define 'appropriate and proper' occasions for suspending pre-existing legal protections to regularize otherwise transgressive transfers of rights and possessions for the 'greater good' of the economic order.

Dr Keren Wang is a rhetorical theorist and political communication scholar. He currently teaches rhetoric and message analysis in the Department of Communication Arts and Sciences at The Pennsylvania State University, USA. His published academic works cover topics such as transnational rhetorics, social change, rhetorics of law, human rights discourse, and political legitimacy.

I0894821

Globalization: Law and Policy

Globalization: Law and Policy builds an integrated body of scholarship that critically addresses key issues and theoretical debates in comparative and transnational law and the principles governance and policy on which they are developed. Volumes in the series focus on the consequential effects of globalization, including emerging frameworks and processes for the internationalization, legal harmonization, juridification, and democratization of law among increasingly connected political, economic, religious, cultural, ethnic, and other functionally differentiated governance communities. Legal systems, their harmonization and incorporation in other governance orders, and their relationship to globalization are taking on new importance within a coordinated network of domestic legal orders, the legal orders of groups of states, and the governance frameworks of non-state actors. These legal orders engage a number of important actors, sources, principles, and tribunals-including multinational corporations as governance entities, contract and surveillance as forms of governance that substitute for traditional law, sovereign wealth funds and other new forms of state activity, hybrid supra national entities like the World Bank and the International Monetary Fund, and international tribunals with autonomous jurisdiction, including the International Criminal Court, the World Trade Organization, and regional human rights courts. The effects have been profound, especially with respect to the role of states, and especially of developed states as their long time position in global affairs undergoes significant transformation. Comparative and transnational law serve as natural nexus points for vigorous and sometimes interdisciplinary approaches to the study of state and non-state law systems, along with their linkages and interactions. The series is intended as a resource for scholars, students, policy makers, and civil society actors, and includes a balance of theoretical and policy studies in single-authored volumes and collections of original essays.

Larry Catá Backer is the W. Richard and Mary Eshelman Faculty Scholar, Professor of Law and International Affairs at the Pennsylvania State University. Previously he served as Executive Director of the Comparative and International Law Center at the University of Tulsa. He has published widely on comparative and transnational law.

Also in the series:

Hostile Business and the Sovereign State
Privatized Governance, State Security and International Law
Michael J. Strauss

Legal and Rhetorical Foundations of Economic Globalization
An Atlas of Ritual Sacrifice in Late-Capitalism
Keren Wang

For more information about this series, please visit:
www.routledge.com/Globalization-Law-and-Policy/book-series/GLOBLP

Legal and Rhetorical Foundations of Economic Globalization

An Atlas of Ritual Sacrifice in Late-Capitalism

Keren Wang

Routledge
Taylor & Francis Group
LONDON AND NEW YORK

First published 2020
by Routledge
2 Park Square, Milton Park, Abingdon, Oxon OX14 4RN

and by Routledge
605 Third Avenue, New York, NY 10017

First issued in paperback 2020

Routledge is an imprint of the Taylor & Francis Group, an informa business

British Library Cataloguing in Publication Data
A catalogue record for this book is available from the British Library

Library of Congress Cataloging-in-Publication Data
A catalog record has been requested for this book

ISBN 13: 978-0-367-72782-6 (pbk)
ISBN 13: 978-0-367-18840-5 (hbk)

Typeset in Galliard
by Taylor & Francis Books

Contents

Illustrations

Figures

Tables

1 Introduction

This work project focuses on one understudied rhetorical dynamic of the late-capitalist global system – its rhetorical inventions of ritual sacrifice. Rituals not only have the capacity to discipline the human body to perform prescribed social transactions, but can also render violent social transactions to appear irresistible, or even palatable. Through three distinct case studies of public takings, this project seeks to examine the subtle ways in which rhetorics of sacrifice are reappropriated into the governance structures of neoliberalism. These case studies also highlight the role ritual plays in the management and normalization of dehumanizing conditions of the prevailing political-economic order. This chapter introduces the research subject, core objectives and mode of inquiry for this work project. This section also provides a preview of the chapters in this work. There are three preliminary research questions for this study: why study sacrifice? Why focus on neoliberalism? Why use a rhetorical approach? Why "atlas?"

Why sacrifice?

Sacrifice, more specifically ritual sacrifice, refers to the prescribed sequence of activities involving the intentional destruction or surrendering of things to a divine patron or other higher purpose. Sacrificial offerings are typically material objects of real or symbolic value, such as food items, libations (liquid beverages) and religious artifacts, but may also involve the killing of livestock or even human beings. To borrow the words of British historian Eric Hobsbawm, the *ritual* component of ritual sacrifice can be understood as a set of symbolic practices, formally organized by explicitly stated or tacitly assumed rules and procedures, and functions in a communal setting to "inculcate certain values and norms of behavior by repetition, which automatically implies continuity with the past."[1]

1 Eric Hobsbawm, *The Invention of Tradition* (Cambridge and New York: Cambridge University Press, 2012), 1–2.

Sacrifices in the form of state-organized rituals have been observed in many societies throughout history.[2] For instance, large-scale, systematic human sacrifice functioned as important political and religious spectacles in Shang dynasty China and in pre-Columbian Mesoamerican societies.[3] Existing scholarship also observed an interdependent relationship between ritual sacrifice and the maintenance of political power in a broad set of historical cases, ranging from Shang dynasty China in 10th century BCE to the witch-hunts in early modern Europe.[4] These violent (both symbolic and real) historical rituals were not simply neutral representations of human psychological conditions, even developmental stages – they are rhetorical in the sense that they were carefully staged political spectacles, stylized in the form of sacred violence for the purpose of shaping and maintaining orders and norms.

It is important to note that ritual sacrifices were far more than simply acts of religious devotion. Historical evidence suggests ritual sacrifices were performed as crisis management devices. Large-scale human sacrifices in the Shang dynasty China and pre-Columbian Mesoamerica would only take place during periods of severe food shortage, usually caused by war or crop failure.[5] Ancient Greece devised the specialized sacrificial forms of *Holokaustos* [6] (total oblation) and

2 Richard E. DeMaris, "Sacrifice, an Ancient Mediterranean Ritual," *Biblical Theology Bulletin* Vol. 43 No. 2 (2013), 60–73. See also, Sigmund Freud, *Totem and Taboo: Resemblances between the Psychic Lives of Savages and Neurotics*, trans. A. A. Brill (New York: Random House, 1961), Chapters II and VI. See also, Michael Rudolph, *Ritual Performances as Authenticating Practices* (Berlin: LIT Verlag Münster, 2008); John Noble Wilford, "At Ur, Ritual Deaths Were Anything but Serene: Science Desk," *New York Times*, October 26, 2009, available: www.nytimes.com/2009/10/27/science/27ur.html. See also, Austine Waddell, *Tibetan Buddhism: With Its Mystic Cults, Symbolism and Mythology, and in Its Relation to Indian Buddhism* (London: W.H. Allen & Co., 1895), 516.

3 Wang Ping and Wolfgang Kubin, 甲骨文与殷商人祭 / *Oracle Bone Inscriptions and Human Sacrifice During the Yinshang Period / Jia gu wen yu Yin Shang ren ji*, Chinese, 1st ed. (Zhengzhou, China: 大象出版社, 2007). *See also, generally*, Vera Tiesler and Andrea Cucina, "New Perspectives on Human Sacrifice and Ritual Body Treatments in Ancient Maya Society," *Interdisciplinary Contributions to Archaeology* (New York: Springer, 2007).

4 Vera Tiesler and Andrea Cucina, *New Perspectives on Human Sacrifice and Ritual Body Treatments in Ancient Maya Society*, 1. Aufl. ed. (DE: Springer-Verlag, 2007); Wang Ping and Wolfgang Kubin, 甲骨文与殷商人祭 / *Oracle Bone Inscriptions and Human Sacrifice During the Yinshang Period* / Jia gu wen yu Yin Shang ren ji, Chinese, 1st ed. (Zhengzhou, China: 大象出版社, 2007). See also, Scarre Geoffrey, John Callow, *Witchcraft and Magic in Sixteenth and Seventeenth-Century Europe (second ed.)* (Basingstoke: Palgrave, 2001); H.C.E. Midelfort, *Witch Hunting in Southwestern Germany 1562–1684: The Social and Intellectual Foundations* (Stanford, 1972)

5 Keren Wang, "Human Sacrifice during Shang Dynasty," updated May 27, 2015, available: https://sites.psu.edu/kerenw/?p=102; Keren Wang, "A Brief Note on Human Sacrifice in Classical Mayan Culture" Rhetorics and Rituals, updated June 2, 2015, available: https://sites.psu.edu/kerenw/?p=142 (accessed March 13, 2017).

6 Sometimes spelled "holocaustos" (ὁλόκαυστος from ὅλος "whole" and καυστός "burnt") ancient Greek term for an exceptional type of animal sacrifice, where the entire animal is burned up as an offering. *See* Liége Ekroth, *The Sacrificial Rituals of*

Pharmakos (scapegoat) as "appropriate responses" to major catastrophes.[7] In the mid-16th century, King Ixtlilxochitl of the Aztec Empire (also known as the Triple Alliance) introduced a highly institutionalized form of ritual warfare, known as the "Flower War" (Nahuatl: *xōchiyāōyōtl*), for the purpose of calendrical population control during periods of famine.[8]

Nonetheless, there is little consensus when it comes to the contemporary implications of these recurring collective memory practices. Much of the existing comparative scholarship on ritual sacrifice draws from the disciplinary frames of cultural-anthropology and social psychology, and thus interpret sacrificial practices primarily from cultural, religious, or mystical points of view. Ritual sacrifices are far more than mere "neutral" representations of mystic superstition or psychological tendencies– they are carefully staged spectacles, often precisely stylized and deployed for specific political ends. Sacrificial rituals of the past should not be considered fundamentally divorced from our modern world: whereas the formal elements of sacrifice of the past may no longer be recognizable, their substantive political functions do remain, with rhetorical overtones that carry into the politics of the present time.

Organized rituals of sacrifice and ideas justifying these acts mutually shape and maintain each other. It is important to note that effects of the dialectical relationship between sacrificial practices and their justifying myths are not contained within the narrowly defined domain of organized religion. Collective ideas, even in the form of "religious superstitions," do not simply emerge from thin air *ad libitum*; rather, they reflect underlying historical conditions and the mode of production of a given society.[9] Rituals, however authentically performed and faithfully embodied, may function as legitimizing rhetoric justifying the continuation of contradictory social conditions. *Mythos,* however poetic and fantastically styled, may function in the domain of the praxis towards reinforcing the ruling ideas of the political sovereign.[10]

The goal for this project is to give due consideration to the politics of sacrificial rites across a broad set of political-theological traditions, hopefully

Greek Hero-Cults in the Archaic to the Early Hellenistic Period (France: Presses Universitaires de Liège, 2002), 215–301, web, http://books.openedition.org/pulg/503 (accessed January 11, 2017).

7 The use of the term 'scapegoat' in the context of sacrifice originated from the Old Testament, where a goat was sacrificed to cleanse the people of their sin. *See generally*, Miranda Aldhouse-Green, *Dying for the Gods: Human Sacrifice in Iron Age & Roman Europe* (Charleston, SC: Tempus Publishing, 2001).

8 Barry L. Isaac, "The Aztec 'Flowery War' A Geopolitical Explanation" (1983), *Journal of Anthropological Research* Vol. 39, No. 4: 416–417. King Ixtlilxochitl's response to the Famine of Year 1 Rabbit (1454).

9 See, for example, Ernest J. Wrage, "Public Address: A Study in Social and Intellectual History" (1947) *Quarterly Journal of Speech* Vol. 33, No. 4: 451–457.

10 Philip Wander, "The Ideological Turn in Modern Criticism=" *Central States Speech Journal* Vol. 34 (1983), 1–18, where Wander also made similar critical remarks concerning the political functions of ideas.

paving the way to a new unifying understanding of sacrificial rhetorics. This research goal revolves around two primary research tasks that are intimately connected. The first is to provide a working interpretative framework for understanding the politics of ritual sacrifice – one that not only accommodates multidisciplinary, interdisciplinary knowledge of ritual practices, but that can also be usefully employed in the integrated analysis of sacrificial rituals as political rhetoric under divergent historical and societal contexts. The second conducts a series of case studies that cuts across the wide variability of ritual public takings in late-capitalism.

Why neoliberalism?

While the term "neoliberalism" emerged from late 19th-century French economic literature, it has since taken on a broad range of meanings in both popular and academic discourse, and therefore requires a more precise treatment in the context of this study.[11]

Neoliberalism can be broadly understood as a political and economic worldview grounded in the notion of the "free market." The concept of the "free market" itself is rooted in the legacies of the Western Enlightenment – most memorably in the economic writings of Adam Smith (e.g. *The Wealth of Nations*) and Richard Cantillon, but also reflected through the works of classical liberal philosophers such as John Locke and Montesquieu.[12] With the historical proliferation of the market economy, the free market ideal has since expanded beyond the domain of economic philosophy, and became saturated in our global economic worldview. Thus, the notion of the free market has effectively become a sacred icon not only for capitalism, but for "modernization" itself.

Once a nomenclature for a particular brand of 19th-century European *laissez-faire* economic worldview, the term "neoliberalism" has since escaped the confines of academic literature, and became an extended metaphor for the post-WWII marketization of the global political economy.[13] The post-WWII, or more precisely the post-1970s energy crisis marketization process is in part driven by the proliferation of a specific modality of the state-market relationship, one that is grounded in a preference for the free movement of goods, capital, services and technology, as well as a managed movement of labor. Marketization and neoliberalism are both marked by an ideological emphasis

11 Gide, Charles (1898-01-01). "Has Co-operation Introduced a New Principle into Economics?" *The Economic Journal* Vol. 8, No. 32: 490–511.

12 See generally, Richard Cantillion, *Essai sur la nature du commerce en general* (Paris: Institut Coppet, 1755); John Locke, *Some Considerations of the Consequences of the Lowering of Interest, and Raising the Value of Money: In a Letter to a Member of Parliament* (UK: Awnsham and John Churchill, 1692).

13 For representative recent academic literatures on the subject of neoliberalism and its relation to global market capitalism, see generally, Joseph E. Stiglitz, *Globalization and its Discontents*, 1st ed. (New York: W.W. Norton, 2002). See also, Thomas L. Friedman, *The Lexus and the Olive Tree* (New York: Anchor Books, 2000).

on a predisposition of market-based behavior management over direct legal or political control of human transactions.[14]

The formal development of neoliberal politics is intrinsically linked to the changing international economic landscape following the global energy crisis of the 1970. This post-energy crisis shift in the global political economy, sometimes known as the Third-Wave Marketization process, marked a growing tendency in terms of the privatization of governance.[15] Subsidiary developments around emergent global neoliberalism transformations included financing in public and private spheres through a matrix of international and transnational institutions.[16] This emergent managerial governmentality has been accompanied by the development of a set of preferential structures for the political organization of states and their economic interactions.[17] With the post-WWII globalization process and the rapid increase in the free movement of goods, capital, and investments across state borders, the vertical state-centric construct is being gradually displaced by the polycentric web of global governance framework which would govern objects and transactions that are no longer containable within a state as they are moving across these borders.

Economic globalization does something very strange—on the substantive level, it catalyzes both the sacrifice of pre-existing rights and the creation of new rights protection frameworks. The acceleration of transnational marketization since the 1970s softened, and sometimes eliminated many state-centric structures (such as national tariffs and centrally planned economy), and triggered the need to develop new hard and soft structures of rules that promote rapid marketization across public and private sectors. Lastly, neoliberalism also suggests the legitimation of the governance authority of non-state actors, principally economic, religious, and civil organizations within private spheres of market-driven and market-managed activities.[18]

As shown in the table below, each of the three historical waves of global marketization brings new economic exigencies. Correspondingly, new human rights discourse and institutional mechanisms have emerged, to manage and contain various antagonistic forces arising from these sweeping economic changes. Neoliberalism, as a historically contextualized rhetorical situation, manifests itself in particular sets of discursive responses to the economic exigencies of the post-1970s energy crisis era – a period which Michael Burawoy formally defines as the "third wave" of global marketization:

14 Matthew Eagleton-Pierce, *Neoliberalism: The Key Concepts* (Routledge, 2007), 114–118.

15 Michael Burawoy, "Public sociology vs. the Market," *Economic Sociology as Public Sociology* (Berkeley, CA: 2006), 356–367.

16 Matthew Eagleton-Pierce, *Neoliberalism: The Key Concepts* (Routledge, 2007), 87–97.

17 Larry Catá Backer, "The Structural Characteristics of Global Law for the 21st Century: Fracture, Fluidity, Permeability, and Polycentricity," *Tilburg Law Review* Vol. 17 (2012), 177–199.

18 Backer, "The Structural Characteristics of Global Law for the 21st Century: Fracture, Fluidity, Permeability, and Polycentricity," 178

Table 1.1 Three waves of global marketization[19]

MARKET-IZATION WAVES	*RESPONSES TO ECONOMIC EXIGENCIES*		
	Rights discourse	*Defense mechanism*	*Representative events*
First wave (*c.*1800s - 1900s)	Labor rights	Labor unions and local communities	1834 Poor Law Amendment Act
Second wave (*c.*1900s - 1970s)	Social and economic rights	State regulations	1944 Bretton Woods Conference
Third Wave(1970 onwards)	Cultural, environmental and developmental rights	Transnational institutions and civil society actors	1970s Energy Crisis

Within these broad definitions, neoliberalism locally articulates itself in diverse and adaptive ways. Expressions and operations of neoliberalism are differentiated contingent on the economic, social, political, cultural and institutional context of the locality. These locally adapted expressions, in turn, shape and contribute to the global neoliberal discourse and its global economic operations. In this context, neoliberalism can be understood as the sum-total ideological assemblage of global market capitalism, operating in a *totalistic-composite* fashion. That is, it is a composite of various localized manifestations; these local expressions contribute collectively towards the totalistic economic logic and its global system of economic production.

This dynamic relationship between the global economy and local expressions produces profound effects on the evolution and operation of neoliberal discourse, which at first glance appears to be a unitary voice, but is in fact a composite of related forces and discourses tending towards convergence.[20] The convergence of global economic transactions thus continues to produce a rich discourse that encompasses voices of discontent as well as voices in search of a more "perfect" form of neoliberalism.

This project focuses on one understudied dynamic of late-modern global capitalism – the rhetoric and practice of ritual sacrifice. At first glance, this theme may appear at odds with the secular-modernist *ethos* of neoliberalism. Indeed, the historical unfolding of a global capitalist system displaced powers of many old religious orders, and in the process made new prophetic declarations for a rational conduct of life and a source of happiness that cut across all human "superstitions." It is through its promises of material comfort and life-fulfillment, and through its rationalist epistemic framework, that neoliberalism justifies its global proliferation. However, we must ask: how could this

19 Table content based on Michael Burawoy's formulation, see Michael Burawoy, "Public sociology vs. the Market," *Economic Sociology as Public Sociology* (Berkeley, CA: 2006), 356–367.

20 Peter Sloterdijk and Wieland Hoban, *In the World Interior of Capital: for a Philosophical Theory of Globalization* (Cambridge: Polity Press, 2013), introduction.

sweeping material promise retain its persuasive force, especially in times when the promised "good life" cannot be delivered without sacrificing it *through the work of destruction and waste and pollution*?[21]

Economic justifications for neoliberalism thus proceeds from the *dóxa*[22] (formulated maxims) of our material lifeworld – it expresses in general, abstract creeds. It is through the political-economic *dóxa* of neoliberalism that many socially and historically shaped material conditions pass as the "natural order" or even "sacred good." When formally expressed *dóxa* of neoliberalism are translated into its local manifestations, as socially embedded *písteis* [23] (faith) pertaining to governance legitimacy, it is then possible to persuade people that by believing mystic properties are intrinsic to tangible objects, the door for believers to become something they otherwise could not open.

The materialist prophecy of neoliberalism effectively returns to a unifying explanatory theology of *ens realissimum* – the prophetic affirmation of the supreme, imminent *realness* of the abstracted market as the ultimate source of value and goodness.[24] Therefore, neoliberalism relies in part on mythical rhetorics and rituals in managing its intrinsic contradictions. Its sweeping claims elevate the political-economic justifications of the prevailing system to the "ontological-objective" logic of "common values" and "historical-telos," and thereby naturalizes experiences of disparities between the make-believe and the lived reality. Thus, the study of the rhetorics of ritual sacrifice in neoliberal discourse may provide a critical angle for understanding the internal tensions of neoliberalism itself.

Jeremy Engels highlighted neoliberalism's tendency to privatize violence and resentment in the rhetoric of its representative figures.[25] What is relatively less-studied, however, is the ritualization of violence under neoliberalism's rhetorics. The governing regime of neoliberalism is heir to a long and diverse set of political, legal, and theological traditions of appropriating rhetorics of sacrifice to justify dehumanizing measures. Whereas many myths and rituals that once served the exploitative rule of god-kings are no longer practiced, it is nonetheless important to remain watchful of their lingering rhetorical resonances in our present time. Given the pervasiveness and multiplicity of neoliberal expressions, an extensive survey that fully captures the global rhetorical landscapes of ritual sacrifice would

21 The italicized portion is a quote taken out of Herbert Marcuse's comment on the intrinsic contradictions of late-capitalist societies in his *Eros and Civilization*. See, Herbert Marcuse, *Eros and Civilization* (Boston: Beacon Press, 1966), xxi.

22 Δόξᾰ (*dóxa*, formulated opinion, conjecture, philosophical *maxims*). See, Project Perseus, "δόξα" available: http://www.perseus.tufts.edu/hopper/morph?l=do%2Fca&la=greek#Perseus:text:1999.04.0057:entry=do/ca^-contents

23 Πίστεις, the plural nominative form of πίστις (*pístis*, good faith, personal trust). See, Project Persus, "πίστις," available: http://www.perseus.tufts.edu/hopper/text?doc=Perseus:text:1999.04.0057:entry=pi/stis

24 For a more detailed discussion on the concept of *ens realissimum*, see, Immanuel Kant, *The Critique of Pure Reason*, trans. Norman Kemp Smith (New York: St. Martin's Press, 1965), A607/B635.

25 Jeremy Engels, *The Politics of Resentment: a Genealogy* (University Park, PA: The Pennsylvania State University Press, 2015), 144–162.

be impractical. Nonetheless, it is important to work towards a better understanding of the manifold appropriations and deployment of ritual sacrifices under the capitalist global system.

This project seeks to study sacrifice through the close interrogation of a small but diverse set of textual objects representative of the neoliberal discourse. I aim to explore the multifaceted ways in which neoliberal discourse appropriates various ritual and theological elements of sacrifice. The investigation also looks into the implications of employing mythical justification for certain political measures of sacrifice, and traces the local rhetorical process of depoliticizing, naturalizing, and ritualizing functions of these problematic measures. Lastly, through critical engagement of selected textual objects, this project also seeks to "map out" the relationship between an explicit rhetoric of sacrifice and tacit underlying tensions stemming from the political-economic system.

The critical analysis in this project will give due consideration to political implications of sacrifice within neoliberal discourse. This study aims to explore new ways of critically interrogating the broader implications of the emergent global economic discourse by engaging its mythical and ritual elements. The question of the *state of sacrifice* under global capitalism fundamentally concerns the radicalization of diverse forms of political regimes, state and non-state actors, into the prophetic "end-of-history/end-of-politics" proclamations of neoliberalism. Perhaps these totalizing mythical assertions in part provide the basis in late-capitalist society to depoliticize, regularize, and ritualize public measures of sacrifices as mere "economic inevitabilities."

Why rhetoric?

Ritual sacrifice is a complex research subject afflicted with an amalgamation of practical, social, and moral implications. One must approach ritual practices from multiple frames of inquiry in order to obtain more a substantive and comprehensive understanding of this subject. Specifically, there are three analytical exigencies this project needs to address – to study rituals as a question of artistry, as a question of science, and as a question of moral implications. To this end, rhetoric may serve as a mode of inquiry that appropriately addresses all three analytical exigencies aforementioned.

The study of rituals is at the most basic level the study of human artistry, or conscious performance of learned faculty. A given practice is identified as "ritual" not only for its tendency towards habitual repetition, but also for its symbolic and formal characteristics. Rituals of sacrifice, like all forms of rhetorics, are strategic symbolic practices formally governed by collectively held rules and knowledge. It is this social-embeddedness of rituals that allows acts of sacrifice to be strategically deployed to exert persuasive effects in a communal setting. In simpler terms, ritual sacrifice is an art with *strategic* and *public* significance. Aristotle famously defined rhetoric as "the faculty of observing in any given case the available means of persuasion."[26] Although the scope of rhetoric has expanded far beyond its classical Aristotelian origin, it is

26 Aristotle, *Rhetoric*, trans. W. Rhys Roberts (MIT Internet Classics Archive, 2009), book I, part 2. Available: http://classics.mit.edu/Aristotle/rhetoric.1.i.html

nonetheless a discipline rooted in the artistry of persuasion in public or communal context. Thus, rhetoric is first and foremost a well-suited approach for addressing the artistic dimension of our research subject.

Addressing the artistic dimension of ritual sacrifice alone is nonetheless analytically insufficient. Rituals occupy a peculiar domain of artistic performance – one that is often shrouded by those seemingly impenetrable veils of spiritualism and mysticism. As rituals tend to be subjectively enclosed within the tacitly embedded normative framework of a given community, it is imperative to develop a *science of ritual* that extends beyond mystification and speculation. In this case, *science* refers to something closer to the meaning of *Wissenschaft*, or the methodological, systematic production of empirically grounded and intersubjective comprehensible knowledge. To this end, rhetoric not only offers the tools to analyze the artistry of representations, it also accounts for the materiality of rhetorical articulation. As Ronald Greene noted, "rhetoric traverses a governing apparatus as a technology of deliberation…makes possible the ability to judge and plan reality in order to police a population."[27] Thus, rhetoric *vis-a-vis* a *science* of persuasion channels a similar realist spirit as found in Machiavelli's *science* of politics – a cold-eyed mindfulness of the gap between the make-believe and material reality. "[I]t appears to me more appropriate to follow up the real truth of the matter than the imagination of it;" as Machiavelli proclaimed in his *Prince*, "for many have pictured republics and principalities which in fact have never been known or seen, because how one lives is so far distant from how one ought to live."[28]

In particular, communal ritual functions both as a system of representation and a practical instrument of the governing apparatus. Simply examining ritual sacrifice as a symbolic or artistic representation of a certain *mythos* runs the risk of overlooking the material consequences of such a practice. Furthermore, focusing on appreciating the persuasive artistry of the ritual sacrifice alone might result in unintended consequences of romanticizing, or even fetishizing what often amounts to materially exploitative and physically violent practices.

To this end, "The Literary Criticism of Oratory" (1925) by Herbert Wichelns is often credited as a landmark essay that defined the early to mid-20th-century revival of rhetorical criticism as a modern academic discipline. Wichelns called for a mode of critique that was already quite popular in literary studies – combining close reading of the written text itself (style, form, genre, rhetoric tactics etc.) with a broad overview of the historical background (e.g. historical effect, authorial biography) relating to the text.

The classically rooted mode of rhetorical inquiry described Herbert Wichelns, often known as the "Neo-Aristotelian" approach, gradually fell into disuse after World War II. Just as early 20th century historical/close-textual rhetorical criticism was developed in accordance with historical constraints of the time, this

27 Ronald Greene, "Another Materialist Rhetoric" *Critical Studies in Mass Communication* Vol. 15, No. 1 (1998), 21.

28 Nicolo Machiavelli, *The Prince,* trans. W. K. Marriott (Project Gutenberg, 2006), Chapter XV.

traditional mode of critique quickly fell out of favor as history progressed. The so-called "Neo-Aristotelian" approach to rhetorical criticism focuses on appreciating the persuasive artistry of the orator, and evaluating the effectiveness of the speech as intended by the orator.[29] Tragedies of the two World Wars and the rapid rise of modern totalitarianism (e.g. the Stalinist USSR, Nazi Germany, and Italy under "Il Duce") have made it increasingly difficult and problematic to simply engage in artistic "appreciation" of the text from a lofty position completely "removed" from political and ideological considerations. "There is no *poetry* after Auschwitz"[30] – it is in this sense that the traditional criticism method has been widely dismissed since the mid-20th century. Many rhetorical scholars, such as Edwin Black, referred to the traditional method as "neo-Aristotelian" – not only for its rigid, formulaic, taxonomist analysis, but also for its failure to substantively address the hidden but deeply entrenched political and material complexities that encumber the subject of analysis.

The rhetoric of ritual sacrifice is not simply "representations" or "artistic faculty" – they are strategically deployed techniques by actors to achieve particular communal ends – the kind of institutionalized rhetoric that often serve to maintain, shape, and break economic and social relations. As such, in addition to addressing the artistic and scientific questions, one must also consider, from a critically distant vantage point, those moral implications that may arise from the rhetoric of sacrifice. As Stephen Browne contended in "Rhetorical Criticism and the Challenges of Bilateral Argument," that critical dimension of rhetorical studies represents "an interpretive practice in which a class of phenomena is identified as rhetorical and judgment is rendered as to the properties and moral implications of those phenomena."[31] This implies that in addition to being an artist and a scientist, a scholar of rhetoric also embodies the persona of a critic. "The key term here is judgment," as Browne noted, "inasmuch as the critic seeks to make sense of the object not simply by describing its several features, but ultimately with reference to the critic's own set of beliefs, values, and commitments."[32]

An interdisciplinary approach is also necessary for this project: the field of rhetoric is a disciplinary latecomer to the study of ritual practices. Ritual practices have long been conceptualized and shaped by religious scholars. Ritual has also been a relatively well-studied subject in a wide range of social science and humanistic disciplines, most notably in historical, sociological, psychological and anthropological fields of inquiry. Meaningful theoretical advancement requires

29 Herbert A. Wichelns, "The Literary Criticism of Oratory" *Annual Bibliography of English Language and Literature* (1925).

30 A quote by Theodore Adorno, referring to the impossibility of language as a "pure" apolitical artistic expression after the events resulting from WWII, from which the totality of society's aesthetic domain has been appropriated by the state apparatus towards political ends. *See* Theodor W. Adorno, *Prisms* (London: Spearman, 1967), 34.

31 Stephen H. Browne, "Rhetorical Criticism and the Challenges of Bilateral Argument," *Philosophy and Rhetoric* Vol. 40, No. 1, 2007: 108–118.

32 Browne, "Rhetorical Criticism and the Challenges of Bilateral Argument," 114.

bringing "news" to the existing body of knowledge. When studying the rhetoric of well-studied social phenomena such as ritual sacrifice, it is helpful to build the rhetorical analysis upon a baseline of interdisciplinary common literacy. This issue of interdisciplinarity will be discussed in greater detail in Chapter 2 of this work.

In summation, the rhetorical approach combines study of artistry with scientific inquiry as well as critical judgment. Rhetorical analysis examines symbolic phenomena from a humanistic-scientific (*Geistwissenschaft*) angle, which duly considers the intertwined complexities between the normative and material dimensions of the human condition. Therefore, rhetoric offers an appropriate response for heuristically addressing the research questions of art, of science, and of moral implications for this study.

Why atlas?

Early comparative studies on human sacrifice were heavily influenced by theories of historical relativism and social evolutionism.[33] Such an approach is exemplified by the works of 19th-century cultural-anthropologists Edward Tylor and Marcel Mauss, both of whom framed practices of human sacrifice as specific iterations of general social features, developed relative to various stages of human historical development.[34]

With the rise of social psychology throughout the 20th century, theories of human sacrifice began to expand beyond the evolutionary framework. The most influential theoretical contribution on the social psychology of sacrifice can be attributed to Sigmund Freud's writings in *Totem and Taboo*, where he grounded ritualistic killings of other human beings as a manifestation of the intrinsic destructive impulse of the human ego. For Freud, human sacrifice, though it may seem like an exceptionally savage type of practice, is in fact a form of collective manifestation of basic human neuroses and insecurities.[35]

Drawing from his own theories on the fundamental structure of the human psyche, Freud claims that even the most brutal forms of ritual sacrifice nonetheless operate as crude measures of social control. Based on his study of those "incomplete reports" of sacrifice customs, Freud identified four main social functions for the ritual taking of human lives: "1. reconciliation with the slain enemy, 2. restrictions, 3. acts of expiation, and purifications of the manslayer, and 4. certain ceremonial rites."[36] Freud also argues that the underlying impulse of ritual

33 Richard E. DeMaris, "Sacrifice, an Ancient Mediterranean Ritual," *Biblical Theology Bulletin* Vol. 43 No. 2 (2013): 60–73. See also, *Max Weber, On the Methodology of the Social Sciences*, trans. Edward A. Shils and Henry A. Finch (Illinois: The Free Press of Glencoe, 1949), 52.

34 Edward Tylor, *Primitive Culture: Researches into the Development of Mythology, Philosophy, Religion, Language, Art, and Custom.* 7th ed. (New York: Brentano's, 1924). See also, Henri Hubert and Marcel Mauss, *Sacrifice: Its Nature and Function*, trans. W. D. Halls (Chicago, IL: University of Chicago Press, 1964).

35 Sigmund Freud, *Totem and Taboo: Resemblances between the Psychic Lives of Savages and Neurotics*, trans. A. A. Brill (New York, NY: Vintage Books, 1961).

36 Freud, *Totem and Taboo: Resemblances between the Psychic Lives of Savages and Neurotics*, Chapter 2, sec. 2–3.

violence has been persistent throughout human civilization, though societies may find ways to redirect compulsive neuroses towards less violent rituals that substitute the functions of human sacrifice. "The original animal sacrifice was already a substitute for a human sacrifice," as Freud notes in *Totem and Taboo*, "for the solemn killing of the father, and when the father substitute regained its human form, the animal substitute could also be re-transformed into a human sacrifice."[37]

Contemporary cultural theorist René Girard also considered the subject of human sacrifice along similar psychological lines, arguing that all sacred rituals are externalizations of violent human tendencies. In this regard, Girard points to our mimetic desire – desiring of what others have that we lack – as the source of human violence.[38]

At a basic level, Girard's argument is a familiar one. The causal relationship between desire and violence has been widely discussed in early Enlightenment political philosophy – most notably by Thomas Hobbes in *Leviathan,* where he famously attributed the "King's violence" to the fundamental and insatiable human desire for power and riches.[39] However, Girard frames such desire in existential and psychological instead of economic/naturalistic terms, arguing that mimetic desire intensifies when the more basic human needs are satisfied. Girard argues that the desiring of others' belongings would often intensify, and transform into violent rituals for its own sake once the basic biological and material needs are fulfilled.[40]

Human sacrificial rituals are differentiated relative to tensions and constraints specific to the historical, temporal and spatial milieu of their corresponding discursive jurisdictions. Understanding differentiated sacrificial practices solely through theoretical abstraction or mystic interpretation runs the danger of washing away the intensely political character of these rhetorical performances. American literary theorist Kenneth Burke addressed the limitations of evolutionary modes of investigation by suggesting a new dramaturgic approach to analyzing symbolic actions.[41] In *Permanence and Change,* Burke proposed that, "[r]ather than thinking of magic, religion, and science as three distinctively successive stages in the world's history, the author would now use a mode of analysis that dealt with all three as aspects of motivation."[42] Note that Burke's emphasis on "motivation" does not suggest a strictly "psychological" orientation; rather, the term "motivation" can be better understood as

37 Freud, *Totem and Taboo: Resemblances between the Psychic Lives of Savages and Neurotics,* Chapter 4, sec. 6.

38 René Girard, *Violence and the Sacred,* trans. Yvonne Freccero (Baltimore, MD: Johns Hopkins University Press, 1977), 156–157.

39 Thomas Hobbes, *Leviathan: Or, the Matter, Form, and Power of a Common Wealth, Ecclesiastical and Civil* (South Australia: The University of Adelaide Library, Rare Books & Mss., 1651), pt. 1, Chapter 9.

40 René Girard, *Deceit, Desire, and the Novel: Self and Other in Literary Structure,* trans. Patrick Gregory (Baltimore, MD: Johns Hopkins University Press, 1965), 155.

41 Kenneth Burke, *Permanence and Change, An Anatomy of Purpose,* 3rd edition (Berkeley, CA: University of California Press, 1984), 29–30.

42 Burke, *Permanence and Change,* xxv.

shorthand for relativized symbolic performances – actions that are "locally" embedded within the framework of a larger *Weltanschauung*.[43]

It is necessary to contextualize Burke's critical interrogation of the mythical within the larger disciplinary context of rhetorical studies. The tragedies of two World Wars and the rapid rise of modern totalitarianism (e.g. Stalinist USSR, Nazi Germany, and Italy under "Il Duce") have made it increasingly difficult for critics to simply "enjoy" the "artistry" of political texts. It became increasingly difficult to engage human discourse as apolitical, purely artistic expressions in the aftermath of WWII, from which the totality of society's aesthetic domain has been appropriated by the state apparatus towards political ends. Theodore Adorno succinctly summarized this modern literary anxiety in *Kulturkritik und Gesellschaft* (1951): "There is no poetry after Auschwitz."[44]

As Kenneth Burke suggested, humans are rhetorical beings. Not only is our embodied *ethos* (identity, class, internalized knowledge, etc.) shaped by others' symbolic actions, we also perform through our internationalized rhetorical characters, and in turn, externalize and shape the lifeworld. Thus, when it comes to symbolic performances, there can be no "pure" ritual that is entirely "apolitical" or "transcendent." When neoliberalism ritualizes and de-politicizes sacrifice via the rhetoric of "market self-corrections," "economic inevitabilities" and "fiscal responsibilities" (the list can go on), this process effectively radicalizes contestable political logic into the incontestable, mystical domain, the "laws of nature/the market." For the purpose of this work, the study of the rhetoric of sacrifice is the study of sacrifice as a form of mytho-political speech.

"Mytho-political speech" refers to political discourse that possesses certain formal characters of mythical speech. Note that mytho-political speech not only articulates itself in explicit voices and writings, but also in its rituals, its ceremonies, its liturgies and sacraments. The mythical component can be understood in the Burkean sense, that the realm of myths and rituals is neither "transcendent," nor is it "beyond" or "prior" to language. Rather, as Burke noted in his *Rhetoric of Religion*, the meanings of mythical expressions are situated within the *logology*, or logic of human language.[45] In a similar vein to Burke's dramaturgical treatment of the rhetoric of religion, Roland Barthes argued in *Mythologies* that critics ought to go beyond the "details of the linguistic schema" in order to give an adequate account of differentiated rhetorics or rituals and sacrifices under neoliberal discourse.[46] Additionally, recent works by Lynda Walsh on the theology of scientific discourse also reflects similar critical attunement, especially in breaking apart modernist assumptions by interrogating those lingering pre-modern mythical practices.[47]

43 Burke, *Permanence and Change*, 25.
44 Theodore Adorno, *Critical Models: Interventions and Catchwords* (New York: Columbia University Press, 1998).
45 Kenneth Burke, *The Rhetoric of Religion: Studies in Logology* (Boston, MA: Beacon Press, 1961), 7–29.
46 Roland Barthes, *Mythologies*, trans. Annette Lavers (New York: The Noonday Press, 1972), 113–114.
47 Lynda Walsh, *Scientists as Prophets: A Rhetorical Genealogy* (New York: Oxford University Press, 2013).

While the dramaturgical analysis as outlined in Burke's works provides a better sensitivity for taking account of the multiplicity of orientations when studying symbolic representations, this approach also has its share of limitations. One critical issue is that our lifeworld is not simply determined by our perceptions. The conclusion of WWII, Cold War struggles, and the rise of transnational capitalism have highlighted a fact about ideology that we can no longer ignore. Public *mythos* or ideology is more than mere beliefs or abstract representations that inform and shape who we are. It forms the legitimation framework for the governing apparatus, and provides organizing principles for the articulations of power and social control. Public *mythos* also gives rise to accompanying public rituals which command repetitions of specific human performances without explicit "persuasion."[48]

Works by James Carey also provide a substantive and analytically helpful update to what Carey refers to as the "ritual view" of communication.[49] Most notably, in his 1994 essay "Communications and Economics," Care first locates the "case of communication" within the context of the prevailing mode of economic production and economic relations.[50] Carey proceeds by echoing the aforementioned Burkean argument. He distills the formal organizing basis of communicative actions, and explains that communication is largely grounded in "ritual and religion."[51] Upon highlighting his ritual view of communication, Carey then translates the formal vocabularies of ritual and religion back into the substantive language of real economic functions: "[i]n this sense, communication can at best act as a control and check upon the economic motive, the motive of self-interest—can prevent self-interest from taking over the entire household of the social."[52]

It is important to note that the "religion" Carey refers to is not simply "superstitious beliefs" or functions of social conditioning and solitary; nor should we reduce "religion" into an abstracted category of social phenomena that can be studied as functional causes or consequences. Proceeding beyond this naive perspective of religion as lingering old superstitions that go against the grain of science and modernity, Carey was perceptive in his works concerning an uncanny resurgence of anti-modern "fundamentalist" rhetorics in our contemporary communicative landscape. Political economist Harold Innis also observed a peculiar and a seemingly contradictory trend in the post-WWII development of global affairs: that the incidents of space-biased communications increase as overall

48 Barthes, *Mythologies.*

49 Eve Stryker Munson and Catherine A. Warren (eds.), *James Carey: A Critical Reader* (Minneapolis: University of Minnesota Press, 1997), ProQuest Ebook Central (accessed August 23, 2017), "Introduction."

50 James Carey, "Communications and Economics," first published 1994, from *James Carey: A Critical Reader*, edited by Eve Stryker Munson, and Catherine A. Warren (University of Minnesota Press: 1997), 69.

51 Carey, "Communications and Economics," 69: "However, primordially and politically, the origin of communication is at one with the origins of ritual and religion: not the transmission of intelligent information but the construction and maintenance of an ordered, meaningful cultural world that can serve as a container for human action— a world of time rather than space."

52 Carey, "Communications and Economics," 60–79.

communication technology improves.[53] It is then increasingly difficult to ignore the prospect that those emergent dark political currents in the 21st century – violent insurrections by the so-called "Islamic State of Iraq and the Levant," the proliferation of "fake news" on new media platforms, and the development new authoritarian philosophical thoughts or political theologies, such as the so-called "fourth political theory" by Alexander Dugin[54] – might be increasingly common responses to a transnational, hyper-fluid, polycentric, yet fragmented global communication landscape.[55]

Works by Giorgio Agamben constituted the most significant 21st-century revival in the study of ritual sacrifice as political discourse. In his *Potentialities: Collected Essays in Philosophy* (1999), Agamben defined the concept of the *homo sacer* (sacred or accursed man) not as a historical particularity or person, as a metaphor for the rhetorical moment which the sovereign declares its power over "bare life" (or life always ready to be disposed).[56] It is a moment where the "experience of history" appropriates the "experience of language," as Agamben suggested, where the collective memory is "saved" by "being transformed into something that never was." The messianic logic also assumes radically different temporality than historical revisionist narratives – it does not merely seek to reshape historical experience of the audience, but to claim the "end of their history." The concept of *kleto* became a major subject of research in Agamben's 2005 book *The Time that Remains: A Commentary on the Letter to the Romans.* In *The Time that Remains,* Agamben identified the messianic rhetoric in the letters of Apostle Paul served to construct a political theology that asserts itself as the end-of-history (and therefore end of political potentialities), by dividing the population along the binary of eternal salvation vs. damnation. Agamben contended that the political implication of Apostle Paul's messianic rhetoric is not trivial – it was deployed as a discursive device for both the perpetual segregation and disenfranchisement of a population.[57]

The "ideological turn" in late-20th-century rhetorical criticism is in part a response to the exigence of searching for better ways to critically evaluate those seemingly "extra-representational" and "pre-symbolic" magical elements that deeply enchant our social world. Initial efforts of materialist analysis in rhetorical studies were heavily influenced by Marxist "dialectical materialist" method and by those "Frankfurt School" critical analysis of late-capitalist culture. It was

53 Harold Innis, *The Bias of Communication* (Toronto: University of Toronto Press, 2008), 28.

54 Dmitry Shlapentokh, "The ideological framework of early post-Soviet Russia's relationship with Turkey: the case of Alexander Dugin's Eurasianism." *Journal of Balkan and Near Eastern Studies* Vol. 18, No. 3 (2016), 263–281.

55 Quentin J. Schultze, "Communication as Religion: In Memory of James W. Carey," *Journal of Media and Religion* Vol. 6, No. 1 (2007): 1–15, at 10.

56 Giorgio Agamben, *Homo Sacer: Sovereign Power and Bare Life* (Stanford, CA: Stanford University Press, 1998).

57 Giorgio Agamben, *Il tempo che resta. Un commento alla Lettera ai Romani* (2000) trans. Patricia Dailey as *The Time that Remains: A Commentary on the Letter to the Romans* (Stanford, CA: Stanford University Press, 2005).

nonetheless a large bracket with a diverse and sometimes mutually-conflicting critical approaches. Representative essays by rhetorical scholars during the early days of the ideological turn (early 1980s), such as Michael McGee's "Ideograph" essay and works by Dana Cloud, represented an overall emphasis on traditional class-struggle analysis. In recent years, rhetorical scholars such as Ron Green and Davi Johnson began to develop a kind of "new-materialism" that goes beyond the Marxist dialectical materialist orthodoxy, instead incorporating many post-structuralist theoretical tendencies.

The "political geography" form of rhetorical analysis as proposed by Davi Johnson provides an important methodological context for this work project.[58] Drawing heavily from the "rhizomatic" analysis outlined in Gilles Deleuze and Félix Guattari's *Thousand Plateaus*, Johnson suggested employing what Deleuze calls "nomadic thought" as the main critical approach for his "geographical" intervention.[59] According to Deleuze and Guattari, "nomadic thought" as a critical framework transcends the epistemological territoriality of the state:

> The space of nomad thought is qualitatively different from State space. Air against earth. State space is "striated," or gridded. Movement in it is confined as by gravity to a horizontal plane, and limited by the order of that plane to preset paths between fixed and identifiable points. Nomad space is "smooth," or open-ended. One can rise up at any point and move to any other. Its mode of distribution is the *nomos*: arraying oneself in an open space (hold the street), as opposed to the *logos* of entrenching oneself to a closed space (hold the fort).[60]

While similar in terms of bare analytical mechanics, the mapping attempt outlined in this work differs from Johnson's new, materialist framework in terms of political focus. The "nomadic" position outlined in the works of Deleuze and Johnson demand an epistemologically indifferent gaze that is radically detached from the "striated territories" of political discourse on the ground. The "nomadic thought" as outlined in their works assumes an undifferentiated plane of analysis that is "extra-political" and "extra-territorial," thereby allowing the nomadic critic to "smoothly" navigate among networks of knowledge-spaces. Deleuze and Johnson's "nomad" playfully assumes a detached neutrality and comfortable indifference towards territorial statehood and political spaces.[61] In contrast, the critical position for this project would better be compared to that of a "fugitive" mode of thinking. More specifically, a fugitive remains in a state of constant exile – always stateless yet remain apprehensively watchful for subtle traces of political power.

58 Davi Johnson, "Mapping the meme: A geographical approach to materialist rhetorical criticism" *Communication and Critical/Cultural Studies* Vol. 4, No. 1 (2007): 27–50.

59 Gilles Deleuze and Félix Guattari, *A Thousand Plateaus: Capitalism and Schizophrenia* (Minneapolis, MN: University of Minnesota Press, 1987), xii–xiv.

60 Deleuze and Guattari, *A Thousand Plateaus*, xiii.

61 Johnson, "Mapping the Meme: A Geographical Approach to Materialist Rhetorical Criticism," 27.

No cartographer can hope to obtain the "God's eye view" removed from the limits of language and symbolic representations, and perfectly transcribes topographical and topological features "the way they are." In addition to identifying relevant features pertinent to the specific theme of the integrative rhetorical analysis, the interpretation and translation of these features are also fundamental challenges for mapping. The unique research topic tasked for this atlas project also adds an additional layer of challenge. The emergence of global capitalism accompanies the proliferation of its totalizing epistemic "fog-of-war" – one that shrouds multitudes of political and historical vicissitudes of everyday life without completely clearing them. Disparities in political variations and economic conditions remain visible at the local level, but these locally embedded tensions would have reduced visibility when examined from afar. When political expressions are "taken hostage" by the all-encompassing economic logic of neoliberalism, it is increasingly difficult locate a stable vantage point to render nuanced understanding of neoliberal discourse.

Driven in part by the interpretative impulse of Kenneth Burke's early critical engagement of mythical speeches, and extending from recent rhetorical works in areas of "political geography" and "ideological assemblage," this project would suggest employing a "rhetorical atlas" approach for its critical analysis. The thematic focus of this mapping effort rests on the discrete and simultaneous tracing of the discursive contours of sacrifice in different local settings. Its aim is to collectively offer a small cross-section glimpse into the multiformity of mythical-ritual practices in the maintenance of neoliberalism governance.

Preview of chapters

The following paragraphs present a basic roadmap for this project.

Chapter 1 presents theoretical discussions and review of relevant academic literature that inform the development of this research project. This chapter begins by establishing a working definition of "ritual sacrifice" – one that conforms to the dominant understandings of the term in current scholarship. This serves as the departure point for further analysis. This chapter then outlines the development of the modern comparative study of mythical and ritual human practices, from its late 19th-century incarnation in Western Europe to the present. The literature review will also highlight three major theoretical turns of the field – from the early dominance of historicism and social anthropology, to the 20th-century turn towards social psychology, and eventually to the late 20th-century intervention from critical-interpretive theoretical perspectives. The latter half of the chapter focuses on examining relevant literature within the field of rhetoric, and highlighting the ways in which this project are informed and influenced by recent developments in rhetorical scholarship. This chapter ends by contextualizing this work project within the current disciplinary landscape of rhetorical study, and explaining the theoretical contributions sought by this project.

Chapters 3, 4 and 5 are the main analytical portion of this work, and collectively constitute the beginning of an effort to construct a rhetorical atlas of ritual sacrifice in late-capitalism. Compiling a rhetorical atlas involves a slightly different method of political mapmaking – one that uses discursive rather than terrestrial contours in tracing and differentiating political realities locally. It is to survey locally expressed politics of sacrifice collectively operating under the global landscape of neoliberalism. For any type of mapping, projecting complex reliefs of the lifeworld onto a finite-sized flat plane would inevitably lead to a certain degree of omission and abstraction. A small-scale map (i.e. world map, map of a continent) can cover a large swath of terrain at the expense of erasing local details. Conversely, a large-scale regional map does a relatively better job transcribing local details, but at the cost of excising the "bigger picture" out of the frame.

The atlas provides a good middle ground that allows for balanced display of both scope and detail, collectively presenting separately mapped localities of a larger region. Given that neoliberalism "speaks" at both global and local levels, it is necessary for this project to study the rhetoric of sacrifice globally without sacrificing attention to its local variations. It is best to capture the manifold neoliberal appropriations of sacrifice in an *atlas* that avoids both over-abstraction and excision of the larger context.

A total of three well-documented bodies of text have been selected as the main objects of analysis for this section. They include three speeches by world leaders, one Supreme Court decision, and one international treaty document. The selection of these objects of analysis is based on the following criteria.

First, the total number of texts to include in this study is based on balancing the needs of scope and depth. Given that neoliberalism "speaks" at both global and local levels, this project needs to look for ways to examine the rhetoric of sacrifice in diverse global settings without excessive sacrifices on the attention to local detail. Thus, a total of three case studies present a realistic middle ground allowing a degree of diversity of examples without sacrificing attention to each individual text. Second, all three text objects are formally organized bodies of speech and/or text produced for public context. For each object of analysis, its operation is confined within the prescribed political and legal parameters, and its textual production revolves around a prescribed set of ritual performances and sequential procedures. Third, the selected texts collectively offer a small but diverse and representative slice of those formal expressions commonly produced by key state and non-state actors in the contemporary global system. Lastly, each of the selected textual objects reveals a subtle yet representative aspect of the multifaceted ways neoliberal politics appropriate and deploy the rhetoric of sacrifice for its productive ends.

The following is a detailed breakdown of the three studies in for analytical Chapters 3–5:

1 *Kelo v. City of New London*, 545 U.S. 469 (2005) – U.S. Supreme Court landmark decision permitting the use of eminent domain by local governments to seize residential properties for private redevelopment. Justice John Paul Stevens wrote the court's majority opinion.[62]

62 Kelo et al. v. City of New London et al., 545 U.S. 469 (2005), available: http://caselaw.findlaw.com/us-supreme-court/545/469.html#sthash.kxJvljNP.dpuf

2 "Complaint to the UK National Contact Point under the OECD Guidelines for Multinational Enterprises," filed by British NGO (non-governmental organization) Survival International on December 2008, in response to the Niyamgiri indigenous land-mining project controversy.
3 Collection of speeches made by Dr. H. F. Verwoerd (1901–1966) – Professor of Sociology and Social Work at University of Stellenbosch, 6th Prime Minister of South Africa, and perhaps most famously remembered as the "Architect of Apartheid."

This work project will attempt to incorporate three separately sketched case studies, or "local maps," in the format of three separate chapters. Each of these analytical chapters will individually latch onto a textual object for close reading and rhetorical analysis. As Kirt Wilson contended, "that twenty-first-century scholars view public address as moments of articulation within rich temporal, spatial, and conceptual contexts."[63] The analysis for each chapter will closely trace relevant contextual dimensions of a given rhetorical moment. Each case study will first sketch out the basic "surface topography" of the rhetorical moment and its immediate contextual landscape. The surface topography introduces the background information of the object of analysis, outlines the setting, the key actors involved, and the stated purpose of the textual artifact. Instances where the rhetoric of sacrifice explicitly appears on the textual surface of the object will be highlighted, then followed by identifying their directly connected political, historical, and institutional contexts.

After surveying the surface topography of the case, the rhetorical analysis proceeds into the ritual and ideological "substrate" of the given rhetorical moment. This substrate analysis involves focused, yet historically deep, excavation of tacitly embedded belief structures that maintain and legitimize ritual sacrifice. The third stage goes beyond surface text and their immediate contexts, and moves towards tracing those tacit political and economic fault lines that run beneath the rhetoric of sacrifice. This involves locating their divergent boundaries, fractures and potential points of rupture. At this stage the cartographer can no longer solely rely on her "bare eyes and senses" from a fixed vantage point. To further survey the sub-textual structures which lay underneath the written and spoken text, the cartographer is tasked with moving freely across the terrain, thus bringing a wide range of instruments and references to trace previously unmapped details. The textual and contextual layers of the text-object will be re-interrogated with the help of divergent vocabularies from past practices of ritual sacrifice. The final stage concludes the textual analysis by bringing the multi-layered mapping from the previous three stages back into the thematic discussion of global, neoliberal discourse.

63 Kirt H. Wilson, "The Racial Contexts of Public Address: Interpreting Violence during the Reconstruction Era" in *The Handbook of Rhetoric and Public Address* (New Jersey, John Wiley & Sons Inc., 2010): 205–228, at 205.

The point of compiling this rhetorical *atlas* is not to stitch together a grand trans-historical "truth;" nor would it seek to establish linear connections between discrete practices sacrifice. Rather, the object of the analysis is to draw from available vocabularies of the public memory to interrogate problematic aspects besieging our present conditions.

Like many other types of atlas collections, the viewer may decide to read these analytical chapters in any order. Each of the chapters will provide a scaled view of a mode of rhetorical practice that is developed within the parameters of its specific operations, and that conforms to the particularities of its local contexts. At the same time, these locally contextualized rhetorical "mappings" will synecdochally refer back to the overall theme of the atlas, which is the *state of sacrifice* under neoliberalism. This hermeneutic process may help the reader to better recognize the multifaceted articulations of ritual sacrifice through neoliberal discourse, and the nuanced re-appropriations of sacrifice towards maintaining the hegemonic economic order.

This study concludes with a brief summary of key findings from the previous analytical chapters, and contextualizes these findings with respect to the larger research questions originally raised in the *introduction*. After a short restatement of the theory, the conclusion moves to a few comments of reservations concerning this project. This includes a review of remaining theoretical weaknesses, methodological constraints, and other lingering issues that demand further attention. The closing remarks will note potential directions for future inquiry.

The next chapter will provide a broad overview of the existing body of scholarship on ritual sacrifice, and to ground the rhetorical analysis upon an interdisciplinary theoretical literacy of its subject of analysis.

2 Interdisciplinary historical overview

This chapter reviews existing theoretical and historical scholarship on ritual practices and human sacrifice. The objective is to find innovative ways to bring interdisciplinarity and integrative analysis into rhetorical research, as well as to support subsequent rhetorical case studies with a baseline interdisciplinary common literacy on the subject of ritual sacrifice.

Raising the issue

Interdisciplinarity is necessary to achieve the research objective of this work. This is in part due to the fact that modern rhetorical studies is a disciplinary latecomer to in the study of ritual. Ritual is historically studied and shaped by various traditions of religious scholarship. Upon the emergence of modern social and humanistic sciences (*Wissenschaft* and *Geisteswissenschaft*), human ritual practice has been systematically examined by a wide range of sociological, psychological, and historical-anthropological disciplines.[1] Substantive theoretical contribution requires bringing "news" to the existing body of knowledge. Therefore, before proceeding to close readings of rhetorical moments, it would be helpful to fortify the rhetorical analytical framework with an interdisciplinary understanding on ritual sacrifice.

The ritual taking of things that are of human value, including the ritual killing of humans, has been continuously practiced for as long as human civilization itself has existed.[2] According to René Girard, "sacrifice is the most critical and fundamental rites…all systems that give structure to human society have been generated from it: language, kinship system, taboos, codes of etiquette, patterns of exchanged, rites, and civil instructions."[3]

1 Karlheinz Stierle, "Ist die Geisteswissenschaft eine Wissenschaft?" *Magazin Forschung 2/2007* (Germany: Kontaktstelle für Wissens-und Technologietransfer: 2007), 37–39.
2 Walter Burkert, René Girard, Jonathan Z. Smith, and Robert Hamerton-Kelly, *Violent Origins: Ritual Killing and Cultural Formation*, ed. Robert G. Hamerton-Kelly (Stanford, CA: Stanford University Press: 1987), at Introduction.
3 René Girard, "Religion and Ritual" in *Violent Origins: Ritual Killing and Cultural Formation*, ed. Robert G. Hamerton-Kelly (Stanford, CA: Stanford University Press: 1987), 7.

American social psychologist Erich Fromm observed in *The Anatomy of Human Destructiveness:*

> It may help to see this point if we think of a modern phenomenon which can be compared with child sacrifice, that of war. Take the First World War a mixture of economic interests, ambition, and vanity on the part of the leaders, and a good deal of stupid blundering on all sides brought about the war. But once it had broken out...it became a 'religious' phenomenon. The state, the nation, national honor, became the idols, and both sides voluntarily sacrificed their children to these idols.[4]

Fromm further noted that not only does the *religious phenomenon* of sacrifice still exist in modern society, but modernity has in many ways amplified the scope, intensity and destructiveness of ritual human sacrifice:

> A large percentage of the young men of the British and of the German upper classes which are responsible for the war were wiped out in the early days of the fighting. Surely they were loved by their parents. Yet, especially for those who were most deeply imbued with the traditional concepts...their love did not make them hesitate in sending their children to death, nor did the young ones who were going to die have any hesitation. The fact that, in the case of child sacrifice, the father kills the child directly while, in the case of war, both sides of an arrangement to kill each other's children makes little difference. In the case of war, those who are responsible for it know what is going to happen, yet the power of the idols is greater than the power of love for their children.[5]

As modern forms of the ritual of sacrifice are disguised behind a thin veil of contemporary mythic justification frameworks, often spelled out in the language of economic, legal, and scientific rationalities, it is helpful to first examine scholarship on historical forms of ritual human sacrifice, so that we may distill an interdisciplinary body of analytical vocabularies for our readings of present movements.

Historical thickness of ritual sacrifice

Although people in modern society seldom consider ritual sacrifice (especially those that involve the slaughter of humans for ritual purposes) as an ongoing practice, it nonetheless remains an organizing element of contemporary institutions of governance.[6] Capital punishment, for instance, is one of the oldest forms of human

4 Erich Fromm, *The Anatomy of Human Destructiveness* (New York: Holt, Reinhart and Winston, 1973), 204–210.

5 Fromm, *The Anatomy of Human Destructiveness*, 206.

6 Roberta M. Harding, "Capital Punishment as Human Sacrifice: A Societal Ritual as Depicted in George Eliot's *Adam Bede*," 48 *Buff. L. Rev.* 175 (2000), 1–72.

ritual sacrifice that is continuously practiced to the present day.[7] Yet the effective modern reenactment of ritual sacrifice runs much deeper than criminal procedures. It is important to note that the defining element for ritual sacrifice is not the act of taking *per se*, but the legitimation of taking through ritual suspension of *nomos* (pre-existing formal and customary social protections). Ritual, in this sense, functions as an audience-adaptation strategy, to regularize those otherwise exceptional and problematic acts of takings.[8] The history of ritual human sacrifice is arguably as long as the history of human civilization itself. One of earliest, and most well-documented example of institutionalized, large-scale human sacrifice regime is Shang dynasty China (*c.*1,600BC – 1,046BC).

The phenomenon of ritual human killings has been present in many societies throughout history; the types of human sacrifice that were practiced in pre-Qin

Figure 2.1 Symbol of the sovereign power of the Shang ruler over the bare life of his subject: Sketch of a bronze ceremonial *yue* axe (钺) from late Shang period China (c. 1200BC – 1046BC), based on an actual artifact excavated from the Suyidu Site-B, Shangdong Province in 1956[9]. The Shang ruling class typically displayed ceremonial Yue axes like the one shown above on top of high poles during ceremonial processions. These were made to physically resemble the type of axe used for human beheadings and dismemberment of the condemned. See Table 2.1 for detailed examples of the uses of *yue* axe for ritual human sacrifice.

7 Harding, "Capital Punishment as Human Sacrifice," 2.

8 Claudio Minca, "Giorgio Agamben and the New Biopolitical Nomos," *Geografiska Annaler. Series B, Human Geography* Vol. 88, No. 4 (2006), 387–403.

9 Original artifact measures 31.7cm x 35.8cm and weighs 4.9 kg, currently in the collection of Anyang Museum of History, Henan, China.

China[10] and pre-Columbian Mesoamerican societies were exceptional in terms of the sheer number of people sacrificed, the frequency at which it was done, and the high degree of formalization of their sacrificial rituals. Large-scale, systematic human sacrifice functioned as political and religious spectacle in the Shang dynasty. Due to ample historical records and surviving archaeological artifacts, human sacrifice during the Shang dynasty and are relatively well-studied despite its historical distance.[11]

The Shang dynasty marked the height of the Chinese Bronze Age, where the dynasty ruled over the fertile Yellow River basin for more than half a millennium, from *c.*1600 BC to 1046 BC. Traditional Chinese historiography has divided periods of Chinese history into 'dynasties' – a formal historical term referring to periods of "unified rule" (天下共主, lit. "One sovereign uniting the world under one Heaven"),[12] where the area we know of as China was ruled by a single sovereign clan. The change of imperial rule signaled a change in dynasty, and also signified a change in the Heaven's Mandate. Officially, of course, imperial rule of China only officially started with the Qin dynasty under Emperor Shihuangdi in 221 BC. Prior to establishment of the Qin dynasty, the previous dynasties – Xia, Zhou, and Shang dynasties – were organized in the form of a confederate feudal state system, in which the state that managed to acquire hegemony via military conquest will be recognized by other feudal clans as having the Mandate of Heaven, and the monarch of that state would be referred to as *Tianzi*, which literally translates as "Heaven's son." The title *Tianzi*, which once referred to those kings of the hegemonic feudoms during Xia, Shang and Zhou dynasties, was carried on as the honorific title of the emperor throughout the imperial China, which lasted from 221 BC until the fall of the Qing dynasty in 1912 AD.[13]

The importance of ritualism in traditional Chinese political theology cannot be understated. The term "ritualism" here more specifically refers to the political, legal and theological system relating to *yinsi* (禋祀, or burned sacrifice rituals of the state) and *sheji* (社稷, or alters of soil and grain). The literal translation for *yinsi* is "burnt sacrifice." *Yinsi* traditionally refers to state-organized sacrifices that were performed first by the feudal rulers during the Ancient Period (*c.*1600 BCE–221 BCE), and later by the emperor during the Imperial Period (221 BCE– 1915 CE). The last imperial *yinsi* ceremony was performed in 1915 by the self-declared "Hongxian Emperor" (Yuan Shikai) at Peking's Temple of Heaven. More

10 A common term in Chinese historiography referring to the period prior to the imperial unification of China by Qin Shi Huang in 221 BC. More specifically, pre-Qin China encompasses pre-classical Shang (*c.*1600 BC–*c.*1046 BC) and Western Zhou (*c.*1046–771 BC) dynasties, as well as the age of classical Chinese antiquity which spans between the Spring and Autumn (771 to 476 BC) and the Warring States (475–221 BC) periods.

11 Wang Ping and Wolfgang Kubin, 甲骨文与殷商人祭 / *Oracle Bone Inscriptions and Human Sacrifice during the Yinshang Period / Jia gu wen yu Yin Shang ren ji, Chinese*, 1st ed. (Zhengzhou, China: 大象出版社, 2007).

12 Chen Qiyun 陈启云, "封建与大一统之间——关于中国传统政体的理论和史实," 学术月刊 /*Xue shu yue kan* 2 (2007).

13 Sun Zhe孙喆, *Tianming wangchao*天命王朝 (Beijing: 中国青年出版社, 2008).

generally, the concept refers to a specific form of Heaven worship involving the complete destruction of offerings via burning. Heaven worship has been the only recognized state religion in pre-modern China, and *yinsi* was performed exclusively by the emperor during major state ceremonies.

Sheji is an ancient political-theological expression which appeared no later than the Warring States period (476 BCE– 221 BCE), and remains in common use in China as a term for the state. The first character "she" (社) in *sheji* refers to the Altar of the Land; and the second character "ji" signifies the Altar of the Grain. The two altars had to be built adjacent to the ancestral temple of the ruling clan, and were used for solemn state rites praying for fecund land and good harvest. The two characters making up the word *sheji* explicitly channel the two-fold significations of the state. That the concept of the state is both materially grounded vis-à-vis necessities and labor, and also theologically maintained through faith and ritual. Thus, the constitutive order of the state understood as *yinsi-sheji* deals with those rituals sanctioned by the sovereign power that are performed in public contexts.

According to official historical records compiled during the Zhou dynasty (1046 BC–256 BC), Shang was the second Chinese dynasty preceded by the quasi-legendary Xia dynasty (*c.*2070 BC–1600 BC). However as there are no conclusive archaeological records proving the existence of the Xia dynasty, Shang is so far the earliest confirmed Chinese dynasty in that the earliest written record were dated to this era. Written artifacts excavated from Shang archaeological sites were predominantly in the form of oracle bone script. These writings were used specifically during state divination ceremonies where the Shang ruler, both acting as a king and as a high priest, would carve scripts concerning matters of state importance (such as military affairs, prayers for bountiful harvest, and matters concerning sacrificial offerings) onto specially prepared tortoise carapaces and cow bones.[14]

The Shang king would then prod the oracle bones with a red-hot bronze rod, which would cause the bones to crack under the intense heat, indicating that the singular supreme deity of the Shang people, Shang-Di (上帝, lit.: "supreme high Lord") had answered the questions inscribed on the bones, and the cracks left on the bones were supposedly Shang-Di's divine answers. Only the Shang king could interpret these and announce them to his people as divine mandates.

Oracle bone script is the earliest known fully developed Chinese writing system.[15] Despite its age, the oracle bone script is nonetheless a highly developed iconographic form of writing, which is partially mutually intelligible with contemporary Chinese characters, and also shares similar syntactical framework with classical-written Chinese. Thus, despite its ancient origin, the oracle script is legible to modern-day archaeological scholars, perhaps due to the fact that it is, like contemporary Chinese, a purely logographic medium that transmits meaning

14 Institute of Archaeology, Chinese Academy of Social Sciences/ 中国社会科学院考古研究所, *Yinxu yu Shang wenhua – Yinxu kexue 80 zhounian jinian wenji* / (Beijing: Kexue Chubanshe / 科学出版社, 2011).

15 Ibid.

without relying on phonetic representation, and therefore has remained relatively static across millennia.[16]

Current understandings of Shang religious practices, mostly based from a large body of surviving written records from Shang and the subsequent Zhou dynasties, suggest that an amalgamation of ancestor worship, natural totemic and shamanistic practices were present in the Shang society. However, the religion practiced by the Shang ruling class was distinctly monotheistic in character, of which the Shang-Di (lit. "Lord above") is recognized as the one and only divine Lord (Di). Shang political theology frames Shang-Di as an incorporeal, omnipresent, and omnipotent metaphysical deity who wields absolute power over all human, natural and spiritual forces. While the Shang people viewed the spiritual domain (e.g. spirit of dead ancestors) as an extension of the human world that was readily accessible, the divine will of Shang-Di was considered radically inaccessible except through the divination of the Shang king.[17]

A sizable portion of the oracle bones uncovered in Shang archaeological sites contain inscriptions, known as oracle bone scripts, specifically concerning ritual human sacrifices performed by the Shang ruling class.[18] These written records are also corroborated by the discovery of numerous mass-graves of human sacrifice victims in these sites. In most Shang sacrificial rituals, only animals and valuable chattel (such as bronze wares) would be used as offerings. There were only two exceptional circumstances where human sacrifices were made: *xunzang* 殉葬 and *renji* 人祭. Xunzang 殉葬 (lit. "suicide burial") refers to the practice in which personal slaves and servants of Shang king, upon the death or their master, were expected to "volunteer" themselves to be buried alive as a form of "honor suicide."

While the practice of "honor suicide" upon the master's death has lingered throughout Chinese history, the second type of human sacrifice, *renji* 人祭 (lit. "human offering") is practiced only during the Shang dynasty period, and also the most massive in scale in terms of the number of people killed in a typical *renji* ceremony. The demographic pattern of Shang sacrificial victims is also quite interesting. Sacrificial burial victims (or supposedly "pious volunteers") were mostly personal slaves (i.e. house servants), and therefore, in sacrificial burial archaeological sites in China, an even mix of male and female human remains could be found. Renji victims, on the other hand, appear to be predominantly male. Unlike sacrificial burial or *xunzang*, the people sacrificed for *renji* were not personal slaves, but mostly prisoners of war and field slaves (keep in mind that Shang field slaves were typically captured from distant lands outside the Shang domain).[19]

16 GAO Ming 高明, *Zhongguo Guwenzi Xuetonglun* 中国古文字学通论 (Beijing: Peking University Press, 1996). *See also*, Chen Qiyun 陈启云, "封建与大一统之间——关于中国传统政体的理论和史实," 学术月刊 2 (2007).

17 *ZHOU Gong*, 周禮 / *Zhou Li* (-1105 BC.), vol. 12, "春官宗伯/Chunguan zongbo" (Chinese Text Project: last accessed July 7, 2017), available: https://ctext.org/library.pl?if=en&res=77333&by_node=36554

18 Wang Ping and Wolfgang Kubin, 甲骨文与殷商人祭 / *Oracle bone inscriptions and human sacrifice during the Yinshang period / Jia gu wen yu Yin Shang ren ji.*

19 Figures 2.2.1–2.2.7: Guo Moruo 郭沫若(ed), *Jiaguwen Heji* 甲骨文合集 (Beijing: 中华书局影印本, 1980–1983), 1079. *See also, generally*, Wang Ping and Wolfgang

Specifically, studies found that Shang dynasty human sacrifice functioned as prayers to Shang-Di to deliver the Shang people from major calamity. This type of sacrifice involving the killing of humans would only take place during periods of severe food shortage, usually due to drought or war (see Table 2.1 below). Hundreds of captured slaves might be executed during a ritual sacrifice ceremony by means of mass executions (see Figure 2.2.6) and/or blood-letting.[20] The corpses of the victims, along with their severed heads, were buried in mass sacrificial pits or collectively incinerated, in order to placate what they thought was an angry Shang-Di.[21]

To pray for the end of the famine brought by Shang-Di's wrath, the Shang king would demonstrate to the supreme deity of their devoutness through the specular spilling of sacrificial human blood. Oracle bone inscriptions refer to such sacrificial human blood as *qiu* (氿, "torrent"), but the precise method for extracting the sacrificial blood remains unknown. The largest recorded human sacrifice of this kind was done by Shang king Wuding, where over 9,000 slaves were slaughtered as offerings to Shang-Di.[22]

It is important to note that the kind of large-scale human sacrifice practiced by Shang rulers, though extraordinary in terms of its high degree of institutionalization at such an early stage of human history, is not historically idiosyncratic. Human sacrifice rituals similar to that of *renji* were also found pre-Columbian Mesoamerica, most notably in Mayan and Aztec societies.[23] Georges Bataille has already performed in-depth analyses on the political economy of ritual human killings in the Aztec empire.[24]

In the mid-16th century, Texcoco King Ixtlilxochitl of the Aztec Empire introduced an highly institutionalized form of ritual warfare, known as the "Flower War" (Nahuatl: *xōchiyāōyōtl*), for the purpose of calendrical population control during periods of famine.[25] In 1519, Spanish conquistador Bernal Díaz del Castillo, who accompanied Hernán Cortés during their expedition into present-day central Mexico, recorded the following conversation between Cortés and two Texcoco nobles on king Ixtlilxochitl's response to the Famine of Year 1 Rabbit (1454):

Kubin, 甲骨文与殷商人祭 / *Oracle bone inscriptions and human sacrifice during the Yinshang period / Jia gu wen yu Yin Shang ren ji.*

20 Guo Moruo 郭沫若(ed), *Jiaguwen Heji* 甲骨文合集 (Beijing: 中华书局影印本, 1980–1983), fragments 1079, 1027 and 32035.

21 Wang Ping and Wolfgang Kubin, 甲骨文与殷商人祭 / Oracle Bone Inscriptions and Human Sacrifice during the Yinshang Period / *Jia gu wen yu Yin Shang ren ji.*

22 Yang Baocheng / 楊寶成, *Yin xu wen hua yan jiu* / 殷墟文化研究 (Taipei: Taiwan gu ji chu ban she, 2004), 20–25.

23 Vera Tiesler and Andrea Cucina, "New Perspectives on Human Sacrifice and Ritual Body Treatments in Ancient Maya Society," *Interdisciplinary Contributions to Archaeology* (New York: Springer, 2007). See also, generally, Diego de Landa, *Yucatan Before and After the Conquest*, Vol. 20 (New York: Dover Publications, 1978).

24 See generally, Georges Bataille, *The Accursed Share: An Essay on General Economy* (New York: Zone Books, 1988).

25 Barry L. Isaac. "The Aztec 'Flowery War': A Geopolitical Explanation," *Journal of Anthropological Research* Vol. 39, No. 4 (1983).

Table 2.1 Examples of Oracle bone inscription on ritual human sacrifice in mid to late Shang period China (*c*.1250BC – 1046BC)

Renji *sacrifice method*	*Oracle bone ID*	*Oracle bone inscription*	*Translation*
Beheading Oracle bone glyph: (*Fá*) 	*Heji* 16131-front[1]	 (Figure 2.2.1)	"Should the King offer human beheadings (for rain)?Affirmed (by ancestral spirit). Humans beheaded and cattle slaughtered on the day of *Yichou*.Divined, it rained on the following day of *Guichou*."
	Heji 456-front[2]	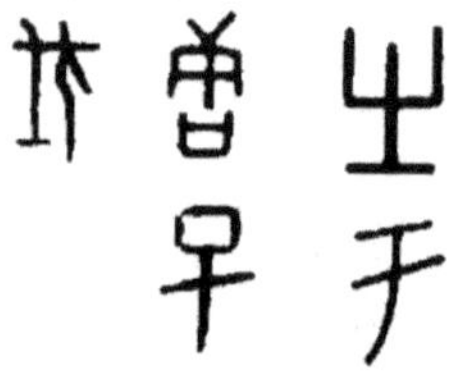 (Figure 2.2.2)	"Should human beheadings be offered to *Tangzi* (name of ancestor)?"
	Heji 1079[3]	 (Figure 2.2.3)	"On the day of *Jiachen*, humans were (beheaded) and buried at the hour of *Wu* (for rain).It rained on the day of *Beingwu*."
Waist chop (severing the body at the waist) Glyph:(*Mǎo*) 	*Heji* 32093[4]	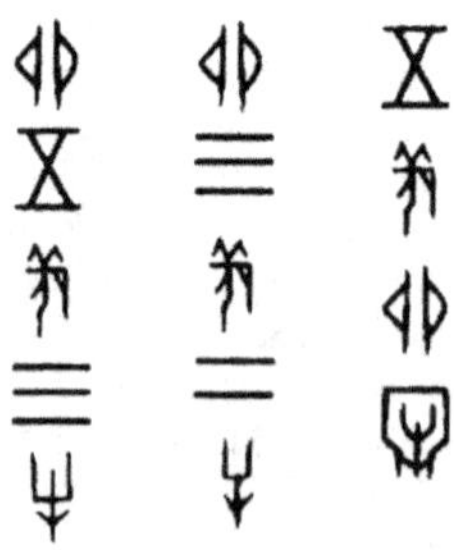 (Figure 2.2.4)	"There are five *Qiang* (nomadic tribes to the west of Shang domain) war captives.Shall we waist chop three captives and slaughter two cattle (as offerings)? Or shall we waist chop five captives and slaughter three cattle?"

Renji *sacrifice method*	*Oracle bone ID*	*Oracle bone inscription*	*Translation*
Dismemberment (*via* chopping) Glyphs:(*Chuí*) 	*Heji* 438-front[5]	 (Figure 2.2.5)	"Divining on the day of *Wuchen*, Lord *Zhen* inquires, should *Qiang* captives be dismembered as offerings to *Bi-geng* (name of ancestor)?"
and (Cè) 	*Heji* 1027-front[6]	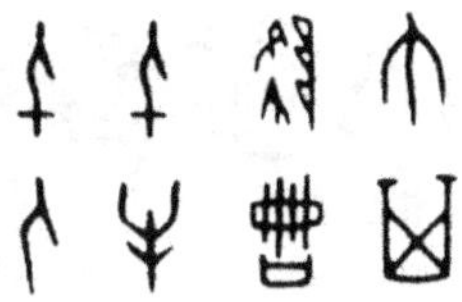 (Figure 2.2.6)	"Shall one thousand cattle and one thousand humans be offered via dismemberment?"
Burning Glyph:(*Jiāo*) 	*Heji* 9177-front[7]	 (Figure 2.2.7)	"Divining now, at day of *Bingxu*, should female servants be burnt as offerings to bring rain?"

1 Guo Moruo 郭沫若(ed), *Jiaguwen Heji* 甲骨文合集 (Beijing: Zhonghua Book Company, 1980–1983), 2227.
2 Guo Moruo, *Heji,* 108.
3 *Ibid.*, at 301
4 *Ibid.*, at 3909.
5 *Ibid.*, 104.
6 *Ibid.*, 288.
7 *Ibid.*, 1331.

The Triple Alliance [Aztec Empire] sometimes defeated them and killed them, and carried off many…for sacrifice, many of the enemy were also left dead…and others made prisoners, and that they [Aztec Empire] never could come so secretly that they [the Tlaxcalans] did not get some warning, and that…they mustered all their forces and with the help of…Huexotzinco they defended themselves and made counter attacks. That as all the provinces…raided by Montezuma and placed under his rule were ill disposed towards the Mexicans…they did not fight with goodwill; indeed, it was from these very men that they [the Tlaxcalans] received warnings,

> and for this reason they had defended their country...[T]he priests...of Mexico-Tenochtitlan said that the gods were angry at the empire, and that to placate them it was necessary to sacrifice many men, and that this had to be done regularly...[26]

Mesoamerican Codices from the early European contact era, such as *Codex Ixtlilxochitl,* are particularly helpful in explaining the ritual practices of pre-Colombian Nahuas, as many of them were both Classical Nahuatl and Spanish.[27] Large-scale human sacrifices depicted in these codices, typically in the form of mass-behead-

Figure 2.3 Ritual bloodletting and land transfer: Mayan ruler Yaxun B'alam IV (752–768) standing over a captive nobleman who is performing non-fatal ritual bloodletting. The bloodletting sealed the capitulation agreement, which formally transferred the territory of the surrendering faction to the winning faction. (Lintel 16 from Yaxchilan ruins, British Museum Collections)

26 Barry L. Isaac, "The Aztec 'Flowery War' A Geopolitical Explanation," 416–417.
27 John B. Glass "A Survey of Native Middle American Pictorial Manuscripts," article 22, *Guide to Ethnohistorical Sources* Part 3; *Handbook of Middle American Indians* (University of Texas Press, 1975).

ings and bloodlettings of war captives, revolve much more closely around spoils of war and conquests rather than arcane "superstition."[28]

Human sacrifice rituals similar to that of Shang dynasty rulers of China were also practiced by the Mayans. To be sure, Mayan political theology was quite different from that of the Shang dynasty China, with each side embodying a heterogeneous set of religious practices. For instance, monotheistic themes that were prevalent in Shang rituals are notably absent in Mayan *mythos*. Furthermore, in contrast with the abundant textual records that remain from the Shang dynasty, much of classical Mayan mythology was destroyed during the Spanish conquest, and the few surviving pre-Columbian Mayan written artifacts remain largely undeciphered. Nonetheless, when looking at mythical rituals in the specific form of large-scale human sacrifices, it is possible to delineate a relatively large set of common elements between the two otherwise distinct civilizations.[29]

Unlike those Shang rulers, whose practice of ritual human sacrifice has long been well-established by historical records, human sacrifice in Mayan culture remained relatively unknown and received little scholarly attention until the late 20th century. Pre-Columbian Mesoamerican human sacrifice only became widely studied after the 1970s, when archaeologists began to uncover large amounts of new textual and archaeological evidence that shed light on Mesoamerican sacrificial practices.[30] Whereas the practice of ritual human sacrifice in pre-Columbian Mesoamerica was previously thought to be limited to the Aztec culture, whose imperial reign over the Valley of Mexico lasted from *c*.1400 AD to 1521 AD, it is now evident that such practices were prevalent in Mayan culture centuries prior to that of Aztecs.[31] Current findings indicate that ritual human sacrifice was continuously present in Mayan city-states throughout the Yucatán regions from the Classic period (*c*.200 AD – *c*.900 AD) up until the arrival of Spanish colonial forces in the 16th century.[32]

Unlike the Shang dynasty, the classical Mayan region has never been unified under the sustained rule of a dominant clan. Instead, Pre-Columbian era Mayan societies existed as multiple mutually independent city-states.[33] Classical Mayan city-states were organized around numerous densely populated and sophistically

28 Francisco Ximénez, Fernando de Alva Ixtlilxóchitl, and Marshall N. Peterson. *The Highland Maya in Fact and Legend: Francisco Ximénez, Fernando Alva De Ixtlilxóchitl, and Other Commentators on Indian Origins & Deeds.* Lancaster, CA: Labyrinthos, 1999.

29 Vera Tiesler and Andrea Cucina, "New Perspectives on Human Sacrifice and Ritual Body Treatments in Ancient Maya Society." See also, generally, Diego de Landa, *Yucatan Before and After the Conquest* Vol. 20 (New York: Dover Publications, 1978).

30 Arthur Demarest, *Ancient Maya: The Rise and fall of a Forest Civilization* (Cambridge and New York: Cambridge University Press), 2004.

31 Robert J. Sharer and Loa P. Traxler, *The Ancient Maya*, 6th ed (California: Stanford University Press, 2006). *See also*, Mary Ellen Miller and Karl A. Taube, *An Illustrated Dictionary of the Gods and Symbols of Ancient Mexico and the Maya* (New York: Thames and Hudson, 1997), introduction.

32 Vera Tiesler and Andrea Cucina, *New Perspectives on Human Sacrifice and Ritual Body Treatment in Ancient Maya Society* (Springer, 2007).

33 Robert J. Sharer and Loa P. Traxler, *The Ancient Maya*.

Figure 2.4 Human sacrifice and wealth transfer: sketch of Stela 6 from Mayan site in Copan, Honduras, collection of Peabody Museum of Archaeology and Ethnology at Harvard University. A typical elite household stela erected for commemorating war victory and the acquisition land and slaves.

developed urban areas. Those urban areas served as centers for politics, commerce and religion, and they were the sites where Mayan priest-kings performed human sacrifice ceremonies. Victims of human sacrifice in Mayan societies were typically war captives and slaves. The stela shown in Figure 2.4 stood inside an elite residential neighborhood of the city due-west of major public buildings. This stela is associated with commemorating warfare, the capture of slaves, and blood sacrifice. The inscriptions on this stela records ritual blood sacrifice on May 8, AD 682. Scholars believe an elite household was awarded the privilege of erecting this monument by the Mayan king. The erection of these sacrificial monuments, as seen from the example of Stela 6 of Copan, was exclusively reserved for those elite households in the Mayan city.[34]

Similar to Shang dynasty China, human sacrifice rites practiced in Mayan city-states were organized as large-scale and elaborately choreographed public spectacles. A detailed first-person account of the Mayan human sacrifice spectacle was written by the 16th century Spanish Catholic priest Diego de Landa, who conducted valuable early studies on Mayan religious practices and public rituals during his tenure as the Bishop of Yucatán:

> When the day of the ceremony arrived, they [the sacrificial victims] assembled in the court of the temple; if they were to be pierced with arrows their bodies were stripped and anointed with blue, with a miter on the head. When they arrived before the demon, all the people went through a solemn dance with him around the wooden pillar, all with bows and arrows, and then dancing raised him upon it, tied him, all continuing to dance and took at him… If his heart was to be taken out, they conducted him with great display and concourse of people, painted blue and wearing his miter, and placed him on the rounded sacrificial stone. …then the falcon executioner came, with a flint knife in his hand, and with great skill made an incision between the ribs on the left side, below the nipple; then he plunged in his hand

34 Cast of Mayan Stela 6 from Copan, Honduras. (*Collection of Peabody Museum of Archaeology and Ethnology at Harvard University*).

> and like a ravenous tiger tore out the living heart, which he laid on a plate and gave to the priest; he then quickly went and anointed the faces of the idols with that fresh blood. At times they performed this sacrifice on the stone situated on the top step of the temple, and then they threw the dead body rolling down the steps, where it was taken by the attendants, was stripped completely of the skin save only on the hands and feet; then the priest, stripped, clothed himself with this skin and danced with the rest. This was a ceremony with them of great solemnity. The victims sacrificed in this manner were usually buried in the court of the temple...[35]

It is also evident from contemporaneous records as well as present-day scholarship that although human sacrifice was of great political and religious importance in pre-Columbian Mesoamerican societies, it was nonetheless performed as occasional spectacle rather than everyday religious ritual. Similar to the case of the Shang, most Mayan religious sacrificial practices only involved non-human offerings such as animals. Ritual mass killings of human beings were reserved only for two types of situations – the killing of enemy captives in victory celebrations, and the mass slaughtering of slaves on those rare "occasions of great tribulation" (such as severe drought or flood).[36]

For the most part of the Mayan history, the predominant technique used in their human sacrifice rituals is decapitation – possibly as reenactment of the Xibalba lords – rulers of the Mayan underworld – decapitating the legendary Mayan ancestor twins Hunahpu and Xbalanque. According to writings from Popol Vuh, the oldest surviving pre-Columbian Mayan mythology, the death of the legendary hero twins *Hunahpu* and *Xbalanque* gave birth to the maize god – the mythological signification of the Mayan staple crop. The myth of sacrifice as a precondition for civilizational growth is displayed in the Classical Period Mayan religious artifacts. A representative example of such depictions can be found on Classic Mayan ceramic pattern on Vessel K1081 from Maya Vase Database, FAMSI, showing mother of the Mayan hero twins, entangled by Mayan maize god's serpent leg, standing before the lords of Xibalba.[37] The well-known "removing the heart" methods were only found to be commonly practiced during the later stages of Mayan civilization, possibly due to rising Aztec influences.

To ground the discussion in further historical context, let us move our focus to the Age of Classical Antiquity in the West. The tale on the *Trick at Mekone* as recorded in the Hesiod's *Theogony*[38] exemplified a "rational-instrumental" ritual ideal type, where the ritual sacrifice itself is explicitly designed and performed as a rhetorical strategy for specific gains. *Mekone* refers to the place where Prometheus and Zeus arranged to meet and settle the matter of dividing sacrificial offerings between gods and humankind.[39]

35 Diego de Landa, *Yucatan Before and After the Conquest*, 51. De Landa also provided more detailed context for the ritual at page 51.

36 Diego de Landa, *Yucatan Before and After the Conquest*, 48–51.

37 Justin Kerr, n.d. Maya Vase Database, FAMSI: available: http://research.famsi.org/kerrmaya.html

38 Hesiod, Theogony, trans. Norman Oliver Brown. Vol.36 (New York: Indianapolis, IN: Bobbs-Merrill Co, 1953), 590–593.

39 Hesiod, *Theogony*, 590–591.

As narrated in the *Theogony*, Prometheus artfully divided a sacrificed ox into two piles– one appears to be a grotesquely bloated stomach with all of the ox's edible meat hidden inside; the other is beautifully glazed with fat but contains nothing more than inedible scraps. Prometheus then invited Zeus to "have the first pick" between the two, and Zeus chose the pile of scraps. Angered by Prometheus's deceit, Zeus took fire away from human world, leaving humans no choice but to eat their meat raw.[40] In the narrative of the mythology, the agency that Prometheus possesses is not merely the knowledge of formal aspects of the ritual. He is also fully aware of the substantive functions those ritual forms and the instrumentality of sacrifice. Prometheus operated on a knowledge basis that provides him the agency not merely to perform sacrifice as a ritual repetition, but also to rhetorically design and deploy the ritual for instrumental gains.

This ritual-instrumentalism expressed in *Theogony* is reflected in the historical schematization of ritual sacrifice during classical Greek period, where two formal modes of sacrifice have been developed: *holokaustos* [41] or apotropaic sacrifice via total oblation, and *Thysia* [42] or "celebrative sacrifice." *Holokaustos,* sometimes spelled "holocaustos" (ὁλόκαυστος from ὅλος "whole" and καυστός "burnt"), is the ancient Greek term for a non-calendrical type of animal sacrifice. They were performed as apotropaic magic to ward off evil, in which an entire livestock animal, usually a goat or ox, is burned up as an offering. *Thysia* (θυσία, celebrative sacrifice) were calendrical festive events where animal offerings were prepared similar to the one by Prometheus in the *Trick of Mekone.* [43] During a *thysia* rite, only the non-edible portion of the sacrificed animal were burnt as offerings to the gods, and the rest of the animal was consumed by the worshippers during a community feast.[44]

The exigential dichotomization of celebratory and apotropaic magic also applies for human sacrifices. There are instances of human *total oblation* where human life itself is the offering to be ritually taken by institutions of power. Capital punishment and warfare are among the most historically enduring (and ritually complex) examples of this *oblative* form of human sacrifice. There are also instances of *modified* human sacrifice that involve ritual taking of human offerings other than biological life itself. Eminent domain is a representative example of a *modified* form of human sacrifice. It is important to note that *oblative* and *modified* forms of human sacrifice differ only in terms of their lethality as formally prescribed by their ritual framework. Both *oblative* and *modified* human sacrifice involve the ritual suspension of *nomos* (pre-existing formal and customary social protections) for the taking and transfer of resources of human value. The ritual in this sense functions as an audience-adoption strategy, to regularize those otherwise exceptional and problematic acts of taking.

40 Hesiod, 592–593.

41 Gunnel Ekroth, *The Sacrificial Rituals of Greek Hero-Cults in the Archaic to the Early Hellenistic Period* (Belgium: Presses Universitaires de Liège, 2002), 215–301, http://books.openedition.org/pulg/503

42 Ekroth, *The Sacrificial Rituals of Greek Hero-Cults in the Archaic to the Early Hellenistic Period*, 11.

43 Sarah Peirce, "Death, Revelry, and 'Thysia'," *Classical Antiquity* Vol. 12, No. 2 (October, 1993), 219–266.

44 Peirce, "Death, Revelry, and 'Thysia'," 220.

These two modes of ancient Greek sacrifice rituals represent the adaptive strategic framing of sacrifice as the "appropriate" strategic response for different communal exigencies. The underlying exigence for *thysia* serves similar ends as all calendrical feasts of religious and traditional nature; that is, to seek to inculcate commonly held values and norms of behavior via predetermined activities revolving around collective food preparation and consumption, thereby automatically implying, via repetition, a collective sense well-being and continuity with their shared memory. As Freud observed in his study of *Totem and Taboo,* "the killing of a sacrificial animal originally belonged to those acts which were forbidden to the individual and were only justified if the whole kin assumed the responsibility."[45] Not only are livestock animals often far too large to be consumed by a single person or family, they are also valuable means of production for the entire community economy. In addition to their direct by-products (e.g. milk, wool), the community also rely on livestock to plow the land and transport goods.[46]

Holokaustos, however, are non-calendrical, solemn ceremonies responding to an entirely different category of public exigence. Historical records show that *holokaustos* rituals were performed primarily as apotropaic magic – to ward off impending catastrophe or impending doom.[47] The ancient Greek differentiation of *holokaustos* and *thysia* sacrifice rituals is also reflected in the stoic dichotomization[48] of catastrophe into *ekpyrosis* (ἐκπύρωσις, lit. "conflagration") and *kataklysmos* (κατακλυσμός, inundation).[49] According to Thomas Rosenmeyer's research on the stoic cosmology, *ekpyrosis* symbolizes the cyclical crisis that burns away ossified elements of the collective memory, and through its destructive force creates a *tabula rasa* for the renewal of the life world. *Kataklysmos* on the other hand is anti-natalistic, signifying the "total destruction of everything that makes life worth living."[50] The interplay between *ekpyrosis* and *kataklysmos* is critical in the rhetorical shaping of ritual response to differently perceived public exigencies.

In substance, *holokaustos* sacrifice typically involves the total destruction of an entire animal, typically a goat via burning, presumably to appease the god(s)' anger over human selfishness. The animal used in this type of sacrifice is known as a "scapegoat." The concept of the scapegoat is far older than Hellenistic civilization

45 Sigmund Freud, *Totem and Taboo: Resemblances between the Psychic Lives of Savages and Neurotics*, translated by A. A. Brill (New York, NY: Vintage Books, 1961), Chapter 4

46 Freud, *Totem and Taboo*, Chapter 4: "The oldest form of sacrifice, older than the use of fire and the knowledge of agriculture, was therefore the sacrifice of animals, whose flesh and blood the god and his worshippers ate together. It was essential that both participants should receive their shares of the meal."

47 Gunnel Ekroth, *The Sacrificial Rituals of Greek Hero-Cults in the Archaic to the Early Hellenistic Period*, 215–301, available: http://books.openedition.org/pulg/503

48 Thomas G. Rosenmeyer, *Senecan Drama and Stoic Cosmology* (Berkeley, CA: University of California Press, 1989), 149.

49 Rosenmeyer, *Senecan Drama and Stoic* Cosmology, 149, available: http://publishing.cdlib.org/ucpressebooks/view?docId=ft7489p15r&chunk.id=d0e7855&toc.id=&brand=ucpress

50 Rosenmeyer, *Senecan Drama and Stoic* Cosmology, 148.

itself. The religious use of the term is clearly recorded in the Hebrew Bible (or the Old Testament), where a goat was sacrificed to cleanse the people of their sin.[51] The historical use of a scapegoat can be traced back to ritual practices of ancient Mesopotamia, where an actual goat was used as a vehicle of evil to be ritually eliminated (via killing or banishment) from the community.[52]

In the context of ancient Greek ritual practices, historical records suggest that a living human sacrifice was sometimes made instead of an animal, and the term *pharmakos* (φαρμακός, lit. "human-as-medicine") in the context of ancient Hellenistic religion refers to those rituals of sacrifice that use the human as the scapegoat.[53] One famous example of *pharmakos* can be found in the writing fragments of Petronius. It describes an indigent man from the city of Massilia (present-day Marseille in France), who offered himself to be sacrificed in order to cleanse the town of the curse of plague. Citizens of Massilia dressed the man in sacred robe and a leaf crown, paraded him through a cursing crowd, and then murdered him.[54]

Scapegoating is a common form of expiation ritual practiced in many societies and cultures.[55] Whereas the specific ritual element may differ, they invariably involve some collective act of mandatory killing as the "appropriate response" against impending major catastrophe for the whole community, usually performed in the name of purifying communal sins, or avoiding retribution from a higher force.[56] Expiation sacrifice is typically performed with a declaration that a sacred covenant or vow is being broken. Furthermore, there are two types of exigencies commonly associated with expiation sacrifices: [1] The belief that there is an inherently angry higher power that needs constant appeasing; and [2] the belief that human subjects are inherently sinful in the eyes of the higher power, and therefore need constant atonement for their sins.

Ritual killing of human scapegoats in the form of apotropaic magic continued beyond classical antiquity. Even this seemingly "primitive" form of ritual human sacrifice continued in early modern Europe and North America between 17th

51 David P. Wright, *The Disposal of the Impurity: Elimination Rites in the Bible and in Hittite and Mesopotamian Literature* (Atlanta: Scholars Press, 1987), 15–74.

52 Wright, The Disposal of the Impurity: Elimination Rites in the Bible and in Hittite and Mesopotamian Literature (ibid.). See also, Miranda Aldhouse-Green, Dying for the Gods: Human Sacrifice in Iron and Roman Europe (Charleston, SC: Tempus Publishing, 2001).

53 Todd M. Compton, *Victim of the Muses: Poet as Scapegoat, Warrior and Hero in Greco-Roman and Indo-European Myth and History,* Hellenic Studies Series 11 (Washington, DC: Center for Hellenic Studies, 2006), Chapter 1.

54 Compton, *Victim of the Muses: Poet as Scapegoat, Warrior and Hero in Greco-Roman and Indo-European Myth and History*, 3–19.

55 Robert Ritner, *The Mechanics of Ancient Egyptian Magical Practice* (Chicago: The Oriental Institute of Chicago, 1988), 14–28. *See also, generally*, James F. Romano, *The Origin of Aha (also called Bes)* (New York: College Art Association, 1978). See also, Hartwig Atlenmüller, *Die Apotopaia und Die Götter Mitteläg̈yptens* (Munich: Ludwig-Maximilians University, 1965); James Ayres, *Domestic Interiors: The British Tradition, 1500–1850* (New Haven, NJ: Yale University Press, 2003).

56 Maev Kennedy, "Witches' Marks: Public Asked to Seek Ancient Scratchings in Buildings," *The Guardian*. Accessed: October 31, 2016.

century to the early 19th century, especially during the period commonly known as the "Little Ice Age," where those living in Europe and North America were subjected to long periods of time without food. According to historian Brian Fagan, agricultural output in Europe during the late 17th century had dropped so dramatically that "Alpine villagers lived on bread made from ground nutshells mixed with barley and oat flour."[57] Works by historian Wolfgang Behringer also suggested connections between periods of intensive "witch-hunting" practices in Europe and the reduced food security during the early modern period.[58]

The practice of sacrificing the poor and powerless during economic crisis is far from being unique to modern industrial age. Early modern Europe and its colonial countries also witnessed a gradual historical transitioning from the traditional "witch-hunt" mode of apotropaic magic, to a more "modern" juridical approach for scapegoating rituals. We have observed, for example, the emergence of a hybrid mode of scapegoating ritual in colonial North America, combining post-Enlightenment common law criminal procedure with late-medieval apotropaic "witch-hunt" magic. The famous case of the Salem witch trials exemplified this hybrid mode of scapegoating ritual, and signaled the historical transition toward the modern rationalization framework for ritual sacrifice.[59]

Another marked example of this modern-medieval hybrid form of human sacrifice is the summary "trials" and executions of slaves and the poor in 18th century colonial New York, most notably the New York "Slave Conspiracy Trials" in 1741.[60] By the 1740s, Manhattan Island had the second-largest slave population of any city in the Thirteen Colonies.[61] In addition to African slaves, which comprised roughly 20 percent of the city's population, indentured servants and other poor working-class whites together constituted the bulk majority of the city's population growth during that time. The population increase, of course, further compounded the city's already severely constrained food and fuel supply.[62]

Large-scale persecution of the city's poor broke out as early as in spring 1741, shortly after a series of fire incidents took place on the Manhattan Island. More than 200 black slaves and dozens of poor whites were arrested by the city's colonial authority for allegedly "conspiring to burn the city down."[63] A total of thirty four people, two white men and thirty two black men, have been executed

57 Brian M. Fagan, *The Little Ice Age: How Climate Made History, 1300–1850* (New York: Basic Books, 2000).
58 Wolfgang Behringer, "Climatic Change and Witch-hunting: the Impact of the Little Ice Age on Mentalities," *Climatic Change* Vol. 43, No. 1 (1999), 335–351.
59 Cotton Mather, M*emorable Providence, Relating to Witchcraft and Possessions*, originally Printed at Boston in N. England: by R.P., 1689 (Ann Arbor, MI: 2003), available: https://quod.lib.umich.edu/cgi/t/text/text-idx?c=eebo;idno=A50139.0001.001
60 Jill Lepore, *New York Burning: Liberty, Slavery, and Conspiracy in Eighteenth-Century Manhattan* (Penguin: Vintage Books, 2006).
61 James Weldon Johnson, *Black Manhattan* (New York: A. A. Knopf, 1930).
62 Weldon Johnson, *Black Manhattan*, ibid.
63 Daniel Horsmanden, *A Journal of the Proceedings in the Detention of the Conspiracy* (Gilder Lehrman Collection, 1744): GLC04205.01

following the crackdown. Daniel Horsmanden, Chief Judge of the New York Supreme Course of Judicature, who presided the New York Slave Conspiracy Trials of 1741, delivered the following opining during the sentencing proceedings for the two white "conspirators:"

> You both now stand convicted of one of the most horrid and detestable pieces of villainy, that ever Satan instilled into the heart of human creatures to put in practice; ye, and the rest of your colour, though you are called slaves in this country; yet are you all far from the condition of other slaves in other countries; nay, your lot is superior to that of thousands of white people. You are furnished with all the necessaries of life, meat, drink, and clothing, without care, in a much better manner than you could provide for yourselves, were you at liberty; as the miserable condition of many free people here of your complexion might abundantly convince you. What then could prompt you to undertake so vile, so wicked, so monstrous, so execrable and hellish a scheme, as to murder and destroy your own masters and benefactors? Nay, to destroy root and branch, all the white people of this place, and to lay the whole town in ashes.[64]

Similar to the earlier Salem witch trials in colonial Massachusetts, those arrested were expressively tried and convicted in the New York Supreme Court of Judicature, and unconventional execution method was used against some of those misaccused.[65] In addition to hanging, which was the typical method of capital punishment of the time, thirteen black men were singled out burned alive at the stake a little east on Magazine Street. Their method of execution was decidedly less juridical, with more than 100 people exiled, hanged, and burned alive at the stake.[66]

Preliminary thesis on the rhetoric of ritual sacrifice

At this point, it might be appropriate to step briefly away from the minutiae of Shang and Mayan mythical practices to instead look at the larger picture of human sacrifice. The practice of human sacrifice and ideas justifying these violent rituals mutually shape and maintain each other. Even if violence is an inherent human condition, personal violent compulsions can only be transformed into collective rituals via collectively shared beliefs. Furthermore, effects of this dialectical relationship between sacrificial practices and their corresponding *mythos* are not contained within the sphere of religious life.

64 Ibid.

65 Historical Society of the New York Courts, "Daniel Horsmanden: Judge and Chief Judge of the New York Supreme Court of Judicature, 1737–1777," available: http://www.nycourts.gov/history/legal-history-new-york/legal-history-eras-01/history-era-01-horsmanden.html.

66 Edwin Hoey, "Terror in New York – 1741," *American Heritage*, June 1974.

Collective ideas, even in the form of "religious superstitions," do not simply emerge from thin air *ad libitum*; rather, they both inflect upon and reflect a given society's political and economic conditions. Preponderance of records and scholarship show that ancient ritual sacrifices in Shang and Mayan societies were not idiosyncratic incidents, but enduring repetitions of strictly regulated and carefully staged spectacles of ceremonial violence. While arguing for explicit manipulative intentions on the part of Shang and Mayan rulers might run the risk of over-instrumentalizing and over-rationalizing their sacrificial practices, it is nonetheless difficult to overlook the powerful functioning of religious ritual in the maintenance of society, even without the presence of such explicit motives.[67]

In theology, *ecclesia* (ἐκκλησία, "ministry") is used to describe local ministries as well as in broader sense all members of a faith organized under a common religious institution. Here I would like to borrow the theological term *ecclesia* precisely because a full-fledged faith society society functions similarly to religious institutions – both require the interdependent presence of formal doctrines and practicing believers.

Consider the following example: imagine you are trying to establish a new local Southern Baptist Church in your local community. The church building must first adopt the basic aesthetic form of a protestant institution. It must ensure its physical design, core mission statement, teachings, and ritual practices adhere to the commonly recognized premises of Southern Baptism and the larger protestant community, for a failure to do so would result in the ministry being seen as illegitimate by its peers. Finally, even when the church building is designed and organized in ways that perfectly conform to protestant taste and Southern Baptist conventions, it is not a functional *ecclesia* without any visiting patrons and attending pastors. Similarly, secular institutions, however perfectly designed, cannot be considered fully functional without a corresponding community that actually believes and practices its legitimacy. The *ecclesia* or legal order of a polity thus represents the integration of constitutional *dóxa* with socially embedded *pístis* (or identification frameworks for persuasion).

Indeed, organized religious communities and secular rule-of-law societies are organized around similar operating principles. Their proper functioning is dependent on two conditions: The first is the "good faith" of the commons – that personal ego and habits are restrained under a self-referencing set of collective core values and beliefs. The second condition is the ritual repetition – that those shared core values are maintained via enforcement of laws that reflect the material condition and pressing needs of the community. The authority of both the ecclesiastical body and the constitutional state are bound by their laws precisely because the laws themselves reflect the set of basic principles that the authority organizes itself upon. This interconnectedness between collective belief, collectively observed

67 James Carey, "Communications and Economics," first published 1994, from *James Carey: A Critical Reader*, edited by Eve Stryker Munson, and Catherine A. Warren (University of Minnesota Press: 1997): "A ritual view of communication is directed not toward the extension of messages in space but toward the maintenance of society in time; not the act of imparting information but the representation of shared beliefs."

rituals, and collective legal consciousness in fact has been succinctly echoed in Rousseau's writings in defense of classical republicanism, where Rousseau used the metaphor of "general will" in describing the sovereignty as a belief community.

While the concept of violence can be extremely broad, context driven, and self-contradictory, it is nonetheless sufficient to say that ritual often functions as a rule-framework for conducting violent social transactions. Historical records have shown that communally practiced ritual sacrifices are often strategically formulated responses to various material exigencies – issues concerning the distribution of resources among community members. A given society has intrinsic material constraints; conflicts arise from allocation, distribution and management of resources within a community. Resources mobilized by a community are primarily factors of production: productive space (land, water, and air), raw material, means of labor (infrastructure, instruments), labor, knowledge. Yet the mobilization of these productive forces also brings corresponding destructive forces: pollution of land/water/air, depletion of raw materials, exploitation and alienation of labor, and the abuse of public security apparatuses to list a few.[68]

Ample historical antecedents suggest an intimate link between ritual sacrifice and organized measures for the allocation, distribution and management of resources in a society. It is reasonable to suspect that the intensification of ritual sacrifice, or what social psychologists identified as the intensification of institutionalized *human cannibalistic tendencies*, constitutes a "dark trajectory" in the historical development of organized political community.[69] As Freud famously observed, the core social element of human cannibalism is not the act of eating, but the *act of taking*: "By absorbing parts of the body of a person through the act of eating we also come to possess the properties which belonged to that person."[70]

Ritual sacrifice, both ancient and contemporary, encompasses a complex set of social phenomena involving the mythic justification and ritualization of collective act of taking. While the ritual acts of taking are organized differently to respond to a broad range of *exigences, audience* and *constraints* that might arise, the substantive nature of the act remains the same. It invariably involves some collective acts of seizure, transfer and/or destruction of things of both symbolic and real human significance, including the capture, confinement, mutilation and slaughter of the human body.[71] By defining ritual as a "collective" social action, it does not imply that the actual performance of

68 Thomas W. Blum, "Social Perspectives of Violence," *Michigan Family Review* Vol. 2, No. 1 (1996), pp. 9–23. See also, generally, Walter Burkert, René Girard, Jonathan Z. Smith and Robert Hamerton-Kelley, *Violent Origins: Ritual Killing and Cultural Formation*, ed. Robert G. Hamerton-Kelley (Stanford, CA: Stanford University Press, 1987).

69 Erich S. Fromm, *The Anatomy of Human*, 179: "One phenomenon that has often been quoted as a proof of man's innate destructiveness is that of cannibalism." See also, Sigmund Freud, *Totem and Taboo: Resemblances between the Psychic Lives of Savages and Neurotics*, Chapter 2.

70 Fromm, *The Anatomy of Human Destructiveness*, 179.

71 Burkert et al., *Violent Origins: Ritual Killing and Cultural Formation*, 8.

taking must be carried out by multiple agents. Rather, it refers to the collective phenomenological *identification* of the act as a "reenactment of a prior event."[72]

In other words, ***ritual sacrifice is the rhetorical reenactment of taking***. It is rhetorical in so far as its ritual speaks to a communal audience via repetition that automatically implies continuity with a collective memory, thereby cultivating and reaffirming certain shared values and habits among the audience community. The ritual situation for the public reenactment of sacrifice can be distinguished as a special articulation of the rhetorical situation. The basic components of exigence, audience and constraints remain present. What is different, however, is that the rhetoric of ritual works by deploying anti-rhetorical tropes. The persuasive power of rituals resides in its pretension of being self-referential and self-justifying, and refuses to be subjected to the constraints of reasoning and debate. On the one hand, ritual sacrifice vis-à-vis the collective act of taking has been continually *reenacted* throughout the development of human civilization.[73] On the other hand, the mythic justification framework for this ancient reenactment continuously reinvents and adapts itself to the changing beliefs, senses and sensibilities of its contemporaneous audience.

Ritualistic elements of sacrifice are rhetorical tropes invented in part to suspend the constraints of taboos, by demarcating the *appropriate and proper* occasion for the community-sanctioned destruction of sacred things. In the study of liminality, rituals are known for its role in regulating and normalizing traumatic human experiences. In the context of public liminality, rituals may also serve institutions of authority, by transforming coercive or violent transactions into something that seems inescapable or even palatable. The ritual taking of things that are of human value, including the ritual killing of humans has been continuously practiced for as long as human civilization itself.[74]

Whereas there are many forms of ritual elements in sacrifice, its rhetorical function largely follows a three-stage ritual process for collective identity transition. The first stage entails preliminal rites that are performed to create a condition of collective uncertainty and disorientation. Preliminal rites would involve the rhetoric invention of an exceptional exigence, typically in the form of a disruptive collective emergency (i.e. *jeremiad* of society's imminent downfall). The emergency itself may be actual (i.e. natural disaster) or

72 Burkert et al., *Violent Origins: Ritual Killing and Cultural Formation*, at page 8, where the authors defined the concept of ritual as the "reenactment of a prior event."

73 Burkert et al., *Violent Origins: Ritual Killing and Cultural Formation*. See also, Richard E. DeMaris, "Sacrifice, an Ancient Mediterranean Ritual," *Biblical Theology Bulletin* Vol. 43, No. 2 (2013), 60–73. See also, Michael Rudolph, *Ritual Performances as Authenticating Practices* (Berlin: LIT Verlag Münster, 2008); John Noble Wilford, "Ritual Deaths at Ur Were Anything but Serene," *New York Times*, October 26, 2009; See also, Austine Waddell, *Tibetan Buddhism: With Its Mystic Cults, Symbolism and Mythology, and in Its Relation to Indian Buddhism* (London: W.H. Allen & Co., 1895), 516.

74 Nicola Perugini and Neve Gordon, "Distinction and the Ethics of Violence: On the Legal Construction of Liminal Subjects and Spaces," *Antipode* Vol. 49, No. 5 (Wiley, 2017), pp. 1385–1405.

constructed, but it is framed in ways to justify the suspension of pre-existing social norms and boundaries.

The second stage of liminal transformation involves rituals that organize fragmented society into an apotropaic emergency entity, or a body exigent, in response to the exceptional exigence. The formation and consolidation of this body exigent often involves rituals mandating exceptional forms of sacrifice as the sola fide route of collective salvation.[75] Liminal sacrifices are characterized by their spectacular staging and destructive tendencies, and are staged with artfully framed anti-rhetoric (e.g. claiming infallible sacred authority). However, once the crisis disappears, a totalistic political body organized around common crisis is radically unstable and self-defeating. Without the explicit reminder impending catastrophe, the body exigent and its corresponding instrumental violence would appear arbitrary and unjustifiable.

The liminal stage concludes with the transformation of the body exigent into a permanent state via a self-referential process of double consecration: first consecrating instrumental violence into a "sacred sacrifice;" the act of sacrifice then consecrates the body exigent into a "sacred union." Thus the emergency entity is rendered into a permanent and self-referencing end *state of sacrifice*. It is through sacrifice that a political order is consecrated, and the sacred polity must be defended with more sacrifices.

Postliminal rites would then follow as the *cultus deorum* for maintaining the "cult" of the consecrated *state of sacrifice*. [76] As Cicero famously declared, that cultivation of the sacred required scientia colendorum deorum, or "the science of giving gods their due."[77] Similarly, the sanctity of the *state of sacrifice* is maintained via legislating laws of sacrifice. Postliminal rites are typically deployed to achieve the rhetorical effect of double imputation. The imputation of the sins of the polity to an extra-human power, and the imputation of the higher power's unquestionable righteousness to the polity.

And on this note, I shall close this chapter with the following two quotes by John Stuart Mill and Joel Feinberg, which together best summarized the rationalization framework adapted for the late-capitalist economic worldview:

> If protection against themselves is confessedly due to children and persons under age, is not society equally bound to afford it to persons of mature years who are equally incapable of self-government? If gambling, or drunkenness, or incontinence, or idleness, or uncleanliness, are as injurious to happiness, and as great a hindrance to improvement, as many or most of the acts prohibited

75 The concept of sacrifice as the sola fide route of collective salvation will be closely examined in Chapter 5.

76 *See* M. Tillius Cicero and Andrew R. Dyck (trans.), *De Natura Deorum. Liber 1* (Cambridge: Cambridge University Press, 2003). Cicero famously defined *religio* as *cultus deorum*," or the "cultivation of the gods."

77 Marcus Tullius Cicero, *De Natura Deorum. Liber 1*, trans. Andrew R. Dyck (Cambridge: Cambridge University Press, 2003), 41. See also, Clifford Ando, *The Matter of the Gods* (University of California Press, 2009), 6.

by law, why should not law, so far as is consistent with practicability and social convenience, endeavor to repress these also? And as a supplement to the unavoidable imperfections of law, ought not opinion at least to organize a powerful police against these vices, and visit rigidly with social penalties those who are known to practise them?

John Stuart Mill, *On Liberty* (1859, p. 47)

A single instance of tax evasion – the harm to any given individual is highly dilute and unnoticeable... do have a tendency, of course, to weaken public institutions in whose health we all have a stake, and if they were allowed to become general, the institutions in question would be undermined to our great collective loss.

Joel Feinberg, *Harm to Others* (1984, pp.10–12)

3 Rhetorical invention of laws of sacrifice

This chapter examines the relationship between American judiciary rhetoric and rituals of sacrifice through the analysis of *Kelo v. City of New London*, a 2005 U.S. Supreme Court (SCOTUS) landmark case concerning the regulatory condemnation and seizure of private residences for private commercial redevelopment. Specifically, it examines the rhetorical invention of new laws of sacrifice in the *Kelo* case, where the SCOTUS greatly expanded the scope for the legitimate use of eminent domain.

The analysis of the *Kelo* regulatory condemnation case shows that the SCOTUS assumed neoliberal ideals of governance as the guiding principle in its interpretation of the constitution, and declared private redevelopment satisfies the "public use" requirement under the Fifth Amendment. The act of judicial "interpretation" in *Kelo v. City of New London* substantively amounted to a radical reinvention of the Takings Clause in the Fifth Amendment. This case study also finds that ritual elements played a central role in the rhetorical mechanism of the Supreme Court. The SCOTUS appropriated a wide range of ritual devices in the *Kelo* decision, rendering its expansion of the "law of sacrifice" to seem inescapable and even palatable.

Case background

> The first man who, having enclosed a piece of ground, to whom it occurred to say this is mine, and found people sufficiently simple to believe him, was the true founder of civil society.
>
> – Jean Jacques Rousseau[1]

When cities have far outgrown their original size, and their revenues have increased, all the citizens have a place in the government … and they all, including the poor who receive pay, and therefore have leisure to exercise their rights, share in the administration.

– Aristotle, *Politics* [2]

1 Jean-Jacques Rousseau, *On the Inequality among Mankind. Vol. XXXIV, Part 3.* Trans. Charles William Eliot (New York: P.F. Collier & Son, 1909)

2 Aristotle, *Politics*, trans. Benjamin Jowett (Batoche Books, 1999), Book 4 at 89.

The ritual taking of things that are of human value, including the ritual killing of humans, has been continuously practiced for as long as human civilization itself.[3] Although people in modern society seldom consider ritual sacrifice an ongoing practice, it nonetheless remains an organizing structure in the contemporary institutions of authority. In "Capital Punishment as Human Sacrifice," Roberta Harding highlighted the judicial embeddedness of modern human sacrifice:

> The ritual slaughter of humans for sacrificial purpose has an ancient provenance. Few members of modern society would be inclined to believe that killing humans for sacrificial purposes continues. Of those, most probably envision it only being practiced by individuals who belong to 'uncivilized,' or non-'First-World' cultures. Upon closer scrutiny, however, it becomes apparent that this is a misconception because the past and present practice of capital punishment includes a thinly disguised manifestation of the ritualized killing of people, otherwise known as human sacrifice.[4]

The effective modern reenactment of ritual sacrifice runs much deeper than criminal procedures. Rituals are known for their role in regulating and normalizing traumatic human experiences. In the context of public liminality, rituals may also serve institutions of authority by transforming coercive or violent transactions into something that seems inescapable or even palatable.[5]

This chapter studies the relationship between American judiciary rhetoric and legal rituals of sacrifice. Specifically, it seeks to highlight the rhetorical invention of laws of sacrifice through analyzing *Kelo v. City of New London*, the 2005 U.S. Supreme Court landmark case concerning the eminent domain taking of private residences for private redevelopment.

The basic facts of the case are as follows. In 2000, the City of New London, Connecticut announced a "comprehensive redevelopment plan" for its economically depressed neighborhoods. The city government invoked its eminent domain power to condemn several privately owned residences in the city, and planned to sell seized properties to private developers. The New London city government argued that the purpose of its regulatory takings was to create jobs and raise tax revenue through redevelopment of the seized land. The city government further claimed that the condemned residential neighborhood existed as a financial burden for New London, and its market-driven redevelopment plan would bring economic growth for the city as a whole. The city government argued that commercial redevelopment of low-income residential neighborhood should be considered a valid *public cause* under the Fifth Amendment of

3 See generally, Sigmund Freud, "Civilization and Its Discontents" (London: Penguin, 2002). See also, Walter Burkert, René Girard, Jonathan Z. Smith, and Robert Hamerton-Kelly. *Violent Origin* (Stanford, Calif: Stanford University Press: 1987).

4 Roberta M. Harding, "Capital Punishment as Human Sacrifice: A Societal Ritual as Depicted in George Eliot's *Adam Bede*," 48 Buff. L. Rev. 175 (2000), 175.

5 Walter Burkert, "The Problem of Ritual Killing" in *Violent Origins: Walter Burkert, Rene Girard and Jonathan Z. Smith on Ritual Killing and Cultural Formation*, ed. Robert Hamerton-Kelley (California: Stanford University Press, 1987), pp. 149–176.

Constitution, which permitted the city to invoke its eminent domain authority. As a reference, Amendment V of the U.S. Constitution reads as follows:

> No person shall be held to answer for a capital, or otherwise infamous crime, unless on a presentment or indictment of a Grand Jury, except in cases arising in the land or naval forces, or in the Militia, when in actual service in time of War or public danger; nor shall any person be subject for the same offence to be twice put in jeopardy of life or limb; nor shall be compelled in any criminal case to be a witness against himself, nor be deprived of life, liberty, or property, without due process of law; nor shall private property be taken for public use, without just compensation. (*U.S. Constitution. Amend. V*)

The petitioners, represented by the lead plaintiff Susette Kelo, sued the city government for condemning their private residences, as well as the larger Fort Trumbull neighborhood for mostly commercial purposes. The city planned to sell all 33.1 acres of condemned Fort Trumbull neighborhoods to private developers. The following table lists all parcels seized by the New London city government, and their proposed uses under the Fort Trumbull redevelopment plan. All seized parcels, with the exception of parcel 1 and 2C, were residential neighborhoods:

The petitioners argued that the city's actions violated the Fifth Amendment's "public use" requirement, which prohibits government from taking private properties except for public use and with just compensation. The Connecticut state court ruled in favor of the city government in 2002, and the case was then forwarded to the Supreme Court of the United States (SCOTUS). On June 23,

Table 3.1 Condemned Fort Trumbull Parcels and their proposed redevelopment

Seized parcel	*Parcel size*	*Proposed uses*
Parcel 1	9.4 acres	Hotel with conference rooms and waterfront access
Parcel 2A	1.7 acres	Residential (approx. 28 units)
Parcel 2B	1.0 acres	Residential (approx. 16 units)
Parcel 2C	1.3 acres	Residential (approx. 20 units)
Parcel 3A	2.6 acres	Competed 88,000 sq. ft. Fort Trumbull Office Building
Parcel 3B	2.6	Residential (approx. 40 units)
Parcel 3C	4.2	Office/commercial/Parking
Parcel 4A	2.5	Office/hospitality/mixed use
Parcel 5A	2.4	Completed 50,000 sq. ft. L&M Medical Office Building
Parcel 5C-1	2.3	Office/commercial
Parcel 5C-2	3.1	Office/commercial

Source: Renaissance City Development Association, "Fort Trumbull Municipal Development" (2014). Available at http://www.rcda.co/parcel-map/

2005, in a 5–4 decision, the SCOTUS affirmed the Connecticut Supreme Court's decision, and once again ruled in favor of New London.

As evidenced in its majority opinion, the SCOTUS in *Kelo* is well-aware of the fact that the New London government intent to sell and lease those taken houses to private businesses, and that private enterprises are the ones directly benefiting from the city's eminent domain takings. Justice Stevens also acknowledged much of the taken land will not even be accessible to the general public. In his own words:

> this is not a case in which the City is planning to open the condemned land–at least not in its entirety–to use by the general public. Nor will the private lessees of the land in any sense be required to operate like common carriers, making their services available to all comers.

Yet the SCOTUS maintained a particularly broad "reading" of the "public use" requirement for exercising eminent domain, as Justice Stevens argued, "*the public end may be as well or better served through an agency of private enterprise.*"[6]

The SCOTUS in *Kelo v. City of New London* sought to justify its controversial ruling based on the assumption that private business growth would lead to more jobs and tax revenue, thus satisfying the public purpose for seizure of private property. The majority opinion also affirmed a major departure from the "use by the public" as the proper definition of "public use," and insisted that anything that the government could argue served "public interest," and even if for purely commercial development purposes, would satisfy the "public use" requirement under the Fifth Amendment. As Justice Stephens wrote, "[i]ndeed, while many state courts in the mid-19th century endorsed 'use by the public' as the proper definition of public use, that narrow view steadily eroded over time."[7]

The analysis of *Kelo v. City of New London* in this study departs from the main legal issue, or "question of law" of the case, and excavates the relevant belief structures as well as the material exigence underpinning the formal legal dispute. "Material exigence" specifically refers to the relevant facts on the ground that inform tensions in economic interests and allocation of resources. Whereas legal analysis of the case's issues focuses on interpretation of specific legal definitions that are subject to debate, the rhetorical analysis would focus instead on what Lloyd Bitzer calls "objective and publicly observable facts in the world."[8] The analysis would highlight the tensions that exist between formal legal dispute and substantive material exigence in *Kelo v. City of New London* through both extensive excavation of tacit elements and close reading of the SCOTUS opinion for the case.

The analysis also looks into the organizing assemblage surrounding the case. The focus will be on those relevant institutional establishments, their power

6 *Kelo v. City of New London*, 545 U.S. 469 (2005).
7 *Kelo v. City of New London*, 545 U.S. 469 (2005).
8 Lloyd F. Bitzer, "The Rhetorical Situation," *Philosophy & Rhetoric* Vol. 1, No. 1 (January, 1968):1–14, 11.

authority, organizing principles, and actors. The goal for looking into the institutional context is to better understand the organizing rule-framework that bestows the court system with both interpretative (e.g. SCOTUS' exercise of judicial review) and interpellative[9] (e.g. city government's assumed eminent domain authority) authorities. The rhetorical analysis will first discuss the socially embedded belief framework that forms the discursive basis for *Kelo v. City of New London*. The discussion seeks to highlight the ritual embeddedness of the judicial rhetoric operating in *Kelo*, and that judicial *dóxa* often operate in ways parallel to the rhetoric of religion. Following the broad historical discussion, the analysis will move closely to the opinions of SCOTUS in *Kelo*, and identify analogous rhetorical elements between the proceedings of the court and rituals of religious sacrifice. The analysis concludes by locating rhetorical implications of the ritual proceedings in the case, and examines the ways which these rituals were deployed to affirm the sanctity of neoliberal economic policies.

This case study finds that the marketization of regulatory takings of private property and the privatization of the *public purpose* in *Kelo v. City of New London* represent a significant expansion of neoliberal economic logic into domains traditionally resistant to economic liberalization. Private ownership and the free movement of goods and capital are two of the core *doxes* of neoliberalism justifying various privatization policies. Self-contradiction among these *doxes* would arise when, in cases like *Kelo v. City of New London*, the implementation of privatization policy would invariably involve the sacrifice of private home ownership, and the promotion of "free market access" would also involve denying people from accessing their neighborhood. The twin tragedies of the commons/anti-commons implied by the *Kelo* decision also represent a widely adaptable argumentative basis for affirming the sanctity of neoliberal policies, even in cases mandating the sacrifice of those very things that neoliberalism considers to be sacred.

Judicial rhetoric and its underlying belief structures

At the technical legal level, *Kelo v. City of New London* concerns the definition of "public use" and the scope of eminent domain within U.S. legal system. However, the dispute in *Kelo* touches on a fundamental exigence that is at the core of human political community – the sacrifice of individual and/or group interests for the good of the "commons."

Even if we accept the Hobbesian premise that political communities are driven by the mutual interest of peace and security, those common needs are not always met with common adherence to the rules of the "commonwealth." In practice, various particularized interests (e.g. individual, familial, local, factional interests) often enter into conflict with the common interest of the larger political

9 See Louis Althusser's definition of the concept of interpellation, from his essay "Ideology and Ideological State Apparatuses (Notes towards an Investigation)." in *Lenin and Philosophy and Other Essays*, translated from the French by Ben Brewster, Monthly Review Press: 1971.

community.[10] The case of *Kelo v. City of New London*, like any other Supreme Court ruling, represents a slice of the "truth-making" power of the judiciary via its formally organized discursive rituals. Specifically in the *New London* case, this is the reinvention of the "truth" concerning the meaning of "fair public use" in mandating private sacrifices for the common good. The analysis herein proceeds not from the formal legal dimension of the Supreme Court ruling, but from the embedded belief structures that gives SCOTUS its rhetorical capacity to radically redefine the threshold for the suspension of one of the most sacred rights under the U.S. constitutional framework.

The belief structures underpinning the judicial review process and the questions of eminent domain and economic redevelopment should not be reduced to mere "ideologies," or sets of abstract representations that inform and shape who we are. Rather, they are more appropriately understood in the frame of religion and ritual.[11] On a similar vein, works by James Carey also provides a substantive and analytically helpful update to what Carey refers to as the "ritual view" of communication. Most notably, in his 1994 essay "Communications and Economics," Carey locates the "case of communication" within the context of the prevailing mode of economic production and economic relations.

This perspective may seem, at first glance, to be incongruent with the neoliberal, market-driven *topoi* of *Kelo v. City of New London*. Indeed, the historical unfolding of a global market-driven governance system displaced powers of many old religious orders, and in the process made new prophetic declarations for a rational conduct of life and a source of happiness that cut across all human "superstitions." This is evidenced in the *Kelo* decision, for example, where Justice Stephens declared the court had already "*embraced the broader and more natural interpretation of public use as 'public purpose,'* "[12] where the implicit goodness of the market-driven policies is signified with the God-term of "natural order."

It is through its promises of material comfort and life-fulfillment, and through its rationalist epistemic framework, that neoliberalism would justify the global proliferation of market-driven governance. However, we must ask: how could this sweeping material promise retain its persuasive force, especially in times when the promised "good life" cannot be delivered without increasing demands for sacrificial offerings – not only in the form of redevelopment regulatory takings in *Kelo v. City of New London*, but also in the pollution and destruction of viable environments?

The *Book of Job* from the Hebrew Bible illuminates two important lessons concerning the relation between our beliefs and the material conditions we live in: First, which human faith, to a large extent, depends on our material conditions, and it is extremely difficult to remain faithful when facing material reality that contradicts our deeply-held beliefs. Consider the governing regime of Democratic

10 The "common interest" here may be real or alleged.

11 James Carey, "Communications and Economics," first published 1994, from *James Carey : A Critical Reader*, edited by Eve Stryker Munson, and Catherine A. Warren (University of Minnesota Press: 1997).

12 *Kelo v. City of New London*, 545 U.S. 469 (2005)

People's Republic of Korea (North Korea) as a 21st-century example for this condition.[13] Second, it is nonetheless possible for humans to remain faithful to certain principles, even at the cost of great hardship and suffering, as long as the promised material prosperity eventually arrives. Ideals, however appealing, will eventually lose their persuasiveness when they are perceived as being in contradiction with our lived experience. Laws, however perfectly written, will lose their legitimacy without implementation on the ground.

Indeed, classical canons of Western political philosophy have long recognized this intimate relationship between the ideal and material in organizing political communities. Consider the debate between Thrasymachus and Socrates on the nature of a "just state" from Plato's Republic – while they offered disparate justifications for the state's existence, both Thrasymachus and Socrates supported their ideological position by pointing to their perceived material reality.[14] Whereas Thrasymachus claimed that "the just is nothing else than the advantage of the stronger,"[15] Socrates rebutted that the just state is "found in the fact that we do not severally suffice for our own needs, but each of us lacks many things,"[16] and from this material necessity arises "the cause of men uniting themselves at first in civil societies."[17]

The principle of organizing a moral community around a set of rule frameworks has been succinctly reflected in the biblical text, from the formal adoption of God's Ten Commandments via the stone tablets in *Exodus,* to the substantive implementation and administration of those divine Commandments in *Deuteronomy.* [18] The basic principle of the rule of law has been reflected in numerous human traditions and is inseparable from the historical development of law and polity themselves.[19] The proper functioning of both religious doctrines and laws of the state not only demand believers or citizens adhere to their constituting core collective ideals and norms, but the laws themselves also need to reflect the material reality and the pressing needs of their subjects. The authority of both the church and the constitutional state are bound by their laws precisely because the laws themselves

13 Mechon Mamre, "Job," *English Bible According to the Masoretic Text and the JPS 1917 Edition*, available: http://www.mechon-mamre.org/p/pt/pt2701.htm

14 See, Plato, *Republic*, trans. Paul Shorey (Cambridge, MA, Harvard University Press; London, William Heinemann Ltd. 1969), book 1.

15 Plato, *Republic*, 338c

16 Plato, 369b

17 Plato, 369c

18 Mechon Mamre, "Job," *English Bible According to the Masoretic Text and the JPS 1917 Edition*, available: http://www.mechon-mamre.org/e/et/et0.htm

19 Similar to the biblical Ten Commandments stone tablets, the Code of Hammurabi from circa. 1760 BCE is one of the earliest examples where stone-carved laws are presented to the public by the ruler, binding the acts of both the ruler and the people under the same set of collectively held rules. There are also rich traditions of Islamic law and Chinese legalism that embraced the governing principle of the supremacy of law. *See* United Nations, Security Council, *The Rule of Law and Transitional Justice in Conflict and Post-conflict Societies: Report of the Secretary-General*, S/2004/616 (August, 23 2004).

reflect the set of basic principles that the authority organizes itself upon. In both cases, the authority's constituting principles or doctrines represent the expression of the singular, indivisible will of the People or God, through the exercise of the popular or divine sovereignty.

Political communities are organized around rules and procedures to help negotiate tensions among competing interests; these rules are often formalized into laws and/or internalized into tacit truth-framework regulating everyday communal transactions. On the most basic level, the phrase "the rule of law" simply stands in contrast with "the rule of personal will."[20] The supremacy of the law, divine or man-made, implies that these collectively maintained legitimation frameworks, or *písteis*, cannot be inferior to the arbitrary rule of an individual or factions within the community.

Furthermore, the *pístis* of the political community would operate to consecrate, via a series of prescribed procedures and rituals, the *dóxa* of the designated authority as "incontestable mandate." The *dóxa* consecrated by the *pístis* of the state may manifest in diverse forms, such as papal decrees, imperial edicts, executive orders, legislative statutes, and, of course court opinions. Formal differences aside, these laws organize the subjects of the political community by ensuring that commonly held rules, not personal will, serve as the basis for the construction and operation of the polity.

Whereas various expressions of the rule of law framework throughout history may have grown out of similar social necessities,[21] the modern discourse on the rule of law is heavily grounded in the formal relationship between the law and the state, namely the *Rechtsstaat* ("law-state"), where the state (*Staat*) is organized within a constitutional framework that is consistent with internationally recognized governing norms, and serves the rights (*Rechte*) and prerogatives of its citizens.[22] Constitutional democracy thus has become the cornerstone for contemporary rule of law discourse.[23]

As the judiciary constitutes a key institutional component of the law-state, state institutions cannot operate without their embedded organizing principles that recognize the absolute sanctity of the constitutional framework. The constitution, in turn, delegates the sacred and incontestable authority of the Supreme Court as

20 Aristotle and Benjamin Jowett, *Aristotle's Politics* (New York: The Modern library, 1943), book 3 sec. 16: "And the rule of the law, it is argued, is preferable to that of any individual."

21 Aristotle, *Politics*, book 4: "So many kinds of democracies there are, and the grew out of these necessary causes."

22 For the UN, the Secretary-General defines the rule of law as: "A principle of governance in which all persons, institutions and entities, public and private, including the State itself, are accountable to laws that are publicly promulgated, equally enforced and independently adjudicated, and which are consistent with international human rights norms and standards. It requires, as well, measures to ensure adherence to the principles of supremacy of law, equality before the law, accountability to the law, fairness in the application of the law, separation of powers, participation in decision-making, legal certainty, avoidance of arbitrariness and procedural and legal transparency." See Report of the Secretary-General: "The rule of law and transitional justice in conflict and post-conflict societies" (2004), available: http://www.unrol.org/doc.aspx?n=2004%20report.pdf

23 Michel Rosenfeld, "The Rule of Law and the Legitimacy of Constitutional Democracy," *Southern California Law Review* Vol. 74:1307, 1352.

the final interpreter of constitutional doctrines and their applications. In this sense, the classical notion of *pístis,* vis-à-vis communally shared legitimation framework, plays a key role in the maintenance of the rule of law. At moments when conflicts-of-interest arise that will not be resolvable via existing rules of interpretation, the intervention of authoritative power (state or otherwise) is triggered to reinterpret or reinvent the meaning of law.

The sacred consubstantiality of the SCOTUS' opinion rests on two belief conditions. First, there is the *pístis* (legitimating framework) of the U.S. constitution that provides the SCOTUS its exclusive authority as the final interpreter of the law. Whereas the particular expressions of the constitution may be subject to interpretation (provided that such interpretation adheres to the rules prescribed by the constitution itself), the basic premise of a constitution must to be seen as sacred and incontestable in order to maintain a legitimate constitutional order. The sanctity of the constitution therefore is imputed upon the SCOTUS, which provides the incontestable organizing principle of the judicial review. When formally expressed *dóxa* of constitutional interpretation are translated into its local applications, and internalized into the pre-existing *písteis* (tacit societal knowledge) affirming constitutional legitimacy, it is then possible to regulate even exceptionally disruptive transactions, such as the seizure of home, as constitutional inevitabilities.

This naturally brings us to the second belief condition, which has to do with the power to issue irresistible sacrifice. As the SCOTUS pronounces its opinion on the dispute brought before the court, its holding not only decides the meaning of the law, but also transforms the "petitioner" and "defendant" into "prevailing" and "losing" parties of the case. Thus, regardless which side of the dispute the SCOTUS favors, its final judgment triggers the inevitable and inescapable sacrifice of the interest of the "losing" party against the "prevailing" claim. SCOTUS's role as the "court of last resort" implies that the losing party must unconditionally acquiesce to the court's opinion. And the absolute certainty, predictability and constitutional legitimacy of court-mandated sacrifice would in turn consecrate and radicalize the *dóxa* of the course as "sacred opinion" (see the diagram in Figure 3.1 below).

In terms of formalized argumentation style, both judicial and religious doctrine-making tend to involve the art of apologetics – the systematic and formalized defense of *dóxa* for the confirmation of a belief framework.[24] It is important to remember that apologetics is not critical reasoning *per se*, but appropriates rhetorical styles of evidence-based critical reasoning for affirming a certain "Good." The "Good" that apologetics argue an abstract, transcendent *Other* that is not subjected to the positive confirmation or negation via empirical reality. This transcendent "Good" that apologetics seek to affirm is not a concrete thing or idea that we attribute as "being-good," but presumed as "Good-itself," or the source of

24 Joseph Torre, *Apologetics: A Justification of Christian Belief John Frame* (P&R Publishing: 2015). See also, Peter Smith, "Apologetics," in *A Concise Encyclopedia of the Bahá'í Faith* (Oxford: Oneworld Publications: 2000), 39–40.

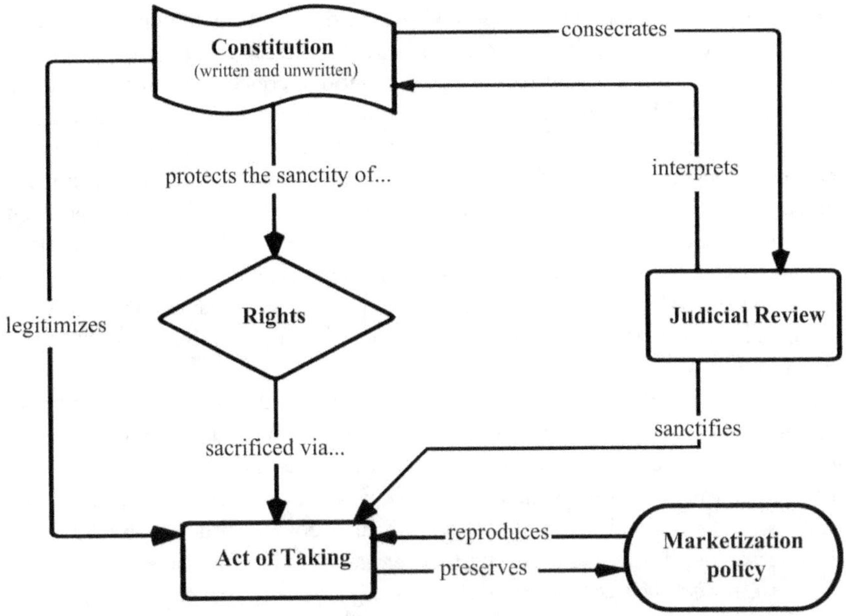

Figure 3.1 Hermeneutic cycle of judicial review process in *Kelo v. City of New London*

other concrete goods. In other words, a rhetoric who engages in apologetics assumes the position as a defender of faith.

As discussed hereinabove, the SCOTUS already generally assumes the apologetics position as the defender of constitutional faith. All constitutional interpretations are presumed to affirm the faith of the constitutional framework. However, in *Kelo v. City of New London*, the SCOTUS also embodied a peculiar second apologetics persona in addition to the general one – it argued with the specific presumption that private redevelopment is a public Good-in-itself that cannot be falsified via material evidence. As Justice Stephens declared:

> Just as we decline to second-guess the City's considered judgments about the efficacy of its development plan, we also decline to second-guess the City's determinations as to what lands it needs to acquire in order to effectuate the project. It is not for the courts to oversee the choice of the boundary line nor to sit in review on the size of a particular project area.[25]

The SCOTUS formally presents itself as a neutral, disinterested interpreter of law. Its decisions are supposedly based on the facts of the case, decided with no predisposition beside the good faith in the constitution itself. Yet in *Kelo v. City of New London*, the majority opinion of the court has made explicit its second

25 Justice Steven's majority opinion in *Kelo v. City of New London*, 545 U.S. 469 (2005).

apologetics persona as the defender of the faith in redevelopment. Aside from departing from its formal constitutional neutrality, the second apologetics persona in *Kelo* also divorces its legal reasoning of economic concepts from their material basis. Economic development, public use, and eminent domain are vocabularies derivative of human economic transactions. Therefore, the goodness of these economic concepts are seldom taken as "Good-in-themselves" *per se*, but qualities subject to the confirmation or disconfirmation of lived material conditions. The separation of economic logic from its material basis in the *Kelo* opinion, in effect, hollowed out the "this-worldliness" of the benefits claimed by the city's redevelopment plan. Material promises of market-driven governance, therefore, are rhetorically transformed into salvation prophecies that are unbound by temporal and empirical constraints.

The SCOTUS in *Kelo v. City of New London* appropriated style of evidence-based reasoning for its judicial opinion (*dóxa*), reasoned that private redevelopment serves the good of public interest. Apologetics in the *Kelo*, similar to its religious counterpart, deployed affirmational argumentative forms of *cataphatics* [26] and *apophatics.* [27] *Cataphatics* seeks to positively defend *dóxa* by providing positive evidence and conformational reasoning, usually *via* connecting the *dóxa* with other totemic signifiers for the good (*e.g. Justice Thomas: "the law of the land … postpone[s] even public necessity to the sacred and inviolable rights of private property.*"),[28] or directly attribute concrete, material benefits to the *dóxa* (*e.g. Justice Stevens: "…the City has carefully formulated an economic development plan that it believes will provide appreciable benefits to the community, including–but by no means limited to–new jobs and increased tax revenue*").[29-] *Apophatics,* [30] conversely, seeks to defend *dóxa* by way of negation, typically via naming the inevitable and insurmountable ills that would stem from the rejection of *dóxa.* Rather than positively define what *dóxa* is, *apophatics* involves pointing to acts of taboos that violate the sanctity of the totemic belief (*e.g. Stevens: "we concluded that the State's purpose of eliminating the 'social and economic evils of a land oligopoly' qualified as a valid public use*" Justice Steven's majority opinion in *Kelo v. City of New London*, 545 U.S. 469 (2005)).

When the legitimation framework for the production of the "truth of law" is at question, it is important to examine rhetoric of judicial etiology, or the "origin

26 George Henry and Robert Scott Liddell, *A Greek-English Lexicon*, revised and augmented throughout by Sir Henry Stuart Jones, with the assistance of Roderick McKenzie (Oxford: Clarendon Press, 1940): κατ⊠ *Cata, "to descend"* + *femi, "to speak.*

27 ἀπόφημι, fut. -φήσω: aor. 1**A.**"ἀπέφησα" Pl.Tht.166a, al.: – *speak out, declare flatly or plainly*, George Henry and Robert S. Liddell (1940) ibid. See also, Plato, *Platonis Opera*, ed. John Burnet. Oxford University Press. 1903 at [360δ]: "καὶ ἐγὼ εἶπον: τί δή, ὦ Πρωταγόρα, οὔτε σὺ φῂς ἃ ἐρωτῶ οὔτε ἀπόφῃς; αὐτός, ἔφη, πέρανον. [Here he could no longer bring himself to nod agreement, and remained silent. Then I proceeded: Why is it, Protagoras, that you neither affirm nor **deny** what I ask you?].

28 See Justice Thomas' dissenting opinion in *Kelo v. City of New London*, 545 U.S. 469 (2005).

29 Ibid.

30 Plato, *Platonis Opera*, ed. John Burnet (Oxford University Press: 1903) at [360δ] *supra* note 164.

myths," that serve as legitimation narratives for the court to declare a more perfect and complete interpretation of the law's "original" meaning. As Justice Stephens wrote in *Kelo*, that "*[w]ithout exception, our cases have defined that concept broadly, reflecting our longstanding policy of deference to legislative judgments in this field.*"

In *Kelo*, both the majority and the dissent opinions professed a coherent etiology for their own "more perfect" interpretation of the original meaning. Justices Stevens (majority), Kennedy (concurrence), O'Connor (dissent), and Thomas (dissent) each and individually presented their cherry-picked collage of judicial precedence, legislative records, and original constitutional intents to tell their own "origin myth" of their version of the legal truth. The petitioner's counter-arguments in *Kelo* also heavily invoke historical originalism in its constitutional interpretation. Similarly, the common law principle of *stare decisis,* the court's decision as a binding precedent, or potential precedent for future cases, can be also seen as a formalized *pístis* (legitimation framework)[31] that provides the persuasiveness of etiology in establishing legal *dóxa* (accepted doctrine).[32]

In addition to the explicitly written *dóxa* by the SCOTUS, it is also important to be mindful of the dynamic relations between those explicit symbolic expressions and tacitly embedded beliefs. Specifically, when judicial disputes arise, a legal *dóxa* often finds itself to be rhetorically dissonant with its socially embedded *pístis.* The former operates within the formal domain of political-legal rhetoric, whereas the latter is tacitly internalized in communal/societal legal-consciousness (or lack thereof). Yet only the majority's etiology prevails as the unambiguous, singularly legitimate "origin myth" of the legal truth in question – that the U.S. Constitution, conveniently, is by design a "living document," and thereby requires constant re-interpretation to meet new policy needs.[33] Similarly, the all four justices offered their own apologetics in arguing their "more perfect" reading of the Takings Clause, but only the majority's argument will be affirmed as the new constitutional truth.

The 5-to-4 split vote among justices, along with the unusual presence of multiple dissenting and concurring opinions in *Kelo* reflects the intrinsic controversial nature

31 The definition of *pístis* (Πίστις) here draws from the general meaning of the term, as "the state of mind produced in the audience." See William M. Grimaldi, "A Note on the *Pisteis* in Aristotle's Rhetoric, 1354–1356," *The American Journal of Philology* Vol. 78, No. 2 (1957): 188–192, at 190.

32 Pierre Bourdieu, *Outline of a Theory of Practice. R. Nice, transl. Volume 16* (Cambridge: Cambridge University Press: 1977), 164.

33 *Kelo v. City of New London*, 545 U.S. 469 (2005), Justice Stephens: "Viewed as a whole, our jurisprudence has recognized that the needs of society have varied between different parts of the Nation, just as they have evolved over time in response to changed circumstances. Our earliest cases in particular embodied a strong theme of federalism, emphasizing the 'great respect' that we owe to state legislatures and state courts in discerning local public needs." See also, *Hairston v. Danville & Western R. Co.*, 208 U.S. 598 (1908), 606–607 (noting that these needs were likely to vary depending on a State's "resources, the capacity of the soil, the relative importance of industries to the general public welfare, and the long-established methods and habits of the people"): "For more than a century, our public-use jurisprudence has wisely eschewed rigid formulas and intrusive scrutiny in favor of affording legislatures broad latitude in determining what public needs justify the use of the takings power."

of the case. Yet despite the appearance of heated debate disagreement among justices, those dissenting opinions are more appropriately understood as ritual performances rather than substantive contestations. The final outcome of the *Kelo* decision, like all other instances of SCOTUS judicial reviews, is not a sum aggregate of the justices' opinions.

Formally speaking, dissenting opinions and justices' voting patterns do not assume any binding legal effect. They do not dilute the strength or the "truthfulness" of the majority opinion. The majority opinion, taken singularly and in totality as the final and incontestable interpretation of the constitutional text, is only subject to being overruled by the Supreme Court itself. Through its constitutional review authority, the *Kelo* decision not only affirmed the legality of the singular act of regulatory takings by the City of New London, but also at the same time radically expanded the scope of the use of eminent domain. By declaring that private commercial redevelopment satisfies the Takings Clause in the Fifth Amendment – "… nor shall private property be taken for public use, without just compensation" – the *Kelo* decision effectively redefined the constitutional meaning of "public use" as to include private commercial development.

Analysis of judicial rituals

> *[T]he law of the land … postpone[s] even public necessity to the sacred and inviolable rights of private property.*
>
> – Justice Thomas, in his dissenting opinion in *Kelo v. City of New London* [34]

The preceding discussion highlighted the fact that legal *dóxa* often operate in ways that are analogous to the rhetoric of religion. This section will move the analysis closely to the text of the court decision, and identify parallel rhetorical devices between *Kelo v. City of New London* and rituals of religious sacrifice.

The U.S. Supreme Court's ruling under the American common law system thus can be understood as a specific mode of rhetorical response to the exigence of resolving customarily non-resolvable societal tensions. For *Kelo v. City of New London*, its particular rhetorical tension revolves around the indeterminateness of the "public-private" distinction. To study the rhetorical dimension of this case is to critically examine the ways in which legal re-interpretation fluidly changes the legitimation framework, or what Foucault referred to as "regime of truth," in regulating the sacrifice of the private for "fair public use."[35]

Whereas the exigence underpinning *Kelo v. City of New London* is grounded in material interest, its rhetorical implication concerns the "truth" of private residences in relation to the predetermined conditions regulating the surrendering of one's private material interest as sacrificial offerings for the common. The Supreme

34 *Kelo v. City of New London*, 545 U.S. 469 (2005), available: http://caselaw.findlaw.com/us-supreme-court/545/469.html

35 Michel Foucault, *Il faut défendre la société Cours au Collège de France. 1975–1976*, ed. M. Bertani and A. Fontana, trans. D. Macey (Paris: Seuil/Gallimard, 1997) *Society Must Be Defended. Lectures at the Collège de France 1975–1976* (New York, Picador, 2003), 145 and 164.

Court, operating within its embedded and publicly recognized rule-of-law *pístis*, would interpret the law and produce a "sacred dóxa (or incontestable opinion)," settling the "truth" concerning the relation of private and common interests.

The Supreme Court's opinion of the case, in terms of its rhetorical objective in *Kelo v. City of New London*, is to establish the legal truth that [1] it is permissible to invoke eminent domain for what the state considers the exigence of economic redevelopment, and [2] that economic redevelopment in itself is considered a "fair public use" of the land. The facticity of these two explicitly stated declarations rests upon existing good faith on the rituality of eminent domain itself, and on the sanctity of "public use." Eminent domain as a ritual practice implies that the state's status as the sole legitimate authority to declare eminent domain is sacred and not subject to questioning, and it is through this sacred authority that the state may perform a prescribed sequence of act of unconditional taking and surrendering. The sanctity of "public use" implies, among many things, that the declaration of its "fairness" by the court effectively consecrates the term, and also closes the legitimate rhetorical space of debating its meaning, thereby automatically triggering the ritual surrendering of private interests as unconditional offerings for sacrifice.

The first ritual device I would like to highlight is *Pharmakos*, or the ritual construction of a human scapegoat. The term "scapegoat" is sometimes used in legal scholarship as a metaphor describing those economically disadvantaged groups facing the burden of regulatory taking as seen in the *Kelo* case.[36] As previously discussed in Chapter 2, the use of the term scapegoat as a metaphor for apotropaic[37] human sacrifice can be traced back to ritual texts of ancient Mesopotamia, where an actual goat was used as a vehicle of evil to be ritually eliminated (via killing or banishment) from the community.[38] The term *Pharmakos* in the context of Ancient Hellenistic religion refers to those rituals of sacrifice that use human as the scapegoat.[39] One famous example of *Pharmakos*, found in the writing fragments of Petronius, describes an indigent man from the city of Massilia (present-day Marseille in France), whom offered himself to be sacrificed in order to expiate the town from the curse of plague. Citizens of Massilia donned the man in sacred robe and a leaf crown, paraded him through a cursing crowd and then murdered him.[40]

Scapegoating is a common form of expiation sacrifice – sacrifices made for warding off evil and avoiding retribution from a higher force. Expiation sacrifice is

36 Kelianne Chamberlain, "Unjust Compensation: allowing revenue-based compensation in regulatory takings," *Wyoming Law Review* Volume 14, Issue 1 Article 8 (2014). http://repository.uwyo.edu/cgi/viewcontent.cgi?article=1021&context=wlr

37 Apotropaic magic (from Greek *apotrepein*) refers to rituals performed to cleanse sins of the community, and to avoid the curse of a higher force.

38 David P. Wright, *The Disposal of the Impurity: Elimination Rites in the Bible and in Hittite and Mesopotamian Literature* (Atlanta: Scholars Press, 1987), 15–74.

39 Todd M. Compton, "Victim of the Muses: Poet as Scapegoat, Warrior and Hero in Greco-Roman and Indo-European Myth and History," *Hellenic Studies Series 11, chapter 1* (Washington, DC: Center for Hellenic Studies, 2006).

40 Compton, ibid.

typically performed with a declaration that a sacred covenant, or after a sacred vow has been broken. Furthermore, there are two types of exigencies commonly associated with expiation sacrifices: (1) The belief that there is an inherently angry higher power that needs constant appeasing; and (2) the belief that human subjects are inherently sinful in the eyes of the higher power, and therefore need constant atonement for their sins.

Upon closely examining the text of *Kelo v. City of New London* decision, it is important to note that these ritual elements of expiation sacrifice also play a key role in the rhetoric of the court. The concept of "economy" was discussed in the *Kelo* decision in similar terms as an "angry God." The SCOTUS framed economy as an abstract, all-encompassing force that is a source of absolute public good, and therefore is a sacred thing that demands constant honoring. The court explains that "promoting economic development is a traditional and long accepted governmental function, and there is no principled way of distinguishing it from the other public purposes the Court has recognized."[41] Like an angry God, the court repeatedly warns that if the economy is not properly cared for, it would inevitably bring unbearable collective curses: "overcrowding of dwellings," "lack of adequate streets and alleys," and "lack of light and air." Thus, both majority and dissenting opinions agreed that *economy* is a sacred object that the government was created to serve, "by employing all means necessary and appropriate for the purpose, including eminent domain."[42]

Resting upon the unquestionable sanctity and wrathfulness of *economy*, the court reinvents the core tenet of the "public purpose" clause for eminent domain as a sacred covenant – that "[s]tates may take account of their special exigencies" to mandate private sacrifices for honoring the constant, all-encompassing need of economic development. "The city's determination that the area at issue was sufficiently distressed to justify a program of economic rejuvenation is entitled to deference."

The rhetoric of economic growth in the *Kelo* opinion was deployed in ways that depart from the practical domain of material necessities. It was framed as a self-justifying, self-referencing ideal. In her dissenting opinion, Justice O'Connor wrote that:

> New London does not claim that Susette Kelo's and Wilhelmina Dery's well-maintained homes are the source of any social harm. Indeed, it could not so claim without adopting the absurd argument that any single-family home that might be razed to make way for an apartment building, or any church that might be replaced with a retail store, or any small business that might be more lucrative if it were instead part of a national franchise, is inherently harmful to society and thus within the government's power to condemn.[43]

41 *Kelo v. City of New London*, 545 U.S. 469 (2005).
42 Ibid., see Justice O'Connor's dissenting opinion.
43 Ibid., see Justice O'Connor's dissenting opinion.

Justice O'Connor pointed out that there is no material evidence suggesting that "eliminating the existing property use was necessary to remedy the harm targeted properties."[44] Furthermore, no fact from the case would suggest that any of the condemned properties "inflicted affirmative harm on society."[45] She noted that the "economic logic" presented in the majority's opinion was not grounded in material realities, but rather in the abstract ideal that "goodness" will arrive.

Writing for the majority's opinion, Justice Stevens was not troubled by the lack of material exigence in the *Kelo* case. Justice Stevens acknowledged that "[t]here is no allegation that any of these properties is blighted or otherwise in poor condition; rather, they were condemned only because they happen to be located in the development area." However, the majority opinion did not see the seemingly arbitrary regulatory taking of private homes in *Kelo* as unjust. Justice Stevens cited the U.S. Constitution as a justificatory framework for the regulatory takings. As the sanctity of the judicial review process derives from the Constitution, SCOTUS must in turn treat the Constitution as a self-contained, self-referencing body of sacred text.

On the one hand, the majority's opinion acknowledged that the notion of private property itself is protected by Constitution and therefore is considered sacred in the U.S. legal system. On the other hand, the court pointed out that "[t]he Constitution of the United States does not require us to say that they are wrong" when taking private properties for public purposes.[46] In the rhetoric of the SCOTUS, the Constitution, just like the logic of abstracted *economy* or the will of the Abrahamic God, implies a certain sacred covenant that is abundant in both mercy and potential *wrath*. Just as articles of religious faith sometimes bind the believer into a sacred vow or covenant that mandates calendrical or exigential sacrifices to a higher power, the Constitution also organizes its political subjects under a similar covenant. The majority's opinion in *Kelo* cited the public takings clause of the Fifth Amendment as the implied "social contract" covenant that places citizens' private properties at the mercy of the state, and is constantly subjected to the possibility of being taken for "public purposes" as determined by the court.

The sacred treatment of the constitution holds true regardless of individual justices' opinion of the case – that both majority and dissenting opinion are being argued as "the most faithful" reading of the constitution. Just O'Connor prefaced her dissenting opinion by stating that "[w]hen interpreting the Constitution, we begin with the unremarkable presumption that every word in the document has independent meaning, that no word was unnecessarily used, or needlessly added."[47] Under the sacred constitutional covenant, the legitimacy and justness of eminent domain itself is not subject to debate. What can be debated in court are

44 Ibid.
45 Ibid.
46 See SCOTUS Majority's opinion by Justice Stevens, 545 U.S. 469 (2005).
47 Ibid.

disputes on the meaning and scope of "fair public use," and on the amount of "just compensation."[48]

Justice Stevens noted that "just compensation" in the *Kelo* case is not an issue for the court as the petitioners only dispute the "public purpose" of the regulatory taking and are not asking for better compensation from the city government. "The question in the case is whether a city's taking of private property for the purpose of economic development satisfies the public use requirement of the Fifth Amendment."[49] Wrote Justice Stevens, and more specifically:

> What protection does the Fifth Amendment's public use requirement provide for individuals whose property is being condemned, not to eliminate slums or blight, but for the sole purpose of 'economic development' that will perhaps increase tax revenues and improve the local economy?[50]

Note that in its elaboration of the legal issue brought before the court, the SCOTUS separated the ends of "eliminate slums or blight" from the means of "economic development" and "improve the local economy." This de-signification process implies that should the court rule in favor of the regulatory taking by the city government, the ruling will also reject the notion that improving living condition and material well-being are not necessary conditions for justifying the "public purpose" of privatization policies. Given that the SCOTUS had already determined that the city's private redevelopment plan is within the "true meaning" already contained in the public use clause, the condemnation of petitioner's properties is therefore "just" and can no longer be subjected to legitimate debate.

Not only does the Fifth Amendment enshrine eminent domain as a "divine right of the state" entirely above the private right of citizens, but it is also arbitrary in the sense that the victims of public seizures are not selected due to any wrongdoing on their part. In this regard, the rhetorical structure regulatory taking resembles the biblical *Jephthah's oath* from the *Book of Judges.* In the biblical account, Jephthah made a ritual sacrifice by declaring:

> *Whatsoever cometh forth of the doors of my house to meet me, when I return in peace from the children of Ammon, shall surely be the* LORD'*s, and I will offer it up for a burnt offering. —Judges 11:31* (KJV)

48 SCOTUS opinion delivered by *Justice Stevens:* "The question presented is whether the city's proposed disposition of this property qualifies as a 'public use' within the meaning of the Takings Clause of the Fifth Amendment to the Constitution," 545 U.S. 469 (2005).

49 545 U.S. 469 (2005). Opinion Announcement by John Paul Stevens (June 23, 2005). Audio file available: Chicago-Kent College of Law at Illinois Tech. "Kelo v. New London." Oyez. https://www.oyez.org/cases/2004/04-108 (accessed September 21, 2016).

50 545 U.S. 469 (2005).

The seemingly arbitrary nature of *Jephthah's oath* provides a sense of equity and fairness in selecting the sacrificial victims – that sacrificial victims are selected not because they have committed a sin, but simply being "in the wrong place at the wrong time." This seemingly unconditional election of the sacrificial victim rhetorically conceals the human agent behind the violent transaction. Similarly, the petitioners in *Kelo* had their properties taken not due to their own wrong-doing, but simply being "in the wrong place at the wrong time." *Jephthah's oath* provides the rhetoric for justifying the selection of "sacrificial properties" for eminent domain.

Notwithstanding the seemingly arbitrary character of regulatory takings, the court in no way considered the apparent "non-wrongdoing" of the petitioner's valid grounds to expatiate them from condemnation.

Just as ritual expiation sacrifices are often performed with an assumption of an inherently sinful human subject (e.g. the concept of *original sin*) in the hands of an angry God, the *Kelo* case was also decided with the assumption of certain *original sin*, encoded as *social constraints* that are intrinsic to human communities. Specifically, the court's argument for the legitimacy of regulatory takings in *Kelo v. City of New London* rests on two particular assumptions of *original sins* or "social inevitabilities:" the first is the *tragedy of the commons*: when everyone shares ownership, no one would have the incentive to manage the property and the resource will be abused in ways that harm the common interest, thus mandating redevelopment via private businesses. The second "inevitability" can be described as the *tragedy of the anti-commons*: when too much private ownership becomes too restrictive for the advancement of the common good, thus mandating the regulatory taking of private residences. As Justice Stevens declares in his majority opinion: "The public end may be as well or better served through an agency of private enterprise than through a department of government."[51]

Chapter conclusion

The New London city government justified its aggressive regulatory seizure of well-maintained private houses with the promise of bringing new jobs and businesses to the city. The actual employment data of New London reveals a very different reality. The unemployment rate of the city skyrocketed from 4.1 percent in 2006 to 8.9 percent in 2010:

The analysis in this chapter concludes with a reconstruction of a political ritual of sacrifice as performed in *Kelo v. City of New London*. The analysis highlights that the judicial process in this case constitutes a ceremonial (or epideictic) framework which organizes material contestations and political debates into a series of prescribed of procedures and ritual repetitions. This process would procedurally seal off the legitimate space for legal contestation, and consecrate both the settled legal *dóxa* as well as the legal "truth" of underlying material exigence. The ritual performance of judicial review in this case preemptively places citizen subjects into

51 *Kelo v. City of New London*, 545 U.S. 469 (2005).

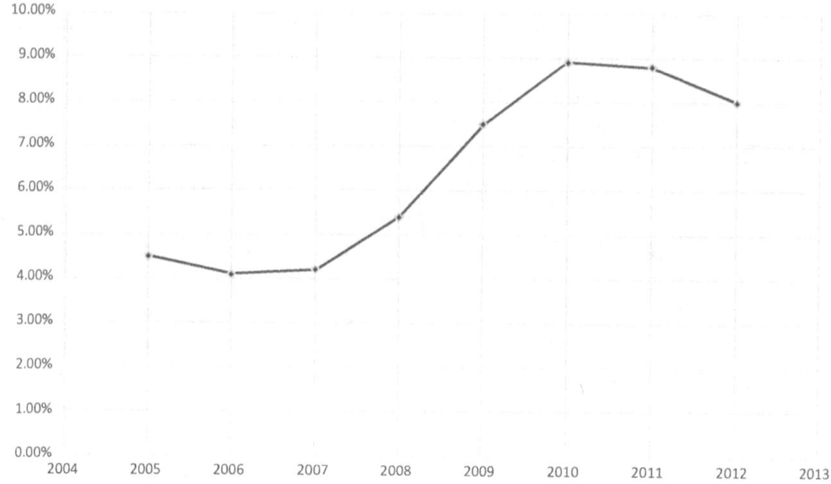

Figure 3.2 City of New London unemployment rate (2005–2012)[52]

binding association with an updated sacred mandate of sacrifice, a vow that promises certain sacrifice, should the sacred association be broken. Whereas purely religious (in the narrow sense) offerings are often entirely symbolic, political ritual often involves offering of real significance (economic or bodily, personal and collective)[52].

At the technical level, the case concerns the definition and scope of "public use" requirement under the takings clause of the Fifth Amendment. However, the dispute in *Kelo* touches on a fundamental exigence that is at the core of human political community – the sacrifice of individual and/or group interests for the good of the "commons." The rhetorical analysis will first discuss the socially embedded belief framework that forms the discursive basis for *Kelo v. City of New London*. The discussion seeks to highlight the ritual embeddedness of the judicial rhetoric in *Kelo*, and that judicial *dóxa* often operate in ways parallel to the rhetoric of religion. Following the broad historical discussion, the analysis will move closely to the opinions of SCOTUS in *Kelo*, and identify analogous rhetorical elements between the proceedings of the court and rituals of religious sacrifice. The analysis concludes by locating rhetorical implications of the ritual proceedings in the case, and examines the ways which these rituals were being deployed in affirming the sanctity of neoliberal economic policies.

On the one hand, these rhetorical "good faith" statements are particular truth-expressions of discursive practices that emerge from distinct historical, social, political and economic conditions of their faith-community, and produce variable

52 Based on data from Federal Reserve Economic Data, "CTNEWL1URN Unemployment Rate in New London County, CT, %, Monthly, Not Seasonally Adjusted," (Federal Reserve Bank of St. Louis: Economic Research Division) available: https://fred.stlouisfed.org.

societal consequences. Yet these locally-contextualized legal doctrines and beliefs invariably serve to define the particular totems and taboos concerning the rituals of sacrifice in a political community. In this regard, the court's ritual re-interpretation in *Kelo v. City of New London*, for better or worse, shapes the legitimation framework regulating people as ***always ready to be sacrificed*** for the sacred goals defined by the state.[53] The rhetorical elements of sacrifice have existed throughout history, thematic in various religious and philosophy texts. We tend to dwell in legal technicalities when looking at the text *of Kelo v. City of New London*, but its structure is historically and materially grounded in tensions that arise from intrinsic contradictions in economic relations.

53 The corresponding tendency to this overdetermined human-as-political-subject is the tendency to reframe and reduce the political subject as "always-already-consenting" to offer oneself for the "always-already-justified" sacrifice mandated by the state. Louis Althusser's theory of ***interpellation*** also expresses similar process in the context of modern states.

4 David and Goliath

Similar to the previous chapter on *Kelo v. City of New London*, this chapter revolves around a case study of state-mandated ritual sacrifice for economic redevelopment. The first half of the chapter provides relevant facts and legal context on the Vedanta controversy – a 2013 land dispute between Vedanta Resources, a British multinational mining company, and a small indigenous tribe in India. The second half of the chapter analyzes the rhetoric of ritual and theological elements underpinning the Vedanta controversy. The ritual analysis in this chapter focuses on the role of legal *pístis* in the ritualization of state-mandated sacrifice, as well as the strategic deployment of rituals as countermeasures, to resist the state authority's monopoly for the legitimate use of ritual public sacrifice.

Background of the Vedanta controversy

> *A primitive Indian tribe which worships its remote jungle mountain as a living god has inflicted a humiliating defeat on one of Britain's wealthiest billionaires over his plans to open a vast aluminium ore mine on their land.* [1]

The above excerpt, taken from the headline of a *Telegraph* front-page news article on August 9, 2013, reported the improbable victory of a small indigenous group in eastern India, known as the Dongria Kondh people, over a land dispute case against Vedanta Resources, a British multinational mining corporation. A small tribe with less than 8000 people in its total membership, whose livelihood primarily relies on subsistence farming, somehow were able to organize a successful campaign to halt a planned multi-billion dollar mining project on their tribal land.[2] This case was dubbed a "David and Goliath victory" by many Western media outlets.[3]

1 Dean Nelson, "Indian villagers defeat British billionaire over plans to mine sacred mountain." *The Telegraph*, last modified August 9, 2013. http://www.telegraph.co.uk/news/worldnews/asia/india/10234314/Indian-villagers-defeat-British-billionaire-over-plans-to-mine-sacred-mountain.html

2 Ibid.

3 Jo Woodman, "India's rejection of Vedanta's bauxite mine is a victory for tribal rights," *The Guardian*, last modified January 14, 2015.https://www.theguardian.com/global-development/poverty-matters/2014/jan/14/india-rejection-vedanta

On April 18, 2013, after nearly ten years of protesting and challenging the plan for an open-pit bauxite mine on Niyamgiri hills, which the Dongria Kondhs claimed to be their "sacred ancestral grounds," the Indian Supreme Court ruled against the controversial mining proposal, and handed the local indigenous communities the right to have a decisive say on future mining proposals in the area.[4]

The Dongria Kondhs (or simply "Dongrias") is a subgroup of the Kondha people, an *adivasi* (indigenous) tribal group in the remote regions of Eastern India. The Dongria Kondhs community is officially recognized as a "scheduled tribe" by the Indian government. "Scheduled tribe" is a legal destination reserved for the most "primitive" and isolated indigenous groups in India. Under Article 342 of the Indian Constitution,[5] scheduled tribes enjoy special protection of their political, social and economic rights.[6] Scheduled Tribes constitute roughly 8.2 percent of India's total population,[7] and like the rest of the groups within this category, the Dongrias almost exclusively reside in wilderness areas like hills and forests, with their livelihood based on subsistence agriculture.[8] Historically, they have maintained only marginal contact with outside communities, and have developed their own distinctive culture, language and religion.[9]

Residing in one of India's most remote regions, the Dongria Kondhs are both culturally and economically isolated. Dongrias predominantly speak Kui, a Dravidian language with a total of 641,662 registered speakers.[10] Kui is officially classified as a threatened language in India, which few people outside of the state of

-mine-victory-tribal-rights*See also*, Kathryn Hopkins, "Indian tribe appeals for Avatar director's help to stop Vedanta," *The Guardian*, last modified February 8, 2010. http://www.theguardian.com/business/2010/feb/08/dongria-kondh-help-stop-vedanta; and "Real 'Avatar' tribe deals fatal blow to Vedanta mine," *Survival International*, posted August 19, 2013: http://www.survivalinternational.org/news/9478

4 Dean Nelson, "Indian villagers defeat British billionaire over plans to mine sacred mountain." *The Telegraph*, last modified August 9, 2013. http://www.telegraph.co.uk/news/worldnews/asia/india/10234314/Indian-villagers-defeat-British-billionaire-over-plans-to-mine-sacred-mountain.html*See also*, Santosh Patnaik, "Dongria Kondhs have shown the way," *The Hindu*, last modified August 21, 2013. http://www.thehindu.com/news/national/other-states/dongria-kondhs-have-shown-the-way/article5044669.ece

5 The Constitution of India, Part XVI, Art. 342, available: https://www.india.gov.in/sites/upload_files/npi/files/coi_part_full.pdf

6 "Report on Socio-economic Conditions of Scheduled Tribes Labour at Vapi, Valsad, Navsari and Sachin (Gujarat) (2006–07)" Labour Bureau, Government of India, Chapter I, available: http://labourbureau.nic.in/SE_Gujarat%2006-07_Contents.htm

7 Ibid.

8 "Subsistence economy" typically refers to forms of non-monetary economic systems that rely on natural resources to provide for basic needs – usually through hunting and gathering, pastoralism, and small-scale agriculture.

9 Ibid. See also, Upali Aparajita, *Culture and development: Dongrias of Niyamgiri* (New Delhi, India: Inter-India Publications, 1994).

10 Bhadriraju Krishnamurti, *The Dravidian languages* (Cambridge: Cambridge University Press, 2003), p. 56.

Odisha (formerly State of Orissa) can understand.[11] What separates the Dongrias from the rest of the Kondh people is their cultural and spiritual connection with the Niyamgiri hills. The Niyamgiri hills in Southern Odisha is the home to roughly 8,000 Dongrias, spread over 90 *adivasi* communities around the mostly undeveloped hills.[12] To be a Dongria Kondh is to live in the Niyamgiri hills – they do not live anywhere else.[13] Dongria Kondh people consider the Niyamgiri hills to be holy, with each mountain representing a deity. Among the hills in Niyamgiri, the Niyam Dongar Mountain is the holiest of the holy – it is the seat of their supreme god, Niyam Raja.[14] The Dongrias do not cultivate on the Niyam Dongar hill top out of respect, and they worship the mountain.[15] The Dongrias believe that Niyam Raja, the "maker of all things," created the Niyamgiri hills as the homeland for the Dongria Kondh people.[16]

The significance of Niyamgiri hills for Dongrias is not only spiritual, but also material.[17] For centuries, Dongrias have based their agrarian livelihood on the rich ecosystem offered by the densely forested hills. "We get everything from the jungle, like the fruits we take to the market. This is like our source of life for our Dongria Kondh people."[18] Niyamgiri forests are historically recognized for their rich wildlife population.[19] More than 75 percent of the hills are covered by thick, primitive forests. The Niyamgiri forest has more than 300 plant species, including about 50 species of valuable medicinal plants; 6 of the plant species are listed in

11 Ibid., see also, Kui reference at *Ethnologue* (17th ed., 2013), http://www.ethnologue.com/language/kxu

12 "India: Generalisations, Omissions, Assumptions: The Failings of Vedanta's Environmental Impact Assessments for Its Bauxite Mine and Alumina Refinery in India's State of Orissa (Executive Summary)," *Amnesty International* (London: Amnesty International UK, 2011) at page 8, available: http://www.amnesty.org/en/library/asset/ASA20/037/2011/en/6006600c-8be3-4495-917f-00584b3efc19/asa200372011en.pdf

13 "The Dongria Kondh," (report) *Survival International*, available http://www.survivalinternational.org/tribes/dongria

14 Damian Grammaticas, "Tribe takes on global mining firm," *BBC News*, last updated July 17, 2008: http://news.bbc.co.uk/2/hi/south_asia/7486252.stm

15 "Report in IA no. 1324 regarding the alumina refinery plant being set up by m/s Vedanta Alumina Limited at Lanjigarh in Kalahandi district, Orissa," The Central Empowered Committee (CEC) 21.09.2005, available: http://www.indiaresource.org/issues/globalization/2005/CECSep2005cancellicense.html

16 Ibid.

17 Damian Grammaticas, "Tribe takes on global mining firm," *BBC News*, last updated July 17, 2008: "We get everything from the jungle like the fruits we take to the market. This is like our source of life for our Dongria Kondh peoples." Available: http://news.bbc.co.uk/2/hi/south_asia/7486252.stm

18 Quote from Jitu Jakeskia, a young Dongria Kondh activist during a BBC interview. See Damian Grammaticas, "Tribe takes on global mining firm," *BBC News*, last updated July 17, 2008: http://news.bbc.co.uk/2/hi/south_asia/7486252.stm

19 Report in IA no. 1324 regarding the alumina refinery plant being set up by m/s Vedanta Alumina Limited at Lanjigarh in Kalahandi district, Orissa," The Central Empowered Committee (CEC) September 21, 2005, available: http://www.indiaresource.org/issues/globalization/2005/CECSep2005cancellicense.html

the IUCN Red Data Book.[20] Since 2004, this area has been designated as an Elephant Reserve by the State of Orissa. Local endangered wildlife species include Asian elephants, sambars, leopards, tigers, and various species of endemic birds.

In the Vedanta controversy, however, it was not the region's biodiversity that was attracting outsiders. The Niyamgiri hills are also rich in bauxite – the raw material for aluminum production. It was the bauxite that brought British mining company Vedanta Resources to the Dongria Kondh homeland in 2003, where it made plans to open a large open-pit mine on top of the sacred Niyam Dongar Mountain.[21]

The other main actor in this land dispute, Vedanta Resources Plc., is a British metals and mining corporation founded and owned by Indian business magnate and billionaire Anil Agarwal.[22] Vedanta is primarily engaged in ore mining for copper, zinc, silver, aluminum, and iron; the corporation also is known for refining, and its stake in the power generation industry. Although headquartered in London, Vedanta is a large multinational conglomerate with most of its assets and operations located in the high growth markets of India, Zambia, Namibia, South Africa, Liberia, Ireland and Australia.

In recent years, Vedanta Resources has come under growing international scrutiny. The company's questionable safety record has generated much public outcry. It contains reports of staggering casualties, 1,247 injuries and 26 deaths in 2007 alone.[23] According to an analysis of deaths of workers at FTSE 100 mining companies during the year 2009, Vedanta had the highest death toll among all 12 London-listed firms.[24] In April 2009, a single construction accident at a Vedanta power plant in Korba, India caused at least 40 deaths.[25] Vedanta is also criticized for having caused environmental damage and contributed to human rights violations, especially with respect to socio-economic and cultural rights.[26] Accusations include repeated breaches of national environmental legislation, illegal production expansions, irresponsible handling of hazardous waste, deplorable wages, hazardous working conditions, and involvement in bribery and corruption.[27]

20 Ibid.

21 Quote from a Dongria villager during a video interview by Survival International, see: http://www.survivalinternational.org/films/handfulsoil at 1:20: "Vedanta has come to destroy the Dongria Kondh and the Niyamgiri mountains, so all Dongrias and our supporters have got together to drive Vedanta out of this place."

22 "Who We Are," *Vedanta Resources* (updated April, 2017, accessed April 22, 2017), available: http://www.vedantaresources.com/who-we-are.aspx

23 "Vedanta Annual Report 2007," (updated April, 2017, accessed April 22, 2017), available: http://www.vedantaresources.com/uploads/VedantaRA07.pdf

24 Simon Bowers, "Vedanta stripped of safety awards in light of Indian site disaster," *The Guardian*, posted August 28, 2010, Available: http://www.theguardian.com/business/2010/aug/29/vedanta-safety-awards-stripped

25 Bowers, "Vedanta stripped of safety awards in light of Indian site disaster," ibid.

26 See "Recommendation of 15 May 2007, To the Ministry of Finance," by the Council on Ethics, The Government Pension Fund of Norway, available: http://www.regjeringen.no/Upload/FIN/Statens%20pensjonsfond/RecommendationVedanta.pdf

27 See report by Amnesty International, supra note 13.

In October 2003, one of Vedanta's subsidiaries, Orissa Mining Corporation (OMC) signed a Memorandum of Understanding with the Orissa state government regarding the establishment of a joint venture company for bauxite mining from Niyamgiri hills. Included in the plan was the establishment of a large open-pit mine on top of the sacred Niyam Dongar Mountain, in order to extract more than two billion USD worth of bauxite deposit inside the mountain. Vedanta also indicated its plans to construct a bauxite refinery for aluminum production and a coal-based power plant in Lanjigarh on the Niyamgiri foothills.[28]

In 2004, an Indian human rights organization, People's Union for Civil Liberties,[29] filed a public interest suit against Vedanta to the Indian Supreme Court sub-committee Central Empowered Committee (CEC), raising concerns regarding the potential environmental impact of the proposed mining project. Subsequent CEC investigations found inadequate environmental clearance for the alumina refinery project,[30] as well as evidence of forcible eviction of local inhabitants of the proposed project site.[31] According to the CEC Report, members of the Dongria Kondh tribe were displaced from their homes through physical eviction by Vedanta employees, with the help of local government in preparation for the mining project:

> Many were beaten up by the employees of M/s Vedanta. The National R&R policy requires that land for land should be given after due process of consultation, particularly in the case of the tribals. Contrary to the above cash compensation was offered to them and which was not acceptable to many. The tribal people living on the plant site are mainly Kondhs who are illiterate and depend completely on their agricultural lands and forest for their subsistence.[32]

The 2005 CEC Report provided shocking revelations on the mistreatment Dongria Kondh people by Vedanta and local authorities, publicly shedding light on the Dongrias' collective struggle against the proposed bauxite mine for the first time:

> [T]hey (the Dongrias) have deep spiritual and cultural attachment to their ancestral lands and settlements. The displacement was opposed vehemently by

28 The Central Empowered Committee (CEC) 2005: *Report in IA no. 1324 regarding the alumina refinery plant being set up by m/s Vedanta Alumina Limited at Lanjigarh in Kalahandi district, Orissa*, 21.09.05, p.7 and p. 50, available: http://www.indiaresource.org/issues/globalization/2005/CECSep2005cancellicense.html

29 "A Short History of PUCL," *Website of People's Union for Democratic Rights* (PUDR) (updated 2010, accessed April 22, 2017), available: http://www.pucl.org/history.htm

30 The Central Empowered Committee (CEC) 2005: Report in IA no. 1324 regarding the alumina refinery plant being set up by m/s Vedanta Alumina Limited at Lanjigarh in Kalahandi district, Orissa, September 21, 2005, at section 32: "The CEC is of the considered view that the use of the forest land in an ecologically sensitive area like the Niyamgiri Hills should not be permitted."

31 Ibid., at section 3, under "Forcible eviction and rehabilitation package."

32 Ibid., at section 3, xvi.

> them despite being offered large cash compensation by M/s Vedanta. In the face of resistance, the District Collector and the company officials collaborated to coerce and threaten them … An atmosphere of fear was created through the hired goons, the police and the administration. Many of the tribals were badly beaten up by the police and the goons. After being forcibly removed they were kept under watch and ward by the armed guards of M/s Vedanta and no outsider was allowed to meet them. They were effectively being kept as prisoners.[33]

The CEC recommended that mining in Niyamgiri should not be allowed, and that were it not for administrative peculiarities the refinery may never have been allowed to be built.[34]

Meanwhile, Vedanta sped ahead with its mining project. In 2005, Vedanta began the construction of its bauxite refinery on the Niyamgiri foothills, and the Niyamgiri Refinery plant became operational in 2006.[35] The Orissa State Pollution Control Board (OSPCB) had documented widespread water and air pollution caused by the Lanjigarh refinery since it opened in 2006. Reports also suggest that those living near the Lanjigarh refinery in Orissa breathed polluted air and were afraid to drink from or bathe in local rivers.[36]

Despite CEC's recommendation against the proposed mining projects, in 2007, India's Supreme Court ruled in favor of Vedanta by allowing its subsidiary to reapply for a license.[37] One year later, the Supreme Court approved Vedanta's mining activities at Niyamgiri hills, including the large open-pit bauxite mine at the top of Niyam Dongar.[38]

The Supreme Court of India is the final court of appeal of the land. After the 2007 Supreme Court ruling in favor of Vedanta, all evidence at the domestic level suggests that the Dongria Kondh people lost their fight against the proposed bauxite mine at their sacred tribal land. However, the domestic struggle took an unexpected global turn in late 2007, when the Norwegian Government Pension Fund, the largest sovereign wealth fund in the world, sold its entire stake in Vedanta for "ethical reasons."[39] The Norwegian Council on Ethics cited

33 Ibid.

34 The Central Empowered Committee (CEC) 2005: Report in IA no. 1324 regarding the alumina refinery plant being set up by m/s Vedanta Alumina Limited at Lanjigarh in Kalahandi district, Orissa, September 21, 2005, p.7 and p. 50, available: http://assets.survivalinternational.org/static/files/behindthelies/CEC_report_smaller.pdf

35 "India refinery 'threatens health of local community,' "*BBC News*, last updated February 9, 2010: http://news.bbc.co.uk/2/hi/south_asia/8505250.stm

36 Ibid.

37 Ibid., at sections 32–33.

38 "Vedanta Resources caught in web of allegations," *The Economic Times*, posted February 8, 2010, available: http://articles.economictimes.indiatimes.com/2010-02-08/news/28391260_1_niyamgiri-mine-bauxite-vedanta-resources See also, Jason Burke, "Indian tribe's Avatar-like battle against mining firm reaches supreme court," *The Guardian*, last modified April 8, 2012, available: http://www.theguardian.com/world/2012/apr/08/indian-tribe-avatar-supreme-court

39 Reuters, "Norway ejects Vedanta Resources from oil fund," *The Indian Express,* last updated November 8, 2007, available: http://www.indianexpress.com/news/norway-ejects-vedanta-resources-from-oil-fund/237296/

Vedanta's environmental damage and human rights violations in India as the primary reasons for its decision to exclude the British mining firm from the investment universe of Norway's sovereign wealth fund.[40] The Council of Ethics specifically referred to the controversial Niyamgiri mining project in support of its claims against Vedanta.[41] The Ethics Council concluded, on the basis of its investigation, that:

> it is highly probable that Vedanta's mining operations in the states of Chattisgarh and Orissa have led to the expulsion of local farmers, and, in particular, tribals, from their homes and land. This constitutes a serious violation of fundamental human rights.[42]

Vedanta Resources share prices dropped 1.6 percent immediately after the announcement by the Norway Council of Ethics.[43]

Up until this point, given the geographical and linguistic isolation of the Dongria Kondh people, their collective struggle is virtually unknown outside of India. The punitive actions by the Norwegian sovereign wealth fund effectively moved the Niyamgiri mining controversy into global discourse.[44] Norway's boycott against Vedanta was quickly followed by other European funds; including the Dutch pension fund PGGM, citing frustration about Vedanta's operations in Niyamgiri.[45]

Most significantly, in 2008, the Dongria Kondh people received a "professional litigator" to assist with their cause. Survival International (SI), a UK based indigenous rights social movement organization (SMO), launched a global campaign targeting Vedanta's mining activity at Niyamgiri.[46] SI refers to itself as the organization "representing the movement for tribal peoples worldwide."[47] Founded in 1969, SI gained international recognition during the 1990s for its indigenous campaigns in South America, when the organization played a crucial role in catalyzing the establishment of Yanomami reservations in Brazil.[48]

40 Norway Council on Ethics, To the Ministry of Finance, Recommendation of May 15, 2007, Vedanta Resources Plc. available: http://www.regjeringen.no/Upload/FIN/Statens%20pensjonsfond/RecommendationVedanta.pdf
41 Ibid., 22–36.
42 Ibid., 36.
43 Ibid., 40.
44 Kavaljit Singh, "Norwegian Medicine for Vedanta," in *Why Investment Matters: The Political Economy of International Investments* (FERN, The Corner House, CRBM and Madhyam Books, 2007).
45 Mark Cobley, "PGGM Joins Norway Fund in Vedanta Boycott, Financial News," posted July 7, 2010. http://www.efinancialnews.com/story/2010-07-07/pggm-vedanta
46 "New Survival campaign targets British company Vedanta – mine set to destroy remote tribe," (Report) *Survival International*, April 29, 2008, available: http://www.survivalinternational.org/news/3272
47 "About us," *Survival International* (updated 2017), available: http://www.survivalinternational.org/info
48 Napoleon, A. Chagnon, *Yanamamo: Case Studies in Cultural Anthropology* (Wadsworth Publishing, 2009), 231–232.

SI kick-started its Dongria campaign by following the Norwegian government's lead, urging shareholders to disinvest in Vedanta.[49] In its first online news post concerning the Niyamgiri mining project, SI did not frame its message towards the general global public, but instead chose to directly address to the major financial stakeholders of Vedanta: "Survival is urging shareholders, including major British companies Standard Life, Barclays Bank, Abbey National and HSBC, as well as Middlesbrough and Wolverhampton Councils, to disinvest unless Vedanta abandons its plans."

A number of British shareholders, including the Church of England and the Rowntrees Foundation, followed the call and divested their holdings in Vedanta.[50] From 2009, SI began to redirect their attention towards publicity campaigns by sending photographers, news reporters and filmmakers to Niyamgiri, translating the struggles of the Dongria Kondh people into narratives for the global audience.[51] In March 2009, SI commissioned British actress Joanna Lumley to narrate their new documentary film titled "Mine: Story of a Sacred Mountain," which depicts the "hidden story of the remote Dongria Kondh tribe in India and their battle to stop a vast bauxite mine destroying their land and way of life."[52] The 11-minute long documentary received more than 800,000 views from the SI website and YouTube,[53] and was subsequently followed by 10 more related mini-documentaries.[54] These mini-documentaries were produced by Michael Tait, a multi-award winning television and film producer, and the multimedia editor for the prominent British news outlet *The Guardian.* [55] Consequently, SI and British news outlet *The Guardian* joined forces to broadcast the battle of the Dongria Kondh people in the domain of mainstream news media.[56]

In 2010, following the international box-office success of the Hollywood sci-fi action film "Avatar," SI published an open letter to film director James Cameron on the *Variety* magazine, comparing the Dongria Kondhs to the Na'vi tribe in Cameron's "Avatar."[57] The open letter reads: "Appeal to James Cameron. Avatar

49 Chagnon, *Yanamamo: Case Studies in Cultural Anthropology*, 231.

50 Hasan Surror, " 'Avatar' actors join protest in support of Orissa tribals," *The Hindu*, last updated July 29, 2010, available: http://www.thehindu.com/news/national/avatar-actors-join-protest-in-support-of-orissa-tribals/article538594.ece

51 See "About us," *Survival International*, available: http://www.survivalinternational.org/info. See also, "The Dongria Kondh," *Survival International* (last updated April 2010), available: http://www.survivalinternational.org/tribes/dongria

52 "Joanna Lumley narrates new film about remote tribe," *Survival International*, March 31, 2009, available: http://www.survivalinternational.org/news/4403

53 "Mine – Story of a Sacred Mountain," *Survival International*, 2009, available: http://www.survivalinternational.org/films/mine

54 Ibid.

55 "Michael Tait," (bio) *The Guardian*, available: http://www.theguardian.com/profile/michael-tait

56 Guy Grandjean, Michael Tait, Surya Shankar Dash and John Vidal, "Tribal survival: the Dongria Kondh," *The Guardian*, posted May 28, 2009, available: http://www.theguardian.com/environment/video/2009/may/28/india-mining-dongria-kondh

57 "Tribal people appeal to James Cameron," *Survival International*, February 8, 2010, available: http://www.survivalinternational.org/news/5529

is fantasy … and real. The Dongria Kondh tribe in India are struggling to defend their land against a mining company hell-bent on destroying their sacred mountain. Please help the Dongria."[58] The "Avatar" analogy was quickly echoed by *The Guardian*, [59] and eventually became a popular mnemonic device or "tag line" used by news media and advocacy organizations to capitulate the Dongria Kondh movement.[60]

In addition to its publicity campaigns, SI also functioned as professional "litigators" for the Dongria Kondh people. Although the Dongrias already exhausted their domestic legal options, SI nonetheless sought means to discipline Vedanta through emerging transnational legal frameworks. In December 2008, SI filed a complaint to the UK National Contact Point for violations of provisions of the OECD Guidelines for Multinational Enterprises[61] with regard to Vedanta's planned mining activities in Niyamgiri.[62] SI posted a 31-page long official complaint on its website.[63]

Specifically, SI claimed that Vedanta breached the OECD Guidelines for Multinational Corporations in that: [1] it failed to respect the human rights of those affected by its activities (Part II, paragraph 2); [2] it also failed to develop and apply effective self-regulatory practices and management systems that fostered a relationship of confidence and mutual trust between enterprises and the societies in which they operated (Part II, paragraph 7); and [3] its failure to engage in adequate and timely communication and consultation with the communities directly affected by its environmental, health and safety policies (Part V paragraph 2(b)). Additionally, SI accused Vedanta of failure to respect the rights of the Dongria Kondh to enjoy their own culture and to profess and practice their own religion (Articles 18 and 27 of the Civil and Political Rights Covenant; Article 12

58 Ibid.

59 Kathryn Hopkins, "Indian tribe appeals for Avatar director's help to stop Vedanta." *The Guardian*, last modified February 8, 2010, available: http://www.theguardian.com/business/2010/feb/08/dongria-kondh-help-stop-vedanta

60 Hasan Surror, "Avatar actors join protest in support of Orissa tribals," *The Hindu*, last updated July 29, 2010, available: http://www.thehindu.com/news/national/avatar-actors-join-protest-in-support-of-orissa-tribals/article538594.ece See also, note 39 above.

61 "UK National Contact Point for the Organisation for Economic Co-operation and Development (OECD) guidelines for multinational enterprises," UK Department for Business, Innovation & Skills, December 2008, available: https://www.gov.uk/uk-national-contact-point-for-the-organisation-for-economic-co-operation-and-development-oecd-guidelines-for-multinational-enterprises

62 "Follow up to Final Statement by the UK National Contact Point for the OECD Guidelines for Multinational Enterprises," UK National Contact Point for the OECD Guidelines for Multinational Enterprises. March 12, 2010, available: http://www.bis.gov.uk/assets/biscore/business-sectors/docs/10-778-survival-international-against-vedanta-resources.pdf

63 Survival International, "Complaint to the UK National Contact Point under the Specific Instance Procedure of the OECD Guidelines for Multinational Enterprises," December 19, 2008: http://assets.survivalinternational.org/documents/96/Survival_complaint_VEDANTA.pdf

of the UN), and their right to be consulted about any project affecting their lands or other resources (Article 8j of the Convention on Biological Diversity; Article 5(e) of the Race Convention; Articles 19 and 32 of the Declaration of Indigenous Rights).[64]

Nine months after the filing of the initial OECD Guidelines complaint, the UK National Contact Point (NCP) for the OECD Guidelines for Multinational Enterprises responded positively to SI's petition against Vedanta.[65] British NCP affirmed all three charges of OECD Guidelines violations lodged against Vedanta by SI. The UK NCP concluded that Vedanta failed to properly inform the affected Dongria Kondh people on the construction of the bauxite mine; it did not adequately consider the impact of their proposed mining project on the rights and freedoms of the Dongria Kondh, and made little effort to mitigate the impact of its activities in the region.[66]

However, OECD Guidelines are "soft law" with limited legal effect, and the UK NCP's response does not have binding legal force. But rhetorically speaking, the NCP's opinions generated significant effect in Great Britain and beyond. Immediately after the NCP's opinions were released, the British government issued follow-up statements reaffirming the NCP's conclusions.[67] In response to the UK NCP's findings, Amnesty International, one of the largest international human rights non-governmental organizations (NGOs), released a report on February 9, 2010 condemning Vedanta's activities at Niyamgiri, where it highlighted Vedanta's breach of the OECD Guidelines, and framed the breach as "violations" of international law.[68]

Mounting international pressures compelled the Indian government to reconsider its previous position. In summer of 2010, the Indian Ministry of Environment and Forests commissioned a special committee to reevaluate the mining activities in Niyamgiri region. The special committee released a report raising concerns over Vedanta's planned projects in Niyamgiri:

> … allowing mining in the proposed mining lease area by depriving two Primitive Tribal Groups of their rights over the proposed mining site in order to benefit a private company would shake the faith of tribal people in the laws of

64 Ibid.

65 "Final Statement by the UK National Contact Point for the OECD Guidelines for Multinational Enterprises," UK National Contact Point for the OECD Guidelines for Multinational Enterprises, September 25, 2009, available: http://www.berr.gov.uk/files/file53117.doc

66 "Final Statement by the UK National Contact Point for the OECD Guidelines for Multinational Enterprises," Ibid.

67 UK Department for Business, Innovation & Skills, "UK National Contact Point for the Organisation for Economic Co-operation and Development (OECD) guidelines for multinational enterprises," available: https://www.gov.uk/uk-national-contact-point-for-the-organisation-for-economic-co-operation-and-development-oecd-guidelines-for-multinational-enterprises#more-like-this

68 Amnesty International, "Don't mine us Out of Existence: Bauxite mine And Refinery Devastate Lives In India," (London: Amnesty International Publications, 2010), available: http://www.amnesty.org/en/library/asset/ASA20/001/2010/en/0a81a1bc-f50c-4426-9505-7fde6b3382ed/asa200012010en.pdf

> the land which may have serious consequences for the security and well-being of the entire country.[69]

The report further suggested several potential violations of law committed by Vedanta in its mining projects in the area, which include violation of Forest Conservation Act,[70] violation of the Environment Protection Act,[71] as well as non-implementation of the Panchayats Extension to the Scheduled Areas Act.[72]

In August 2010, in response to the special committee's report, Jairam Ramesh, India's Minster of State at the Ministry of Environment and Forests said that Vedanta had shown a "shocking and blatant disregard for the rights of the tribal groups," and announced the move by the Ministry to block Vedanta's controversial mining plan at the Niyam Dongar Mountain.[73] In October, the Environment Ministry rejected Vedanta's plan to expand the Lanjigarh refinery below the Niyamgiri hills, and demanded immediate improvements to environmental conditions of the existing plant.[74]

Vedanta moved quickly to file an appeal to the Indian Supreme Court against the Environment Ministry's ministerial decision.[75] As the functioning of the Lanjigarh aluminum refinery was dependent on the establishment of the bauxite mines on nearby Niyamgiri hills, in September 2012, Vedanta announced that it would close its Lanjigarh refinery by December 2012 unless the Supreme Court granted Vedanta the permission to mine Niyamgiri hills once again.[76] This time around, in addition to supports from international SMOs, an alliance of local tribes formed

69 N. C. Saxena, S. Parasuraman, Promode Kant, Amita Baviskar, "Report of the four member committee for investigation into the proposal submitted by the submitted by the Orissa Mining Company for bauxite mining in Niyamgiri," Ministry of Environment & Forests, Government of India. August 16, 2010, available: http://moef.nic.in/downloads/public-information/Saxena_Vedanta.pdf

70 Ibid., p.71: "The company is in illegal occupation of 26.123 ha of village forest lands enclosed within the factory premises ... This is an act of total contempt for the law on the part of the company and an appalling degree of collusion on the part of the concerned officials."

71 Ibid., p.73: "The company M/s Vedanta Alumina Limited has already proceeded with construction activity for its enormous expansion project that would increase its capacity sixfold from 1 Mtpa to 6 Mtpa without obtaining environmental clearance as per provisions of EIA Notification, 2006 under the EPA. This amounts to a serious violation of the provisions of the Environment (Protection) Act."

72 Ibid., p.73.

73 "David v. Goliath: Indian tribe in 'stunning' victory over mining giant," Survival International, August 24, 2010, available: http://www.survivalinternational.org/news/6385

74 "Troubled Vedanta loses appeal for controversial refinery," Survival International, October 21, 2010, available: http://www.survivalinternational.org/news/6605

75 Jason Burke, "Indian tribe's Avatar-like battle against mining firm reaches supreme court," *The Guardian*, posted April 8, 2012, available: http://www.theguardian.com/world/2012/apr/08/indian-tribe-avatar-supreme-court

76 "Victory: Vedanta to close Orissa refinery." Survival International, September 13, 2012, available: http://www.survivalinternational.org/news/8670

around the Dongria Khondhs for the common purpose of defending their socio-economic and cultural rights.[77]

In April 2013, the Indian Supreme Court today rejected an appeal to allow Vedanta Resources to mine the Niyamgiri hills. The court further held that those indigenous people affected by the proposed mine should have a decisive say in whether the project should continue, that all issues concerning religious and cultural rights of the indigenous people must be heard in the decision-making process.[78] Additionally, the court recognized the Dongria Kondh tribe's right to worship their sacred mountain, and held that their right to worship must be protected and preserved.[79]

It is important to remember that the OECD Guidelines are "soft law" with limited legal effect, and the UK NCP's response does not have binding legal force. But rhetorically speaking, the NCP's opinions generated significant effect in Great Britain and beyond. Immediately after the NCP's opinions were released, the British government issued follow-up statements reaffirming the NCP's conclusions.[80] In response to the UK NCP's findings, Amnesty International released a report on February 9, 2010 condemning Vedanta's activities at Niyamgiri, where it highlighted Vedanta's breach of the OECD Guidelines, and framed the breach as "violations" of international law.[81]

The mounting international pressures compelled the Indian government to reconsider its previous position. In summer of 2010, the Indian Ministry of Environment and Forests commissioned a special committee to reevaluate the mining activities in Niyamgiri region. The special committee released a report raising concerns over Vedanta's planned projects in Niyamgiri:

> ... allowing mining in the proposed mining lease area by depriving two Primitive Tribal Groups of their rights over the proposed mining site in order to benefit a private company would shake the faith of tribal people in the laws of

77 Ibid.

78 John Perkins, "A New Age of People Power: Lessons from the Dongria Kondh," *YES! Magazine*, posted September 3, 2010, available: http://www.yesmagazine.org/peace-justice/a-new-age-of-people-power-lessons-from-the-dongria-kondh

79 Dean Nelson, "Indian villagers defeat British billionaire over plans to mine sacred mountain." *The Telegraph*, last modified August 9, 2013, available: http://www.telegraph.co.uk/news/worldnews/asia/india/10234314/Indian-villagers-defeat-British-billionaire-over-plans-to-mine-sacred-mountain.html

80 See UK Department for Business, Innovation & Skills, "UK National Contact Point for the Organisation for Economic Co-operation and Development (OECD) guidelines for multinational enterprises" (December 2009), available: https://www.gov.uk/uk-national-contact-point-for-the-organisation-for-economic-co-operation-and-development-oecd-guidelines-for-multinational-enterprises#more-like-this

81 Amnesty International, "Don't mine us out of existence: bauxite mine and refinery devastate lives in India." (London: Amnesty International Publications, 2010), available: http://www.amnesty.org/en/library/asset/ASA20/001/2010/en/0a81a1bc-f50c-4426-9505-7fde6b3382ed/asa200012010en.pdf

> the land which may have serious consequences for the security and well-being of the entire country.[82]

The report further claims suggested several potential violations of law committed by Vedanta in its mining projects in the area, which include violation of the Forest Conservation Act,[83] violation of the Environment Protection Act,[84] as well as non-implementation of the Panchayats Extension to the Scheduled Areas Act.[85]

Legal ritual analysis

> *As for the Dongria Kondh themselves, a question: Has anybody even told them that their god may be sacrificed to make weapons of DEATH?*[86]

First we shall examine the ritual significance of the disputed mining site, the Niyam Dongar hill in Niyamgiri. This site bears multiple layers of material and symbolic significance. It is considered "sacred" not only by the Kondhs tribe, but also by the Indian government as well as by the Vedanta Corporation.

The ritual significance of the disputed land to the local Dongria Kondh tribe is first and foremost grounded in its material dependency on the densely forested Niyamgiri hills. The ecosystem of the Niyamgiri hill range, centered on its highest peak, the Niyam Dongar Mountain, is critical in sustaining the small area of available arable land of the region. Being a subsistence farming-based community in a remote and economically less developed region of India, the local tribespeople entirely rely on the Niyamgiri hills for food security. Thus, members of the Dongria Kondh community are bound by their shared existential stake in their tribal land, and consider the Niyamgiri hills to be holy, with each mountain representing

82 N C Saxena, S Parasuraman, Promode Kant, Amita Baviskar, "Report Of The Four Member Committee for Investigation into the Proposal Submitted by the Orissa Mining Company for Bauxite Mining in Niyamgiri," Ministry of Environment & Forests, Government of India. August 16, 2010, available: http://moef.nic.in/downloads/public-information/Saxena_Vedanta.pdf

83 Ibid., p.71.

84 N C Saxena, S Parasuraman, Promode Kant, Amita Baviskar, "Report of the four member committee for investigation into the proposal submitted by the Orissa Mining Company for Bauxite Mining in Niyamgiri," Ministry of Environment & Forests, Government of India. August 16, 2010, p.73.

85 Ibid., p.73: "[I]n addition to the implementation of FRA, the state government also has to ensure the compliance of the following provisions of PESA: Section 4(i): The Gram Sabha or the Panchayats at the appropriate level shall be consulted before making the acquisition of land in the Scheduled Areas for development projects. Section 4(d): every Gram Sabha shall be competent to safeguard and preserve the traditions and customs of the people, their cultural identity, community resources and the customary mode of dispute resolution; Section 4(m) (iii), according to which Gram Sabha has the power to prevent alienation of land in the Scheduled Areas and to take appropriate action to restore any unlawfully alienated land of a Scheduled Tribe."

86 Ahni Schertow, "Niyam Raja sacrificed," posted August 11, 2009, available: https://intercontinentalcry.org/niyam-raja-sacrificed/

a inviolable deity. Among the hills in Niyamgiri, the Niyam Dongar Mountain is the holiest of the holy – it is the seat of their supreme god Niyamraja.[87]

Vedanta Resources certainly does not share those animistic beliefs of the Dongrias; nonetheless, the disputed mining site bears its own sacred meaning for the British mining corporation. Similar to the case of local tribe, the ritual significance of the Niyam Dongar Mountain for Vedanta is grounded in the material value of the land. The sacred mountain contains a key factor to Vedanta's economic production – the bauxite deposits. Unlike the local tribe, the stakeholders of the multinational mining conglomerate do not rely on those hills for their basic food security. Instead, Vedanta identifies the economic value of the disputed land via an entirely different self-referencing belief system – the corporate creed to maximize capital returns for its stakeholders.

For both Vedanta and the indigenous tribe, the ritual significance of the Niyamgiri hill range is grounded in the fact that the disputed land functions as an elementary factor of production for both parties. In other words, the local land sources are objects transformed by human labor in the creation of valuable goods. However, Vedanta operates on a much more abstract belief framework than the local tribe in enshrining and ritualizing the material value of these land resources. Local tribespeople are the direct stakeholders in their land, being both laborers and the direct benefactors of their land resources. The Niyamgiri hill range provides the necessary objects to be transformed by the labor of the tribespeople (e.g. water, arable land and livestock), their labor products (e.g. food, beverages, animal products) are of direct use-value for themselves.

For Vedanta, its stakeholders are not the laborers of their land resources, nor do they directly benefit from the use-value of land products. Instead, Vedanta's shareholders derive the value of mining operations via the transforming real products of the land with use-value (minerals) into abstracted financial capital (currencies and securities), and in turn re-invest the financial capital to result in more value accumulation. The laborers of Vedanta, on the other hand, are not its stakeholders in the sense that they do not enjoy the value created by their labor products. Instead, they engage in labor via a salary contract that only provides a calendrical fixed-amount cash payment that is entirely disjointed from the real value of their labor production. Those stakeholders of the mining company, who do not perform the labor in transforming land resources into goods, and do not derive use-value from the goods of the land, still maintain themselves as the sole recipients of sum total value generated by the productive forces of the company.

Vedanta's mode of labor organization is fairly standard for a contemporary multinational corporation. Yet when looking at the material characteristics alone, this "standard" mode of corporate labor relations stands out as being both inexplicably circuitous and grotesquely disproportionate, in terms of its distribution of resources among laborers and stakeholders. There is not much of a materially rational explanation that can be made for the apparent transnational proliferation and persistence of this mode of corporate economic relations. The corporate mode

87 Ibid.

of labor relation discussed here contradicts fundamental principles of labor-value relation that are recognized across Marxist and classical-liberal schools of economy.

It follows that the real value of economic production, when stripped of purely subjective factors such as the consumer perceptions of demand and supply, equals the sum of labor time (average skill and productivity performed in producing the finished commodities during the period) plus the constant capital (i.e. machinery, upkeep cost, raw materials, land rent) involved in producing the product. This basic principle can be more elegantly summarized as the following material relation: *W (real value of production) = c (constant capital) + L (labor time).* [88] It is difficult to imagine such an unusual mode of labor relations could possibly emerge "organically" or out of material necessity alone, and much less become the dominant mode of "corporate responsibility" that governs our contemporary economic worldview. It is only possible with the support of an exceptionally well-maintained faith community, one that calls for unquestioning "good-faith" of its members to accept or embrace self-sacrifice as ritual obligations, especially when it comes to the distribution of communal resources.

Thus, the ritual significance of the disputed mining site, for both the local tribe and Vedanta, as well as for the Indian government authority, are grounded in the shared material exigency concerning the distribution of valuable land resources among competing parties. However, each side chants this shared material exigence in their own language of self-referencing values, thereby giving rise to very different ritual identifications among the parties. Furthermore, this ritualized significance of the bauxite mining project is enclosed within a threefold cage of conflicting mythologies: the tribal sacred ground for their supreme deity; the government's eminent domain authority under the supremacy of the rule-of-law; and the corporate creed to maximize returns for its stakeholders. The conflicting ritual identification among different parties to the proposed mining site suggests each party assumes their claim over the site is undisputed, and self-evident.

In addition to conflicting ritual identification, there is also the issue of competing ritual procedures underpinning the Vedanta mining controversy. As already discussed in the previous *Kelo v. City of New London* chapter, judicial review procedures function as a ritualized mechanism to *automatically* resolve social contestation, and to produce a *final* settlement that is foreclosed to further political contestation and deliberation. In the Vedanta case, specifically, the procedural

88 Ian Steedman and Judith Tomkins, "On measuring the deviation of prices from values," *Cambridge Journal of Economics* Vol. 22, No. 3, May 1998, pp. 379–386. Edward N. Wolff, "The rate of surplus value, the organic composition of capital, and general rate of profits in the U. S. economy, 1947–1967," *American Economic Review*, March 1979, pp. 329–341. See also, generally, V. K. Dmitriev, "The Theory of Value of David Ricardo," in *Economic Essays on Value, Competition, and Utility* (edited by D. M. Nuti) (Cambridge University Press, 1974); Pierangelo Garegnani, "Quantity of Capital," in *The New Palgrave: Capital Theory*, edited by John Eatwell, Murray Milgate, and Peter Newman, Macmillan, 1990; Adam Smith, *An Inquiry into the Nature and Causes of the Wealth of Nations*, 1776.

element in this case revolves around the presence of multiple mutually unintelligible rule frameworks, each claiming to be the sole legitimate ritual-apparatus to automatically settle the contestation in the allocation of collective resources.

Recall the ritual mechanism of "regulatory taking" in the *Kelo v. City of New London* case from the previous chapter. Although the sanctity of the private domicile is embraced by most, if not all, organized human societies, this seemingly universal totemic ideal is nonetheless contingent to myriad forms of ritual suspension. It follows that, irrespective of their ritual significance, both private domicile and tribal farmland define some of the most essential resources for livelihood within the socio-economic order from which they operate. Although different societies devise different means to organize and manage resources among their members, they all face a similar violent dilemma should competing interests arise for the allocation of resources. Niccolò Machiavelli described this dilemma succinctly in *Prince*: "You must know there are two ways of contesting, the one by the law, the other by force; the first method is proper to men, the second to beasts; but because the first is frequently not sufficient, it is necessary to have recourse to the second."[89]

Machiavelli's point on the fragile line that separates peaceful and violent contestation is also reflected in Thucydides' famous account of the Melian dialogue, in the *History of the Peloponnesian War*. When the Athenian forces decided that persuasion was insufficient to bring Melians to a quick, unconditional surrender, the Athenians did not hesitate to resort to mass violence. It is predictably difficult to convince people to sacrifice their means of livelihood to others, particularly when the terms of the sacrifice are materially unfair and one-sided. Ritual systems, like the Aztec Flower Wars and the Salem witch trials, are deployed as liminal "buffer" rituals between peaceful contestation and unhinged collective violence. Through more sophisticatedly developed social institutions and rationalization frameworks, the ritual system of regulatory taking by design effectively conceals the material and power disparity of the transaction, and the mythic acquiesce to the state's creed of eminent domain prevails.

Through the ritual system of regulatory taking, the contestation of resource among parties is presumed to be confined within the rule-of-law framework of the state, where the state government singularly wields the authority to decide the prevailing party of the dispute. The prevailing party that emerges from the state judiciary procedures, in both the *Kelo* and Vedanta cases, are enshrined into the sacred authority of the state and its rule-of-law. The dramatic enactment of regulatory taking and the subsequent judicial review process rhetorically erases the inequitable resource transfers that actually took place, thereby transforming a violent and materially disruptive event into a palatable dramatic ritual sacrifice.

89 Nicolo Machiavelli, *The Prince*, Chapter XVIII, translation by W. K. Marriott (Project Gutenberg: 2006, last updated August 26, 2016), available: https://www.gutenberg.org/files/1232

There are, however, key differences in the deployment of ritual procedures between the *Kelo* and *Vedanta* cases. In *Kelo v. City of New London* discussed in the previous chapter, although private domicile is considered both culturally and legally sacred, and is under constitutional protection, it is the very same constitution that also prescribes the laws allowing for the "appropriate" occasion where the private shall be sacrificed, for the higher "public good." Thus, for *Kelo*, should a citizen, being a member of the U.S. constitutional *ecclesia* in good faith, assume the legitimacy of the constitutional framework along with its rights protections, this same believer must also accept the conditions of ritual sacrifice of his or her rights mandated by the same constitutional framework. The U.S. constitution, like most written constitutions, effectively asserts itself as an absolute and singular covenant that its followers must accept in whole. Being a citizen automatically predestines one to be subjected under this constitutional covenant, and those organizing rules and principles within the constitutional framework, both written and assumed, must be applied in their totality, and cannot be compartmentalized or selectively followed.

However, in the Vedanta dispute, the Dongria tribe did not automatically acquiesce to the state's act of regulatory taking. Even more unusual is that the local tribe did not cease their petition against the land grab even after the Indian Supreme Court had reached its final ruling against the tribe. This is in part due to the existence of a counteracting public faith community within the supposedly monocentric constitutional civic *ecclesia* of the modern Indian Republic. Given their material dependency on the Niyamgiri hills, the Dongria community regarded the sanctity of their homeland to be inviolable, but at a time of crisis to stand independently from the state constitutional authority of land sacrifice. In other words, in the Vedanta dispute, the Dongria people assumed their own self-referential *ecclesia* (or communal "faith") that existed within yet autonomously from the state-centric constitutional *ecclesia*. However, given the vast power disparity between the Indian government and the Dongria Kondh tribe, the tribal community's act of doctrinal resistance against the monopolizing legitimacy of the state judicial process ran the risk of being labeled a "heretical" anti-state sect (i.e. labeled as "outlaw"), thereby potentially triggering a more violent response from the state apparatus.

Indeed, the Indian Supreme Court in the Vedanta case ruled in favor of the regulatory taking of tribal land similar to that of the *Kelo v. City of New London*. The highest court of India, like the SCOTUS in the *Kelo* decision, argued that economic development conforms to the "public purpose" doctrine for eminent domain takings, even if the taken land is transferred to a private, party for for-profit activities. In *Kelo v. City of New London*, Justice Stevens, who authored the SCOTUS' majority opinion, was well-aware of the fact that the city government intent to sell and lease those taken houses to private businesses, and that private enterprises are the ones directly benefiting from the city's eminent domain takings. He also acknowledged much of the taken land will not even be accessible to the general public. In Justice Stevens' own words:

> this is not a case in which the City is planning to open the condemned land–at least not in its entirety–to use by the general public. Nor will the private lessees of the land in any sense be required to operate like common carriers, making their services available to all comers.

Yet SCOTUS maintained that, again in Justice Stevens' quote: "the public end may be as well or better served through an agency of private enterprise." Justice Stevens' arguments in *Kelo v City of New London* were primarily grounded upon the logic that private business growth would lead to more jobs and tax revenue, thus satisfies public purpose of takings. The majority's ruling even abandoned the "use by the public" as the proper definition of "public use," and insisted that anything that the government can argue serves "public interest," even if for purely commercial development purposes, would satisfy the "public use" requirement under the 5th Amendment. As Justice Stevens wrote: "Indeed, while many state courts in the mid-19th century endorsed 'use by the public' as the proper definition of public use, that narrow view steadily eroded over time."[90]

Under the traditional state-centric transnational legal *pístis*, which assumed the monopolizing authority of the state within its sovereign legal structure, the Indian Supreme Court's decision would mark a hard stop for the contestability of the regulatory taking. To elevate the apparent legality and authoritativeness of its allegations, it was necessary for SI not only to draw from various rule frameworks in support of its claims, but also to present the claims in a coherent and unified fashion that is easily recognizable under the global legal *pístis*. To achieve this, SI employed the following strategies: [1] stylistically frame the format of the document to resemble a "legal complaint" rather than a typical "OECD inquiry;" [2] brush over the legal distinctions between cultural rights, socio-economic rights and civil-political rights by avoiding rights-categorization and referring them collectively as "human rights;" [3] frame violations of corporate social responsibility and OECD Guidelines as breaches of *international law*. The relationships between various rule frameworks, types of rights, and the presentation styles of the document with respect to their perceived legality and authoritativeness under the global legal *pístis* can be demonstrated in Table 4.2 (in a simplified and generalized fashion).

Although the complaint document revolves around allegations of "human rights violations" and the breach of "international law," its claims are problematic in as the [1] OECD NCP structure formally provides no legal remedies; [2] violations of socio-economic and cultural rights are often considered outside of the purview of "human rights," and [3] human rights themselves are not part of the traditional international law structure. To overcome these intrinsic difficulties, the document framed its language in ways that would be more recognizable and identifiable in relation to the global legal *pístis.* [91]

90 See *Kelo v. City of New London* (04–108) 545 U.S. 469 (2005), available: https://www.law.cornell.edu/supct/html/04-108.ZS.html

91 See Survival International, "Complaint to the UK National Contact Point under the Specific Instance Procedure of the OECD Guidelines for Multinational Enterprises,"

What is the role of legal *pístis* in the context of the Vedanta controversy? To answer this question, we must first consider the meaning of *pístis* within theology. Whereas *Pístis* (Πίστις) was the personification of good faith and trustworthiness in Greek mythology, this term was later appropriated in both rhetoric and Christian theology to describe the general conditions for persuasion, or more precisely the "affect and effect rather than on the representation of the truth."[92] In this sense, legal *pístis* refers not to legal arguments themselves, but on the embedded interpretative and normative frameworks on which the audience would rely to determine the persuasiveness of the legal argument. In other words, one way to understand legal *pístis* is that it is a general and rather abstract term that describes some sort of legal culture or custom within a society. Legal *pístis* understood as such is the substantive social knowledge that regulates and defines social relations. However, "legal *pístis*" does not have to exist in a purely abstract and psychological form.

Indeed, the state of mind of a given audience with regard to legal perception is often a reflection of the formal legal structure that already exists in a society, and legal culture can also affect the way legal institutions form. In this sense, a state's formal legal structure, or its municipal law, can also in some way be viewed as being part of its legal *pístis.* As we are dealing with "human rights" legal *pístis*, and assuming by "human rights" we are not referring to the culture of any single state, but rather a set or norms that all state and non-state actors are expected to adhere to. The notion of *pístis as* socially embedded knowledge framework for human rights gives legitimacy for specific *dóxa* (teachings) of human rights, such as right to bear arm or right to basic income. The legal *pístis* is mostly tacit and consubstantively assumed. It should not be taken as referring to any particular set of explicitly stated legal *dóxa* or written law, but rather the general legal culture/custom that is commonly associated within the human rights discourse.

A helpful starting point for our analysis on this matter is look at the Statute of the International Court of Justice (ICJ), Article 38.1. It is often considered as the principal statute dealing with the sources of the international law. The statute stipulates:

> The Court, whose function is to decide in accordance with international law such disputes as are submitted to it, shall apply: (a). international conventions, whether general or particular, establishing rules expressly recognized by the contesting states; (b). international custom, as evidence of a general practice accepted as law; (c). the general principles of law recognized by civilized nations; (d). subject to the provisions of Article 59, judicial decisions and the teachings of the most highly qualified publicists

p.10. http://assets.survivalinternational.org/documents/96/Survival_complaint_VEDANTA.pdf

92 Roger Dennis Cherry, *A Rhetoric of Doing Essays on Written Discourse: Pístis, Expression, and Belief* (Carbondale, IL: Southern Illinois University Press, 1992) at 133–135.

of the various nations, as subsidiary means for the determination of rules of law.[93]

ICJ Article 38.1(a) provides that "international conventions" can be a source of international law. Although the concept of the human rights legal *pístis* itself can be very abstract, if the relevant parties decide to enter into a treaty that defines the meaning of human rights, then this seemingly abstract concept of legal *pístis* will be reified into treaty or an international convention, and it can become a formal source of international law under ICJ Statute Art. 38.1(a). It is not unprecedented for states to transform their common legal *pístis* into a binding treaty. The Lisbon Treaty, or the Treaty on the European Union (TEU) is an example where member states entered into a binding agreement that is designed partly to promote their common European values.[94]

TEU Article 1 provides that: "The Union is founded on the values of respect for human dignity, freedom, democracy, equality, the rule-of-law and respect for human rights, including the rights of persons belonging to minorities. These values are common to the member states in a society in which pluralism, non-discrimination, tolerance, justice, solidarity and equality between women and men prevail." Also, Art. 6, ind. 3 of TEU states that "fundamental rights … as they result from the constitutional traditions common to the Member States, shall constitute general principles of the Union's law."

ICJ Article 38.1(c) also recognizes "general principles of law recognized by civilized nations" as a possible source of international law. There are two different views as to the concept of "general principles of law recognized by civilized nations." One is that it refers to the general principles of law recognized by all civilized nations. If this view is taken, and assuming that India and UK are considered "civilized nations," then this 38.1(c) should be only referring to the general principles in the most-broad terms, and the localized or culturally-specific concepts of human rights would seem irrelevant as their fundamental legal conceptions should be already included in that broad reading. The alternative view on 38.1(c) is that the "general principles of law" is referring to general principles of municipal jurisprudence.[95]

If this view is taken, and if the "*human rights generally*" is referring to the municipal legal jurisprudence of India and UK, then such legal *pístis* may be seen as applicable under public international law. Paragraph (d) of Article 38

93 United Nations, *Statute of the International Court of Justice*, April 18, 1946, Art. 38.1 (c) (accessed April 28, 2017), available at: http://www.refworld.org/docid/3deb4b9c0.html.

94 European Union, *Treaty on European Union*, 2012/C 326/01 (accessed April 28, 2017), available at EUR-Lex: https://eur-lex.europa.eu/legal-content/EN/ALL/?uri=celex:12012M/TXT

95 Municipal jurisprudence refers to the legal rule framework specific to sub-national legal system, such as the state law of California.

provides that subject to the provisions of Article 59 (which stipulates that the decision of the ICJ has no binding force except between the parties and in respect of that particular case), authoritative legal discourse, that is, judicial decisions and the teachings of the most highly qualified publicists of the various nations, as subsidiary means for the determination of rules of law. If there are abundant precedents of judicial decisions and the teachings of the most "highly qualified" legal writers made reference to human rights standards, then those concepts of jurisprudence may have a place in the international law under Art. 38(d).

Most importantly, ICJ Article 38.1(b) refers to "international custom" that can be used as evidence for international law. Scholars have identified four elements to the customary international law, and they are: duration, uniformity, generality, belief of legal necessity (*opinio juris et necessitatis*).[96] As for the duration, although a long practice would certainly add weight to the evidence supporting the applicability of the custom in international law, as long as the uniformity and generality elements are fulfilled, the ICJ does not usually emphasize the time element as a prerequisite. The common "human rights" legal *pístis* as we know today, especially relating to socio-economic rights, is commonly seen as a by-product of the waves of civil rights movements and international political discussions during the 1960s and 1970s, which are not particularly long in history. Lastly, *opinio juris et necessitatis*, that is, recognition by the parties of a certain practice as obligatory, and the given practice is required by, or consistent with prevailing norms of international law. The notion of human rights, as an outgrowth of Western notions of civil-political rights and the reflection from the tragedies that savaged the world during World War II, has become an anchor of the international legal system.[97] However, there is lack of global consensus on the parameter of human rights standards, and whether socio-economic and cultural rights are protected by any prevailing formal frameworks of international law.

The advent of socio-economic rights and cultural rights have elicited the talks of fragmentation in human rights norms—that those traditional Western civil and political rights are first generation human rights, and socio-political rights being the second generation (some consider right of development, right of sustainable living environment, and right to standard of living as 'third generation' human rights).[98] This schism between civil-political rights and socio-economic rights has profound political, ideological, and cultural implications. In her article "The Minimal Core for Economic and Social Rights," Katharine Young puts this generational divide succinctly:

96 Ian Browlie, *Principles of Public International Law* (Oxford University Press, October 22, 2008), 7.

97 Alexandra R. Harrington, "Don't Mind the Gap: The Ride of Individual Complaint Mechanisms Within International Human Rights Treaties," *Duke Journal of Comparative and International Law* Vol. 22 (2012), p.153, 177.

98 Ian Browlie, *Principles of Public International Law* (Oxford University Press, October 22, 2008), pp.519–604

> The lack of consensus on human rights norms is due in part to the late secularization of the protection of collective material interests in human rights history compared with other categories of rights. It is also a feature of the ideological disagreements of the Cold War period, when Western governments worked actively to demote the importance of economic and social rights and when the human rights nongovernmental organizations headquartered in the West, including Human Rights Watch and Amnesty International, followed suit. Yet even with the end of this polarization, consensus continues to lead to conservative and abstract expressions of the content of economic and social rights.[99]

The idea of incorporating socio-economic and cultural rights under the umbrella term of "human rights" has been met with considerable resistance from legal scholarship. Many have expressed skepticism on the fundamental validity of socio-economic rights, arguing that the so-called economic and social rights are in fact "entitlements" that justify the development of "welfare states."[100] Some even go as far to suggest socio-economic rights as the antithesis of human rights.[101] The schism between civil-political and socio-economic rights in international legal discourse is exemplified by the continued U.S. resistance against the incorporation of the right to safe drinking water, a socio-economic right, as an UN-recognized human right.[102]

Table 4.1 Three generations of human rights under the state-centric legal *pístis*

	3rd gen. human rights (i.e. basic income, basic living standards)	**2nd gen. human rights** (economic, social and cultural)	**1st gen. human** rights (civil-political)
Legal ritualization	informal, non-legal, customary	Semi-formal, quasi-legal, "soft law"	Formal, "hard" law
Belief doctrines:	corporate social responsibility	OECD Guidelines, UN Guiding Principles on Business and Human Rights	National and International law
Formal enforcement:	Self-regulation + civil society actors	State + civil society actors	State legal apparatus

99 Katharine Young, "The Minimum Core of Economic and Social Rights: A Concept in Search of Content," *The Yale Journal of International Law* Vol. 33 (2008), p.113

100 See Alex Kirkup and Tony Evans, "The Myth of Western Opposition to Economic, Social, and Cultural Rights? A Reply to Whelan and Donnelly," *Human Rights Quarterly* 31 (2009), 221–238.

101 Amartya Sen, "Human Rights and Asian Values," *The New Republic*, July 14-July 21, 1997.

102 Amnesty International, "Document - United Nations: General Assembly Makes Progress on the Human Rights to Water and Sanitation, But Only so Far as the USA Permits," November 26, 2013 IOR 40/005/2013.

The three-generation schematization of human rights as shown in the table above cannot be considered independent from the historical development of neoliberalism. Historians of modern political economy have similarly identified three waves of the global marketization process, each new wave propelled by the crisis generated from the previous wave.[103] Each wave comes with accompanying ritual inventions at both the state and communal levels, to address new contradictions that emerge from the market:

Table 4.2 Three waves of marketization and ritual inventions against the market

	First wave: 1800s - 1914		**Second wave:** 1944 - 1973	**Third wave:** 1973 onwards
Formal ritual inventions (protections for the market)	labor rights	**Thirty-years of crisis: WWI & WWII**	Civil-political rights	2nd and 3rd gen. human rights
Societal ritual responses (defenses against the market)	Labor unions		Civil and political rights movements	Civil society actors
Representative historical event	UK Poor Law Amendment Act of 1834		1944 Bretton Woods Conference	1973 Oil Crisis

These ritual inventions at both formal and societal levels reflect the evolving tensions between "state" and "transnational" norm structures that are intrinsic to the development of neoliberal legal *pístis*. The so-called "neoliberal legal pístis" is not a monolithic and stable one, but rather a historical process of crisis management. While neoliberalism reified in the form of a global legal *pístis* an amalgamation of both provincial and global values, those values are nonetheless subject to the hierarchy of recognition – that economic ideals enshrined in the language of market and development became transnationally recognized as authoritative legal justifications for ritualized taking. It can be said that the neoliberal legal *pístis* of the world enables a kind of "race towards universal identification," not only for the laws of ritual sacrifice, but also for strategic ritual responses against these universalized sacrifices.

In this sense, the complaint document from SI ritually embraces the language of neoliberal legal *pístis* to strategically resist the regulatory taking of tribal land. This strategic deployment of neoliberal legal *pístis* allows the civil society actor to position itself and the state authority under the same neoliberal *ecclesia*, thus creating the necessary stasis ground to challenge the regulatory taking as a legal rather than political issue. This means that by embracing the

103 Michael Burawoy, "Public sociology vs. the market," *Socio-Economic Review* (2007), at 256–361. *See also*, Donald Mackenzie, *Material Markets: How Economic Agents are Constructed* (Oxford, UK: 2009): 85–109.

common neoliberal legal *pístis* as the state, SI is able to reopen the otherwise foreclosed legal debate without fundamentally challenging the legitimacy of the state authority. This strategic framing by SI ritually reorients the conflict between the Dongria tribe, Vedanta, and the state into a technical question concerning the proper jurisdiction of transnational rule frameworks. SI's strategic ritual response also erases the revolutionary potential of its petition, as it is obligated to affirm in good faith the legitimacy of the common neoliberal *pístis* with which its rituals are governed. This strategic compromise would also make the civil society actor, as well as its indigenous tribal "clients" appear less "dangerous" from the perspective of the state authority.

A close reading of the complaint text filed by SI reveals the deployment of "appropriate" ritual terms that have been blessed by the marketization process, and strategically by drawing from various differentiated norm systems concurrently in a unified fashion, transforming parochial norms into authoritative global rules, effectively elevating the otherwise non-legal document into a functional legal complaint. The strategic framing is evident from the very first page of the document, when SI decided to use the word "complaint" in the document title "Complaint to the UK National Contact Point under the Specific Instance Procedure of the OECD Guidelines for Multinational Enterprises." It is well-understood that observance of the Guidelines by enterprises is voluntary and not legally enforceable. Consequently, according to the filing procedure of The Guidelines, reports of guideline violations should not be called "complaints." Rather, the report should be filed as "inquiries" in "specific instances" seeking "clarification of the Guidelines."[104] Although it is no longer the case, for many years the OECD even prohibited "inquiries" from naming the corporations whose conduct gave rise to the allegation of guideline violations.[105] The term "complaint" is commonly recognized as a legal term, which carries the connotation of allegations pertaining to legal violations – the nonobservance of rules that expect strict observance. By titling the document as a "complaint" rather than an "inquiry," this seemingly minor deviation from OECD's formatting requirement effectively intensified the expectation of observation with regard to the alleged violations, and helped to set the legal-sounding tone for the rest of the document.

More importantly, the complaint document deals with the recognition difficulty associated with socio-economic and cultural rights by simply grouping all alleged rights violations under the widely recognized umbrella term of "human rights." For instance, when looking at the document's table of contents, specific allegations of rights violations are arranged as follows:[106]

104 Larry Catá Backer, "The Structural Characteristics of Global Law for the 21st Century: Fracture, Fluidity, Permeability, and Polycentricity," *Tilburg Law Review* Vol. 17 (2012), 177–199.

105 Survival International, "Complaint to the UK National Contact Point under the Specific Instance Procedure of the OECD Guidelines for Multinational Enterprises," p.1.

106 Ibid., p.1.

CONTENTS

… …

……

1

Note that the traditional (Western) understanding of human rights only includes individual natural rights (e.g. religious freedom) and civil-political rights (e.g. equality before the law), whereas the rights of "means of subsistence" and to be consulted and to give or refuse their FPIC (Free, Prior and Informed Consent) of an indigenous people typically belong to the contested domain of socio-economic and cultural rights.[107] Against this inconvenient rights-fragmentation, the document unproblematically presented all of its references – socio-economic, cultural, and civil-political rights – as fundamental "human rights" that are equally protected under international law. Likewise, under the "Summary of complaint" section, the document narrated its allegation of rights violation in a similar unified framework:[108]

Summary of complaint

… …

21. The human rights to which the host government has made international commitments but which Vedanta has failed to respect are the rights of the Dongria Kondh:

(1) to enjoy their own culture and to profess and practice their own religion…

(2) to equality before the law…

(3) not to be deprived of their means of subsistence…

(4) to be consulted about any project affecting their lands or other resources and to give or refuse their free, prior and informed consent to the project before it is permitted to proceed…

… …

8

107 UN General Assembly, *Universal Declaration of Human Rights*, December 10, 1948, 217 A (II), available: http://www.un.org/en/documents/udhr/index.shtml

108 Survival International, "Complaint to the UK National Contact Point under the Specific Instance Procedure of the OECD Guidelines for Multinational Enterprises," pp.7–8.

Often, cases of indigenous populations being deprived from their "means of subsistence" due to development projects without their FPIC are framed as "economic or contractual disputes" rather than "rights violations," despite the grossly asymmetric balance-of-power between small native tribes and multinational enterprises.[109] This seemingly trivial terminology distinction carries major legal and semantic implications – consider the difference betwixt "economic disputes *between* Vedanta and Dongrias," and "rights violations committed by Vedanta *against* Dongrias." It is evident that the use of the term "economic dispute" often masks the underlying power disparity between the parties involved. Furthermore, the phrase "economic dispute" in itself only signifies the presence of *difference* between negotiating parties; it does not suggest any damages or injuries suffered. Whereas the invocation of "rights violation" implies underlying damages and injuries, it does not refer to any specific rule framework for addressing and disciplining the alleged violations. The frame of "human rights violation," however, triggers both the rhetorical exigency of underlying injuries, as well as situating the exigency within the well-established normative framework of international law.

Lastly, while it is unlikely that SI is unaware of the non-binding nature of the OECD Guidelines, the document was nonetheless drafted in such a way that frames The Guidelines as "international law." This framing effort, *prima facie,* appears to be paradoxical. International laws are recognized as such because they embody "general principles of law and customs" that transcend state and institutional boundaries, and are widely recognized by the citizens of the world.[110] The OECD Guidelines on the other hand can almost be seen as the antithesis of internal law – it is a set of newly introduced intra-organizational recommendations that receives little widespread recognition.

The subsistence and substance of international law rest within the prevailing transnational legal *pístis,* which is manifested through the intersubjective recognition of others' *living-in-the-world-ness.* There is no international law *a priori* recognition, and there is no recognition *a priori* the exchange and circulation of meanings. Many foundational principles of international law today were once little more than neologistic jargon articulated by those Enlightenment philosophers, in the hope of persuading people to adopt and extend those obscure ideas into common values.[111] In this sense, the emergent global legal *pístis* is in fact the result of individuals and groups attempting to interpellate[112] others, through the circulation of meanings, into seeing the new and different meanings of the relations in the world, hopefully breaking out of the ossified limitations that bind the transaction of meanings. Though the transformation and proliferation of meanings

109 FPIC stands for "Free, Prior and Informed Consent."

110 United Nations, *Statute of the International Court of Justice*, April 18, 1946, Art. 38.1 (c).

111 Paul Patton, "Concept and Politics in Derrida and Deleuze," *Critical Horizons,* 02/2010 Vol. 4, No. 2, 157.

112 Louis Althusser, "Ideology and Ideological State Apparatuses (Notes towards an Investigation)." *Lenin and Philosophy and Other Essays* (New York: Monthly Review Press: 1971).

are in part driven by historical and social forces that are outside of the manageable domain of any single individual or organization, there is nonetheless a practical need for organizations like SI to catalyze knowledge creation by strategically framing neologistic expressions as an integral part of a larger set of well-accepted value frameworks.

The "Introduction" section of the complaint document already presupposes that one of the key functions of the document is to address violations of international law:[113]

> **I. Introduction**
>
> … …
>
> 8. …They [the Dongria people] should be allowed to follow their own path in their own time, and that they should not have a new one foisted upon them by Vedanta or anyone else.
>
> 9. International human rights law fully endorses this position, recognising as it does that the free, prior and informed consent ("FPIC") of an indigenous people must be obtained for any project likely to affect its lands…
>
> … …
>
> 14. In the meantime Vedanta should agree to stop work on the mine and its infrastructure…
>
> 15. This approach accords not only with well-established principles of international law but with commercial good sense.

As the introduction orderly presents the summary of the substantive content of the rest of the 32-page-long document, it problematically juxtaposes the invocation of "international law" (indents 9, 15) after the statements of specific demands (indents 8, 14), implying that the demands are clearly backed by well-established principles of international law. The introduction therefore gives the appearance that from the very beginning the document was drafted within the context of international law, and expects an interpellated reader who is already a subject of the normative recognition of international law.

Throughout the remainder of the OECD complaint document, the complaint does not address the fundamental question of whether those alleged violations really in fact pertain to international law—as such question should be already "evident" from the introduction of the document. The theme of international law is further reinforced through the frequent highlighting of "human rights" violations throughout the document, without separating those rights that are less recognized under traditional international law from the "human rights" frame. Finally, all the alleged violations of international law listed in the document refer

113 Survival International, "Complaint to the UK National Contact Point under the Specific Instance Procedure of the OECD Guidelines for Multinational Enterprises," pp. 2–7.

back to the singular body of OECD Guidelines, which in turn implicitly frames the OECD Guidelines as an inseparable and integral Part of the international law cosmos.

Conclusion: a myth at last

> *If the NCP cannot persuade Vedanta to do this, the Dongria will have no other means of securing their right to be heard. Denied that right, they may feel driven to use every means available to them to resist and disrupt Vedanta's operations. This cannot be in the long term interests of anyone.* [114]

From the case study and the analysis of the complaint document filed by SI, we can see that the OECD Guidelines for Multinational Enterprises have opened a possibility for a framework through which standards of human rights and corporate social responsibility could be applied directly to private entities by states enforcing transnational norms under their treaty obligations. The apparent strength of the OECD Guidelines was especially important because they provided a quasi-judicial mechanism through which non-state actors could bring complaints against multinational enterprises for mandating irresistible sacrifices for its private interests. The OECD Guidelines effectively provide a "safer" language of resisting sacrifice, one that fully conforms to the core values and principles of neoliberal rhetorical theology. The previously transgressive act can be reframed with the blessed language of "socio-economic and cultural rights violations," thereby providing new space for contestation-under-good-faith that are previously unprotected under traditional human rights standards.

Technically, the system is not "hard law" – it is neither binding on states and corporations, nor incorporated into their domestic; but they could affect the judgment of individuals and investors that might persuade either state or private entities to adhere to these customary human rights norms. More importantly, these systems may have legal effect, regardless of whether or not they conform to the classically understood notions of "law." The SI case also demonstrates an effective process of operationalizing soft law to produce the "hard law" effects beyond national borders without directly challenging state authority. The output of quasi-judicial and interpretive statements, like those from the SI, will continue to contribute to the institutionalization of transnational systems of human rights enforcement, while at the same time further universalizing the legal *pístis* of neoliberalism.[115]

114 Survival International, "Complaint to the UK National Contact Point under the Specific Instance Procedure of the OECD Guidelines for Multinational Enterprises," December 19, 2008, p.30.

115 "UN 'Protect, Respect and Remedy' Framework Guiding Principles," Business & Human Rights Resource Centre, 2011 (accessed April, 2017), available: http://www.business-humanrights.org/SpecialRepPortal/Home/Protect-Respect-Remedy-Framework/GuidingPrinciples

More broadly, this case also demonstrates the capacity of neoliberal discourse not only to enforce ritual sacrifices for advancing the marketization process, but also to open up new ritual spaces for resisting against the dehumanizing measures of the "market." This seemingly self-compromising ritual mechanism of neoliberalism serves as a highly effective crisis-management mechanism. Not only is neoliberalism driven by recurring economic crises that are intrinsic to its marketization process, it is also strengthened by organized resistance efforts against the ills of its marketization. By "universalizing" the neoliberal legal *pístis* as the sole legitimate transnational rule framework for both mandating and appealing ritual sacrifice, it closes the viability for alternative forms of political *ecclesia* that do not conform to the rhetorical theology of neoliberalism.

The adaptive ritual-invention capacity of neoliberal rhetoric not only preserves its governmentality, but also strengthens its economic enforceability. The seemingly successful petition by the indigenous tribe in the Vedanta controversy was proved to be a short-lived victory. After the *Vedanta* ruling by the Indian Supreme Court, the Odisha government re-submitted its bauxite mining proposal through the state-owned OMC. The Supreme Court allowed the Odisha government to form its own commission to review all in-state mining proposals.[116] In 2018, the Odisha government approved its own plan to mine bauxite from the controversial Niyamgiri deposit, and immediately sold its Niyamgiri mining rights back to Vedanta Resources.[117]

David and Goliath: a myth after all.

116 Meera Mohanty, "Odisha new Bauxite linkage policy to benefit Vedanta," *The Economic Times* (updated: February 12, 2018, accessed April 11, 2018), available: //economictimes.indiatimes.com/articleshow/63018502.cms?utm_source=contentofinterest&utm_medium=text&utm_campaign=cppst

117 Subhashish Mohanty, "Capacity boost for Vedanta: Naveen nod to Lanjigarh refinery expansion," *The Telegraph India* (posted April 9, 2018, accessed April 12, 2018), available: https://www.telegraphindia.com/states/odisha/capacity-boost-for-vedanta-221986

5 Messianic rhetoric of Apartheid

The use of civic ritual to legitimize deprivation of personal rights is nothing new. Even the modern *Rechtsstaat* incarnation of ritual takings, better known as *eminent domain*, has been in use for more than a half-millennia. We can trace the humanistic legal formulation of eminent domain back to the Protestant Reformation era, most notably in the writings of Armenian theologian and legal philosopher Hugo Grotius.[1] What is new is the appropriation of the logic of the market and the faith of development as the legitimation frame, or in "Burkean" terms, the *terministic screen*, co-substantiating public ritual takings. This chapter traces back to one of the earliest post-World War II examples of a major world leader who predominantly relied on "economically-liberal" justifications for radically illiberal policies. Our person of interest is Dr. Hendrik Frensch Verwoerd (September 8, 1901–September 6, 1966). He was Professor of Sociology and Social Work at University of Stellenbosch, 6th Prime Minister of South Africa, perhaps most famously remembered as the "Architect of Apartheid."[2]

The rhetorical analysis in this chapter focuses on *Verwoerd Speaks* – a comprehensive collection of speeches by H. F. Verwoerd. This 730-page long edited volume is by far the largest and most complete collection of Dr. Verwoerd's published speeches, covering the entire span of his political career from 1948 to 1966.[3] It is impossible to accommodate the original line-by-line analysis of the entire *Verwoerd Speaks* collection within the pages of this chapter. Given practical limitations, only a small selection of the most representative excerpts from the Verwoerd collection will be highlighted in this chapter, presented as a distilled summary of key finds from the full reading.

1 Hugo Grotius, *The Law of War and Peace*, originally published in 1625, trans. Francis Kelsey (Carnegie edition, 1925), 28.

2 Catherine M. Cole, *Performing South Africa's Truth Commission: Stages of Transition* (Bloomington, Indiana: Indiana University Press, 2010) pp. 31, 226. See also, Annie E. Coombes, *History after Apartheid: Visual Culture and Public Memory in a Democratic South Africa* (Durham, NC: Duke University Press, 2003) at p.22.

3 *Verwoerd Speaks* records a total of 58 speeches made by H. F. Verwoerd between 1948 and 1966. All speeches in the collection, with the exception of his "Speech on the Occasion of the First Quinquennial Celebration of the Republic of South Africa" on May 31, 1966 (which was delivered months before his assassination) have been edited by Dr. Verwoerd himself.

After examining all 58 speeches transcribed in the *Verwoerd Speaks* collection, this study has reached the following conclusions:

[1] The analysis affirms the existing understanding that Apartheid South Africa, as envisioned by Dr. Verwoerd, epitomized the racial totalitarian state in terms of its effective operation. That is, the Apartheid state was conceived by Dr. Verwoerd as a "scientifically-engineered" management apparatus, optimized for the efficient and total enforcement of racial segregation doctrines in all aspects of public and private transaction.
[2] In his public remarks, Dr. Verwoerd consistently eschewed explicitly racist vocabulary, and avoided narratives that immediately resembled authoritarian personalities commonly recognized in the West. Instead, Dr. Verwoerd framed his brand of racial totalitarian state as a "more perfect realization" of liberal democratic ideals – specifically to bring "unity, prosperity, and happiness" for all South Africans.[4] Furthermore, Dr. Verwoerd was arguably the first post-World War II world leader who made serious attempts to synthesize totalitarian political measures with liberal economic principles.
[3] Throughout his public remarks, Dr. Verwoerd consistently cultivated a subtle, yet rhetorically powerful cult of personality around his scientist/expert persona, delivering "extra-political" messianic gospel for the future of South Africa. His brand of messianic cult of personality can be understood as a significant departure from the heroic-*Übermensch* type of cult of personality which was associated with European fascist leaders.
[4] His use of messianic rhetoric played a central role in his rhetorical invention of a new brand of totalitarian state masked under thin veils of "development" and "economic self-determination." Interestingly, his messianic rhetoric employed similar rhetorical strategies as those used by 16th century jurist and Reformed theologian John Calvin, albeit for radically different ends.
[5] Lastly and most importantly, this study has identified five interacting core doctrines underpinning the political theology of Dr. Verwoerd. These core doctrines together frame Apartheid as the appropriate ritual response to his manufactured public exigence. They are: (i) *Total depravity* of the status quo for racial/ethnic relations; (ii) *Unconditional* segregation of populations for no reason other than their assigned racial or ethnic category; (iii) *Limited realization* of development benefits under Apartheid; (iv) *Irresistible* forced racial segregation in all aspects of public and private life; and (v) *Perseverance* of the Apartheid system as the sole route towards "true democracy."

Conceptual overview

The previous two chapters have examined two prominent and relatively recent controversies concerning the use of administrative taking of private dwellings for economic redevelopment. Although *Kelo* and *Vedanta* are two distinct rhetorical

4 H. F. Verwoerd, "Day of the Covenant Address at Blood River, December 16th, 1958." *Verwoerd Speaks*, 206.

moments which took place in disparate political and cultural settings, they nonetheless share similar underlying exigencies (alleged need for economic redevelopment) and similar responses (administrative taking of private homes, with judicial enforcement). The government authorities in *Kelo* and *Vedanta* also faced similar rhetorical constraints, in terms of the difficulty to radically shift the acceptable threshold for public takings, as well as in the remarkable "insubordination" of their sacrificial subjects. Both *Kelo* and *Vedanta* represented certain continuations and departures of pre-existing norms of eminent domain. They are continuations in the sense that both cases proceeded from long-established civic rituals that substantiate *legitimate* forms of public sacrifice (the use of eminent domain). Phenomenologically, this legitimation process functions as formal repetition and collective identification of civic rituals, through which acts of taking would automatically assume certain continuity in past collective memory. They are also departures in terms of their attempts to apply familiar civic rituals to radically unfamiliar circumstances (private redevelopment purposes). In both the *Kelo* and *Vedanta* cases, the rhetorical contestations had to do with not only the controversies at hand, but also on the scope and boundaries of the laws of public sacrifice.

Although the outcomes of the two previous case studies are quite different, the authority employed similar justification frameworks in affirming their expansion of eminent domain – that private development in itself is an indispensable public good without the need for further empirical justification. Indeed, the arguments presented by respective authorities in *Kelo* and *Vedanta* are hardly "new." The appropriation of the *logos* of economic liberalism as a God-term justifying public takings has been a familiar phenomenon in the post-World War II proliferation of market-driven governmentality. Consider, for example, those "mining friendly" – but environmentally costly – policies of Peruvian president Alberto Fujimori, as well as the ongoing (as of 2018) mass displacement of low-income city populations in China due to a sweeping urban redevelopment effort to boost GDP growth. The list goes on, but this rhetoric of "predestined" public sacrifice for the sake of "indispensable" market-driven development is something that is both historically particular (post-World War II emergent), as well as transnationally prevalent.

Political scientists have often used the term "new authoritarianism" to denote a shift in the post-Reagan (or more precisely, post-1970s energy crisis) era transnational political discourse, characterized by the growing tendency of appropriating economically "liberal" narratives to promote politically illiberal policies like the ones mentioned previously. The precise cause, scope, and nature of this shift towards "new authoritarianism" are still subject to debate among academics; nonetheless, this tendency has been most frequently observed in highly developed (U.S. and Great Britain) and emerging (post-Soviet Russia and Eastern European states, "Asian Tigers," post-1980s China) market economies. While it is difficult to pinpoint the precise origin of new authoritarian discourse, Dr. Hendrik Verwoerd, former Minister of South Africa from 1958–1966, stood out as one of the earliest, if not the first, post-

World War II world leader who systematically deployed economically liberal justifications for authoritarian/totalitarian politics.[5]

Clarifications must be made with regard to parameter and scope of the findings from the rhetorical analysis in this chapter. Similar to the analyses in previous chapters, theological concepts are used in this chapter as analytical tools for effective rhetoric, not as literal allegations of religiosity in a narrower sense. The personal religious beliefs and practices of Dr. Verwoerd are not an area of concern for the analysis in this chapter. Provided, it is well-known that Dr. Verwoerd had been a lifelong member of the Dutch Reformed Church of South Africa (NGK), which is a Reformed Christian denomination of the Calvinist tradition.[6] It is also true that the NGK as well as the larger "Afrikaner Calvinism" (a term referring to the historical development of Reformed Christianity in South Africa that combined traditional Calvinist teachings with elements of modern Afrikaner nationalism) has been criticized for providing "religious nourishment" to the roots of the Apartheid system.[7] That being said, the historical impact and political implications of Apartheid are far larger than Dr. Verwoerd's personal state of mind. It would be unhelpful and myopic to focus on the particularities of organized religion in its narrowly construed form, while overlooking the much broader appropriations of the rhetorical strategies of religion, and the redeployment in other domains of social transactions. Therefore, references to messianic rhetoric and John Calvin's theology in this chapter serve to highlight functional parallels in terms of effective rhetorical operations, and should not be mistaken as literal speculations about Dr. Verwoerd's religious character.

Furthermore, the analysis in this chapter does not suggest that the messianic rhetoric as employed by Dr. Verwoerd is necessarily a direct consequence of his religious affiliation or of Calvinism at large, nor does this study seek to establish any causal link between Apartheid South Africa and any particular religious doctrine or theology. Correlation does not imply causation. By highlighting parallel rhetorical strategies between John Calvin and H. F. Verwoerd, this study simply seeks to promote a more nuanced understanding of the appropriation of religious rhetorical techniques towards problematic political ends. In no way does this study suggest any direct causal link between Calvinism (or any religious teaching) and Apartheid. With regard to the broader relationship between Protestant ethics and capitalist political

5 Examples of academic discussions about "new authoritarianism," *see* David Held, "From Postwar Stability to Political Crisis: The Polarization of Political Ideals," *Models of Democracy*, 3rd ed. (Stanford, CA: Stanford University Press, 2006), 185–215. *See also, generally*, Dennis Compton Canterbury, *Neoliberal Democratization and New Authoritarianism* (Aldershot: Ashgate Publishing, Ltd., 2005); Ivan Krastev, "Paradoxes of the New Authoritarianism," *Journal of Democracy*, vol. 22, no. 2 (2011): 5–16.

6 The Reformation Society, "Calvinism in Africa," South Africa: Reformation Society (posted 2010, accessed February, 12 2018), available: http://www.reformationsa.org/index.php/history/65-calvinismafrica?format=pdf

7 Bruce Buursma, "Apartheid's Roots Nourished by Religion," *Chicago Tribune* (published January 19, 1985).

economy, it is already an extensively examined subject in social sciences, dating back to the seminal works by Max Weber.[8] Representative examples of recent studies on this subject include the works by Steven J. Overman, *The Protestant Ethic and the Spirit of Sport: How Calvinism and Capitalism Shaped America's Games* (2011), Gordon Marshall, *In Search of the Spirit of Capitalism: An Essay on Max Weber's Protestant Ethic Thesis* (1982), Jean Comaroff, "Privatizing the Millennium: New Protestant Ethics and the Spirits of Capitalism in Africa, and Elsewhere" (2000), Teemu Mikkonen, Tere Vadén and Niklas Vainio "The Protestant Ethic Strikes Back: Open Source Developers and the Ethic of Capitalism" (2007), J. Barbalet, *Weber, Passion and Profits: 'The Protestant Ethic and the Spirit of Capitalism' in Context* (2008) and so on.[9]

What rhetorical insight can be distilled from this relatively large body of existing research? They highlight ethical frameworks that emerge from religious teachings and can be farther reaching than organized religious practices themselves. More importantly, these studies found that religious ethical frameworks, including the Protestant work ethic, are preserved in their social embeddedness. The expansion and reproduction of Protestant work ethic does not necessarily require the organized religion itself to expand.[10] Given the abundance and overexposure of existing scholarship on the deep-seated connection between Protestant ethics and capitalist economies, it would be tautological to rehash these points at length in this chapter, and the findings of this study are broadly consistent with the Weberian conclusions aforementioned.

8 See generally, Max Weber, *The Protestant Ethic and the "Spirit" of Capitalism and Other Writings*, originally published in 1905 (Penguin, 2002); *The Theory of Social and Economic Organization*, originally published in 1915 (Simon and Schuster, 2009); *Economy and Society: An Outline of Interpretive Sociology*, Vol. 1 (Stanford, CA: University of California Press, 1978); *The Sociology of Religion* (Beacon Press, 1993), and most notably, in his *General Economic History*, originally published in 1924 (Transaction publishers, 1981).

9 Steven J. Overman, *The Protestant Ethic and the Spirit of Sport: How Calvinism and Capitalism Shaped America's Games* (Macon, GA: Mercer University Press, 2011). Gordon Marshall, *In Search of the Spirit of Capitalism: An Essay on Max Weber's Protestant Ethic Thesis* (New York: Columbia University Press, 1982). Jean Comaroff and John Comaroff. "Privatizing the Millennium. New Protestant Ethics and the Spirits of Capitalism in Africa, and Elsewhere." *Africa Spectrum* (2000): 293–312. Teemu Mikkonen, Tere Vadén, and Niklas Vainio. "The Protestant Ethic Strikes Back: Open Source Developers and the Ethic of Capitalism." *First Monday* 12, no. 2 (2007). Peter Baehr, "The 'Iron Cage' and the 'Shell as Hard as Steel': Parsons, Weber, and the Stahlhartes Gehäuse Metaphor in the Protestant Ethic and the Spirit of Capitalism" *History and Theory*, 40: 153–169 (2001). Rogene A. Buchholz, "The Protestant Ethic as an Ideological Justification of Capitalism." *Journal of Business Ethics* Vol. 2, No. 1 (1983): 51–60. J. Barbalet, *Weber, Passion and Profits: 'The Protestant Ethic and the Spirit of Capitalism' in Context* (Cambridge; New York: Cambridge University Press 2008). Herbert L. Mirels, and James B. Garrett. "The Protestant Ethic as a Personality Variable." *Journal of Consulting and Clinical Psychology* Vol. 36, No. 1 (1971): 40.

10 Ibid.

From theologian to social psychologist

The purpose of analyzing speeches by Dr. H. F. Verwoerd is to study the strategic use of mythical rhetoric within the domain of formal political discourse, and to examine the articulations of these mythical elements in the invention and legitimation of Apartheid – an elaborate civic rite for the automatic execution of mass sacrifice along racial lines. The rhetorical analysis in this chapter focuses on the collection of speeches made by Dr. Verwoerd, presented in a 735-page, single volume text titled *Verwoerd Speaks.* [11] *Verwoerd Speaks* was published in 1966 – the same year of Dr. Verwoerd's assassination.[12] The edited volume offers the most complete published collection of Dr. Verwoerd's formal public oratory. A total of 58 speeches were included in *Verwoerd Speaks*, which covers the timespan of his entire political career in South Africa.

The *Verwoerd Speaks* collection begins with his September 3, 1948 parliamentary address "The Policy of Apartheid" – a speech Dr. Verwoerd delivered almost immediately after becoming a newly elected member of the South African Senate. "The Policy of Apartheid" was the speech that marked the national political debut of Dr. Verwoerd, who previously served as the Professor of Sociology and Social Work at the University of Stellenbosch.[13] It was in this speech that Dr. Verwoerd, in his usual calm and pedantic voice, coined "Apartheid" as the official brand-name for the National Party's (NP) policy of "total segregation."[14]

Dr. Verwoerd was, and remains a deeply controversial political figure in South Africa. Self-styled as "Dr. Verwoerd" even during his premiership, the personal biography of H. F. Verwoerd delineates a life of many contradictions. Despite his politics of radical Afrikaner nationalism, Verwoerd is the only foreign-born prime minister in South Africa's history. Verwoerd was born in the Netherlands on September 8th, 1901, into a family that Verwoerd himself described as middle class and "deeply religious."[15] Verwoerd moved to South Africa with his family in 1903, where they resided in Wynberg, a relatively wealthy and predominantly English-speaking suburban neighborhood of Cape Town. In 1912, Verwoerd moved with his family to the city of Bulawayo in the British colony of Southern Rhodesia (present-day Zimbabwe), where his father, Wilhelmus Johannes Verwoerd, worked as an assistant evangelist in the local Dutch Reformed Church.[16] While in Bulawayo, Verwoerd attended the prestigious Milton High School. It was reported that Verwoerd received top marks at Milton High, and his education

11 H. F. Verwoerd, *Verwoerd Speaks: Speeches 1948–1966.* Ed. A. N. Pelzer (Johannesburg: APB Publishers, 1966).

12 David Goodman and Paul Weinberg, *Fault Lines: Journeys into the New South Africa* (Berkeley, CA: University of California Press, 1999), p. 154.

13 H. F. Verwoerd, *Verwoerd Speaks: Speeches 1948–1966*, "Introduction" at pp.XII–LVII

14 Verwoerd, "The Policy of Apartheid, September 3, 1948," p.21.

15 H. F. Verwoerd, *Verwoerd Speaks: Speeches 1948–1966*, "Introduction" at pp. XII–LVII.

16 Pieter W. Grobbelaar, *This was a Man* (South Africa: Human & Rousseau, 1967), 1–14.

expenses were fully covered by a scholarship financed by British diamond magnate Alfred Beit.[17]

Verwoerd became a theology student at the University of Stellenbosch in 1919. After completing his undergraduate degree with honors in 1921, Verwoerd applied to continue his graduate study in theology at University of Stellenbosch. However, for unknown reasons, Verwoerd withdrew his Theology School application, and instead opted to study philosophy at Stellenbosch, where he received his Ph.D. in philosophy in 1924. From this point until his assassination in 1966, H. F. Verwoerd had maintained "Dr. Verwoerd" as his preferred form of address.

Dr. Verwoerd accepted post-doctoral scholarships to study the emerging field of social psychology abroad, first at University of Oxford in 1924, then left for Germany in 1926 to further his study in the field of social psychology. From 1926 to 1928, Dr. Verwoerd enrolled in three successive post-doctoral programs at University of Hamburg, University of Berlin, and University of Leipzig.[18] While in Germany, Dr. Verwoerd worked with some of the biggest names in social psychology at the time – including Felix Krueger, Otto Lipmann, Wolfgang Köhler and William Stern.[19] This period also marked the most productive years for Dr. Verwoerd in terms of academic publications. Dr. Verwoerd ended his German study abroad trip in 1928 and returned to South Africa, after receiving his first tenured position as the Chair of Applied Psychology and Psycho Technique at his *alma mater* University of Stellenbosch. By 1933, most of the German professors Verwoerd was working with were banned from teaching due to the rise of Nazi Party. Some of the academics who worked with Dr. Verwoerd in Germany indicated that Verwoerd showed increasing interest in eugenics studies during his years abroad, studying in Germany.[20]

A cursory search through academic publications by Dr. Verwoerd during this period does not yield any direct evidence of eugenics' influence on his work. Most of his publications between 1925 and 1933 involved experimental psychology involving and laboratory-controlled studies of human subjects. Dr. Verwoerd also invented a laboratory device which he named "The Memory Apparatus," with which he designed to conduct a wide range of behavioral feedback experiments that involved the selective delivery of painful electric shocks to human test subjects.[21] The following excerpt, taken from his 1926 paper "A Method for the Experimental Production of Emotions," provides a snapshot of the type of

17 Beyers, C. J. (1981). *Dictionary of South African Biography*, Vol. 4, Durban: Butterworth, pp. 730–740; P. W. Grobbelaar, Man van die Volk, 13–15 (1966).

18 "Hendrik Frensch Verwoerd Collection" *South African History Online*, Archive 7, documents 9, 11 (updated September 20, 2016, accessed January 4, 2018), available: http://www.sahistory.org.za/collection/9202

19 "Hendrik Frensch Verwoerd Collection" ibid.

20 A. Burke, "Mental health care during apartheid in South Africa: An illustration of how 'science' can be abused," in Gozaydin en Madeira (ed,) *Evil, Law and the State* (Oxford: Interdisciplinary Press, 2006), 117–133.

21 H. F. Verwoerd, "A Method for the Experimental Production of Emotions," *The American Journal of Psychology*, Vol. 37, No. 3 (July, 1926), pp. 357–371.

research Dr. Verwoerd was engaged with, as well as his "bone dry" academic writing style, something he retained throughout his political career:

> "The *Os* are told that yellow, red and purple will succeed one another at intervals and that a severe shock (of the painfulness of which the Os are given a foretaste) will be applied whenever purple appears in the slit of the memory apparatus ....The *Os* are punished with a painful shock whenever they are entrapped. Usually, before blunting takes place, keen disappointment, and sometimes regret, is felt incorrect reactions at the trap, and exaltation or elation in the few cases when an *O* is not caught in the trap. Satisfaction is felt at the usual correct reactions at the true reaction-positions and is especially pronounced after the *O* has been entrapped several times in succession."[22]

It is also important to note Dr. Verwoerd did not produce any academic publications after 1930. In 1934, Dr. Verwoerd was appointed as the Professor of Sociology and Social Work at University of Stellenbosch. It was also during this time that Dr. Verwoerd became increasingly involved with social work helping poor, white South Africans affected by the global economic depression of the 1930s.[23]

Architect of Apartheid

In 1937, Hendrik F. Verwoerd, then a full-time academic faculty at University of Stellenbosch, made the highly controversial move by accepting the editorship position for the newly established *Die Transvaler* – a "newspaper" functioned as the propaganda mouthpiece for the Transvaal branch of National Party of South Africa (NP).[24] Transvaal was a South African province which existed from 1910 to 1994, with Pretoria being its capital city. This move signaled the definitive turn towards political activism for Dr. Verwoerd, but also marked an ironic return to his theological "roots." Rather than working as an evangelist of the Reformed Church like his father did, Dr. Verwoerd instead took up the role as the chief evangelist for the NP in Transvaal Province. Under the editorship of Dr. Verwoerd, *Die Transvaler* aggressively preached a radical brand of Afrikaner nationalism that incorporated elements of *völkisch* populism, anti-communism, and economic nationalism.[25]

At this time, the National Party occupied a relatively fringe position on the national political stage, in part due to the sudden radicalization of the political

22 Verwoerd, "A Method for the Experimental Production of Emotions," 364.

23 J. J. Venter, "H. F. Verwoerd: Foundational Aspects of His Thought," *Koers* Vol. 64, No. 4, 1999: 415–442.

24 "Hendrik Frensch Verwoerd Collection" *South African History Online*, Archive 7 (updated September 20, 2016, accessed January 4, 2018), available: http://www.sahistory.org.za/collection/9202

25 Harris M. Lentz III, *Heads of States and Governments* (Jefferson, NC: McFarland & Company, Inc., 1994), 451–452.

positions of the NP during the 1930s, especially in terms of increasingly hardline positions on racial policies. This radical turn to the far-right drove moderate conservatives out of NP. Thus, the 1938 General Election proved to be a disaster for the NP – who secured only 6.3 percent of the total votes and less than one-fifth of the parliament seats (House of Assembly). On the other hand, the politically center-right, anti-segregationist United Party (UP) scored a landslide victory in the 1938 election, securing a 74 percent absolute parliamentary majority.[26]

The General Election of 1948 was a watershed moment for post-World War II South African politics. After two consecutive disappointing election performances in 1938 and 1943, the far-right NP delivered a shocking victory and became the largest political party in the House of Assembly, the lower house of Parliament. The center-right UP in fact won far more popular votes in the 1948 election than the NP (the UP received 49.2 percent of the popular votes, the NP received 37.7 percent). However, due to electoral gerrymandering in South Africa which disproportionately favored rural white voters, the NP nonetheless received more seats (70 seats) than the second-party UP (65 seats).[27] The newly formed NP House majority also picked Daniel F. Malan, former Dutch Reformed Church minister and hardline Afrikaner nationalist, as the Prime Minister of South Africa. This is also the year when Dr. Verwoerd took public office for the first time as a member of the Senate. Note that the Senate was the upper house of the bicameral parliamentary system in South Africa prior to 1981, where Senators were indirectly elected by an electoral college consisting of members of the House of Assembly plus members of the Executive Councils of the four South African provinces.

The political career of Dr. Verwoerd proved to be a highly successful one, and one which Verwoerd and his NP remained consistently and singularly focused on advancing what he called the "total segregation" which he first outlined in 1948.[28] Dr. Verwoerd was appointed as the Minister of Native Affairs in 1950 – a position in which he remained until his appointment as Prime Minister in 1958. From 1958 to his assassination in 1966, Dr. Verwoerd was known for his instrumental role in the design and development of the Apartheid system, primarily implemented through series of "apartheid legislations." Some representative examples of these legislations are: *Promotion of Bantu Self-Government Act* of 1959, which severed fiscal responsibilities between better developed, predominantly white, urban areas and those less-developed interior, rural areas in South Africa, and reorganized those less-developed regions into fiscally-independent "Bantustans" reserved for non-whites.[29] *The Bantu Investment Corporation*

26 *Keesing's Contemporary Archives 1937–1940* (London: Keesing's Limited, 1931–), pp. 3074–3075. Available: https://search.lib.virginia.edu/catalog/u747425

27 Ibid. Figure 3: Published by Universal Studios, via Wikimedia Commons (Public domain: 1960), available: https://archive.org/details/1960-12-31_News_Highlights_of_1960

28 H. F. Verwoerd, *Verwoerd Speaks: Speeches 1948–1966*. Ed. A. N. Pelzer (Johannesburg: APB Publishers, 1966): "The Policy of Apartheid" (1948).

29 Act No. 46 of 1959, commenced June 19; subsequently renamed the Promotion of Black Self-government Act, 1959 and later the Representation between the Republic of South Africa and Self-governing Territories Act, 1959

Act of 1959, which formed the "Bantu Investment Corporation," allowed the NP-led South African government to capitalize on development opportunities within the so-called "Bantustans."[30] The *Extension of University Education Act* of 1959 mandated total segregation in all institutions of higher education in South Africa (total segregation as mandating separate universities for white and non-white students, as opposed to intra-university segregation).[31]

An attempt was made on April 4, 1960 to publicly assassinate Dr. Verwoerd, during his opening address at the Union Exposition in Milner Park, Johannesburg, to mark the Jubilee of the Union of South Africa. A gunman suddenly emerged from the attending crowd and ran towards the podium where Dr. Verwoerd speaking. The gunman shot Verwoerd twice at point-blank range with a hand gun before being subdued by the security personnel. Dr. Verwoerd received two gunshot wounds on his right cheek, but his injury proved to be superficial and non-life-threatening. The assassin, David Pratt, was arrested as the scene, but later ruled not guilty by reason of insanity. Pratt was forcibly committed to a mental institution where he committed suicide in 1961.[32] After surviving the 1960 assassination attempt in, Verwoerd soon introduced two additional Apartheid legislations further streamline the "total segregation" process: The *Coloured Persons Communal Reserves Act* of 1961, which furthered territorial, political, economic and social segregation between white South Africa and "Coloured Persons Settlement Areas,"[33] and the *Preservation of Colored Areas Act* of 1961, which rendered all previous temporary segregation laws permanent.[34] These legislations under Verwoerd altogether constituted the Apartheid South Africa which persisted in history with infamy.

Dr. Verwoerd remained as prime minister until the afternoon of September 6, 1966, when he was assassinated at the front entrance of the House of Assembly in Cape Town.[35] Dr. Verwoerd was stabbed multiple times with a concealed knife by Dimitri Tsafendas, who worked as a parliamentary staff and former member of the South Africa Communist Party.[36] Tsafendas was arrested immediately at the crime scene. However, just like the 1960 assassin David Pratt (who non-fatally shot Dr. Verwoerd but was found not guilty by reason of insanity), Tsafendas was also

30 Union of South Africa, Bantu Investment Corporation Act, Act No. 34 of 1959, available: http://disa.ukzn.ac.za/sites/default/files/pdf_files/leg19590603.028.020.034.pdf

31 O'Malley, Padraig. "1959. Extension of University Education Act No 45." Nelson Mandela Center of Memory and Dialogue, accessed May 3, 2010.

32 Loammi Wolf, "David Beresford Pratt: die Mens Agter die Sluipmoordpoging," *LitNet Akademies*, Vol. 9, No. 3 (1998), 102–107.

33 Union of South Africa, Coloured Persons Communal Reserves Act, Act No 3 of 1961, available: http://disa.ukzn.ac.za/leg19610303028020003

34 Parliament of South Africa, Preservation of Coloured Areas Act, Act No 31 of 1961, available: http://nifty.works/about/EN6Or9Ql0jwrklVG/preservation-of-coloured-areas-act-act-no-31-of-1961#topic-article

35 David Goodman and Paul Weinberg, *Fault Lines: Journeys into the New South Africa* (Berkley, CA: University of California Press, 2002).

36 Ibid.

declared not guilty by reason of insanity. Tsafendas nonetheless remained in state custody for the rest of his life (until his death in 1999) under an emergency security bill.[37]

Messianic rhetoric of total segregation

H. F. Verwoerd was instrumental for advancing "total segregation" in all spheres of life within South Africa via "apartheid legislations." The concept of "total segregation" was first introduced by Dr. Verwoerd in his 1948 speech "The Policy of Apartheid," which was his address to the national parliament as a newly appointed senator. Dr. Verwoerd began the speech by framing the racially segregated political order as an undeniable ideal for development: "Nobody will deny that for the Native as well as for the European, complete separation would have been the ideal if it had developed that way historically."[38] Dr. Verwoerd presented this ideal assumption as a self-justifying article of faith. He did not list any material evidence in supporting this political ideal in the speech. Most of the speech content argued against, in his words, "the lack of faith" among MPs for successfully achieving total segregation in South Africa. From that premise, Dr. Verwoerd defined his policy of total segregation in very a concrete, precise three-point policy frame:

1. That Native should not be allowed to own land among white people, but that so far the ownership of land is concerned the should be confined to the various Native reserves;
2. That Natives and coloured people in our towns and villages should not live in European residential areas, but that there should be separate residential areas for them, that is to say separate Native and coloured villages; and
3. That in our factories, etc. Europeans and non-Europeans should not be allowed to work among one another, but separately, and that certain sorts of work should be reserved for the Europeans.[39]

Dr. Verwoerd's three-point policy for total segregation, within a span of 15 years, have materialized into what are commonly known as Apartheid legislations. See Table 5.1 for a more complete collection of Apartheid legislations, arranged in the order of their date of ratification.[40]

After close examination and analysis of all 58 speeches contained in *Verwoerd Speaks*, this study made the following conclusions. First, the analysis affirms existing understanding that the Apartheid, as envisioned by Dr. Verwoerd, epitomizes

37 Ibid.
38 H. F. Verwoerd, *Verwoerd Speaks: Speeches 1948–1966*. Ed. A. N. Pelzer (Johannesburg: APB Publishers, 1966): p.13
39 Ibid.
40 The content of this table is developed based on the list of key Apartheid legislations originally compiled by Joe Naumann, Professor of Geography at University of Missouri, St. Louis Available: www.umsl.edu/~naumannj/.../Apartheid%20Legislation%20in%20South%20Africa.do...

Table 5.1 Representative Apartheid legislations under the Verwoerd regime

Apartheid legislation	*Description*
Dr. Verwoerd appointed to the national Senate, April 1949	
Prohibition of Mixed Marriages Act of 1949 [1]	Banned marriages between "Europeans" and "non-Europeans," also invalidated pre-existing inter-racial marriages in South Africa.
Dr. Verwoerd became the Minister of Native Affairs in 1950	
Immorality Amendment Act of 1950 (amended in 1957) [2]	Banned of all sexual interactions between "white people" and "non-white people" in South Africa.
Population Registration Act of 1950[3]	Mandatory classification of all South African citizens into officially pre-scribed race and ethnic groups. Forced physical separation between races in public areas.
Group Areas Act of 1950 (subsequently amended in 1957 and 1966)[4]	Expanded mandatory physical separation between races in all public and private spaces. Subsequently amended in 1957 and 1966 to further strengthen mandatory physical separation between racial groups.
Suppression of Communism Act of 1950[5]	Provided sweeping power to the executive government to ban organizations, publications and individuals that are considered to be involved in "communistic activities."[6]
Native Building Workers Act, Act of 1951[7]	Restricted the places in which "non-Europeans" construction workers are allowed to work.
Separate Representation of Voters Act 1951[8]	Stripped "non-Europeans" of their voting rights via banning them from the common voters roll registration.
Prevention of Illegal Squatting Act of 1951[9]	Provided Verwoerd, then Minister of Native Affairs, the power to use police force to remove non-whites from public and private lands, and to establishment concentration camps for displaced non-whites. Also restricted judicial repeals for these forced relocations.
Bantu Authorities Act of 1951[10]	Abolished all political representations of "non-Europeans" in the South African central government, also imposed severe restrictions for "Blacks" from residing in better-developed urban areas.

Apartheid legislation	*Description*
Natives Laws Amendment Act of 1952[11]	Restricted property ownership for non-white South Africans in cities and towns.
Natives Act of 1952[12]	Commonly known as the Pass Laws, forced "non-European" South Africans to carry identification cards, or "passes" with them at all times. Failure to produce an identification pass upon police request was an arrestable offense.
Native Labour Act of 1953[13]	Prohibited strikes and other labor rights litigations by "non-European" South Africans.
Bantu Education Act of 1953[14]	"This Act provided for the establishment of a separate educational system run by the Department of the Native Affairs under the minister Dr. H. F. Verwoerd and was in fact penned by Dr. Verwoerd."[15]
Reservation of Separate Amenities Act of 1953[16]	Imposed mandatory segregation of all public amenities, buildings and transports.
Natives Resettlement Act of 1954[17]	Gave executive government power to remove remaining "non-Europeans" from the city of Johannesburg.
Group Areas Development Act of 1955[18]	Officially "Act to provide for the control of the disposal and for the acquisition of immovable property in group areas and other areas defined under the Group Areas Act, 1950, and for the proper development of such areas, and for the said purposes to establish a board and to define its functions, and to provide for matters incidental thereto."[19]
Natives (Prohibition of Interdicts) Act of 1956[20]	Stripped the judicial due-process rights of "non-Europeans," and their right to appeal forced removals.
Dr. Verwoerd became the 6th Prime Minister of South Africa, September 1958	
The Natives Taxation and Development Act of 1958[21]	Imposed unequal tax schemes between "Europeans" and "non-Europeans."[22]
Bantu Investment Corporation Act of1959[23]	Forced segregation of financial services.

Apartheid legislation	*Description*
Extension of University Education of 1959[24]	Mandated separate higher education institutions for different races and ethnicities, excluded non-Europeans from the best universities in South Africa.
Promotion of Bantu Self-Government Act of 1959[25]	Further divided black South Africans into eight "ethnic groups" with segregated "homelands" to each group.
Assassination attempt on April 4, 1960, Verwoerd survived with non-fatal injuries	
Coloured Persons Communal Reserves Act of 1961[26]	"The Act was to apply the Mission Stations and Communal Reserves Act 1909, of the Cape of Good Hope, to coloured persons settlement areas within the meaning of the Coloured Persons Settlement Areas (Cape) Act."[27]
Preservation of Coloured Areas Act, 1961[28]	Strengthened Apartheid land legislation by allowing the eminent domain seizure of mortgaged land owned by non-whites, with compensation paid to a white "Guardian" of the taken land.
Urban Bantu Councils Act, 1961[29]	Created separate municipal councils and administrative apparatus for "non-Europeans."
Terrorism Act of 1962[30]	Provided sweeping power to the executive authority to identify "terrorist" and "terrorist organizations," and to detain suspected terrorists indefinitely without trial. Similar to the Suppression of Communism Act of 1950, this legislation provided extremely broad definition for "terrorism."
Dr. Verwoerd assassinated on September 6th, 1966	
Terrorism Act of 1967[31]	Allowed for indefinite detention without trial for people detained by the internal state security apparatus of South Africa.
Bantu Homelands Citizens Act of 1970[32]	Forced annulment of South African citizenship for all black South Africans, marked the total "outlawing" of all non-whites under the South African Constitution.

1 Union of South Africa, Act No 55 of 1949Available: https://en.wikisource.org/wiki/Prohibition_of_Mixed_Marriages_Act,_1949

2 Union of South Africa, Act No 21 of 1950, Available: https://en.wikisource.org/wiki/Immorality_Amendment_Act,_1950
3 Union of South Africa, Act No 30 of 1950, available: https://en.wikisource.org/wiki/Population_Registration_Act,_1950
4 Union of South Africa, Act No 41 of 1950, available: https://blogs.loc.gov/law/files/2014/01/Group-Areas-Act-1950.pdf
5 Union of South Africa, Act No 44 of 1950, available: https://en.wikisource.org/wiki/Suppression_of_Communism_Act,_1950
6 The legislation used an extremely broad and discretionary definition of communistic activities. *See* Act No. 41 1950, Art.1.1.
7 Union of South Africa, Act No 27 of 1951, "Legislation: 1950s." South African History Online. (Retrieved 3 May 2010): http://www.sahistory.org.za/pages/governence-projects/liberation-struggle/legislation_1950s.htm
8 Union of South Africa, Separate Representation of Voters Act, Act No 46 of 1951, available South African History Online: https://www.sahistory.org.za/archive/separate-representation-of-voters-act%2C-act-no-46-of-1951
9 Union of South Africa, Act No 52 of 1951, available South African History Online *supra*.
10 Union of South Africa, Act No 68 of 1951, South African History Online *supra*
11 Union of South Africa, Act No. 54 of 1952, ibid.12
Union of South Africa, Act No 67 of 1952, ibid.
13 Union of South Africa, Act No 57 of 1981, ibid.
14 Union of South Africa, Act No 47 of 1953, ibid.
15 Ibid.
16 Union of South Africa, Act No 49 of 1953, ibid17
Union of South Africa, Act No 19 of 1954, ibid
18 Union of South Africa, Act No 69 of 1955, available: https://en.wikipedia.org/wiki/Group_Areas_Development_Act,_195519
Ibid.
20 Union of South Africa, Natives (Prohibition of Interdicts) Act, (Act No 64 of 1956), (22 June 1956).
21 Act No 38 of 1958, ibid.
22 Union of South Africa, Natives (Prohibition of Interdicts) Act, (Act No 64 of 1956), 22 June 1956. Available DISA Archive at: https://www.sahistory.org.za/collection/30327
23 Act No 34 of 1959, ibid.
24 Act, Act 45 of 1959, ibid.
25 Act No 46 of 1959, ibid.
26 Act No 3 of 1961, available: http://www.aluka.org/stable/10.5555/al.sff.document.leg19610303.028.020.00327
Ibid.
28 Act No 31 of 1961, "Apartheid Legislation 1850s–1970s," South African History Online, Archive 1, available: http://www.sahistory.org.za/article/apartheid-legislation-1850s-1970s.
29 Act No 79 of 1961.30
No 83 of 1962, ibid.
31 Act No 83 of 1962, *South African History Online Archive*, available: http://www.sahistory.org.za/article/black-homeland-citizenship-act-1970
32 Edited list based on the research originally compiled by Joe Naumann, Professor of Geography at University of Missouri, St. Louis, available: http://www.umsl.edu/~naumannj/Geography%201002%20articles/Sub%20Saharan%20Africa/Apartheid%20Legislation%20in%20South%20Africa.doc.

a racial totalitarian state in terms of its effective operation. That is, the Apartheid was a "scientifically engineered" management apparatus, optimized for maximally efficient enforcement of racial segregation doctrines in all aspects of public and private transaction. The rise of totalitarian states in the 20th century can be broadly described as reactions against the inner contradictions of democratic liberalism. Yet paradoxically, in his speeches, Dr. Verwoerd consistently discussed his racial totalitarian politics as being perfectly compatible with modern liberal ideals. Furthermore, Dr. Verwoerd framed his brand of totalitarianism as a more perfect realization of those economic promises of liberalism. His ideal frame perhaps had been best summarized in the opening lines of Verwoerd's "First Speech as Prime Minister in the House of Assembly" on September 18, 1958: "I am not using this occasion as a platform for putting forward ideas other than those which I hope will help to bring unity, prosperity, and happiness to South Africa."[41]

The ritual situation for the public reenactment of sacrifice can be distinguished as a special articulation of the rhetorical situation. The basic components, exigence, audience and constraints remain present. What's different, however, is that the rhetoric of ritual works by deploying anti-rhetorical tropes. The persuasive power of rituals resides in its pretension of being self-referential and self-justifying, and its refusal to be subjected to the constraints of reasoning and debate. A ritual response to the rise of a given material exigence is predicated upon two structural conditions. The first is a collectively embedded and self-referencing belief-framework, one that serves as the basis for the "good faith" of the commons, as well as the rule framework for the regulation of personal ego and habits. The second condition is the act of ritual repetition. That is, symbolic actions that are deployed to inculcate commonly held values and standards of behaviors, via repetitions, that automatically invoke collective memory and values.

The material exigence underpinning Dr. Verwoerd's rhetorical response stems from the colonial history of South Africa. European colonial domination in South Africa was maintained, at least in part, through its ideological and governance apparatus that enforced unequal economic relations via racial distinctions. This race-based social stratification scheme, similar to that of the caste system of India, perpetuates economic relations via a two-prong signification process. The affixation class status to kinship practices on the one hand, and the strict enforcement of segregation and endogamy among kinship groups on the other hand. The end of formal colonialism did not bring the end of racial segregation South Africa. Aphorisms of the European colonial kinship construct, organized around narratives of "white" vs. "non-white" distinctions persisted in post-World War II South Africa, despite the nominal end of the British colonial regime. Also persistent were the practices and antagonisms intrinsic to colonial class/race relations. The re-emergence of economic liberalism and market-driven governance ideals in the post-World War II global order, however, did provide a rhetorical opportunity for segregationist politicians to provide an updated justification framework for the colonial race-class stratification.

41 H. F. Verwoerd, *Verwoerd Speaks: Speeches 1948–1966*. Ed. A. N. Pelzer (Johannesburg: APB Publishers, 1966): p.164.

In his public remarks, Dr. Verwoerd consistently eschewed narratives that were explicitly associated with pre-World War II authoritarianism and white-supremacy. Instead Dr. Verwoerd framed his brand of racial totalitarian state as a more perfect realization of liberal democratic ideals – specifically to bring “unity, prosperity, and happiness” for all South Africans.[42] Furthermore, Dr. Verwoerd was arguably the first post-World War II world leader who attempted to synthesize totalitarian political measures with liberal economic ideals. A distinguishing and perhaps paradoxical theme throughout Dr. Verwoerd's speeches for Apartheid is his concurrent embracement of both pre-World War II totalitarian and post-World War II neoliberal ideals.

Consider, for example, the following excerpt from the “Address on the Occasion of Convention for the Promotion of Export Trade,” May 16, 1962, where Dr. Verwoerd made the following explanation for the apparent inequality of resource distribution among populations in South Africa:

> South Africa is beginning to realize that its economic growth ought to be large and fast if it wants to supply all the needs of its whole population. We have huge problems – in a certain sense bigger problems than other countries in the world. In order to triumph we must supply employment to our own population and to an immigrant population which we desire to have for the sake of the White man insofar as we feel that we have to strengthen ourselves. At the same time we have many non-Europeans from various population groups who are basically dependent on us and will remain thus no matter how politically independent they become. … Thus we have to build up industry, whether it be I the existing industrial areas or along the borders of Bantu areas or wherever it may be. We have to build up an industrialism which will create the widest background for supplying the needs for employment and subsistence of all those people. When this is the object, it can be reached partly by the expansion of the home market.[43]

Note that Dr. Verwoerd made the comment above to foreign trade delegates during a time of mounting international economic sanctions against Apartheid South Africa. Dr. Verwoerd extensively appropriated vocabularies that implied conformity with the emergent post-World War II liberal political economy as popularly conceptualized in the “democratic West.” At the same time, his policies that promoted “unity, prosperity and happiness” were all predicated upon, without exaggeration, assertion of the total and all-encompassing authority of the Euro-colonial segregationist regime to all public and private transactions. In other words, the policy vision that Dr. Verwoerd explicitly outlined in his speeches transforms pre-existing *petty Apartheid* into a total state. Racial segregation is no longer simply applied as new laws or policies. *Apartheid* vis-à-vis “separate development,” as elaborated by Dr. Verwoert, is an

42 Ibid.

43 H. F. Verwoerd, *Verwoerd Speaks: Speeches 1948–1966*, ed. A. N. Pelzer (Johannesburg: APB Publishers, 1966), 704.

extra-political, self-referencing, and singular rule framework for the organization of the South African state, its institutions and people.[44]

Most importantly, the use of messianic rhetoric played a central role in Dr. Verwoerd's rhetorical invention of his "new-totalitarianism." Specifically, his messianic rhetoric employed similar rhetorical strategies as employed by 16th-century jurist and Reformed theologian John Calvin. Throughout his public remarks, Dr. Verwoerd consistently cultivated a more subtle yet powerful cult of personality – one that assumes a messianic-scientist persona in contrast to the heroic-*Übermensch* cult of personality which was associated with European fascist leaders.

The rhetorical style of Dr. Verwoerd has been characterized as matter-of-fact and "Kantian" rationalist.[45] Despite the fact that Dr. Verwoerd made no academic publications after 1930, he nonetheless maintained the title "Doctor" as his preferred form of address.[46] Combing through news archives from the time of Verwoerd's political career, it is evident that both domestic and international news outlets commonly addressed Verwoerd the politician as "Doctor Verwoerd."[47] Available records of public remarks and newspaper correspondences by Dr. Verwoerd demonstrated that he maintained a fairly consistent style resembling academic writings, characterized by his "bone dry" prose and "fact based" *logos.* [48] His stylistic consistency, even when explicitly advocating racial policies that were extremely controversial in his own time, did not resemble emotionally charged demagoguery commonly associated with authoritarian personalities.[49]

The "Kantian-rationalist" rhetorical style of Dr. Verwoerd bears a striking resemblance to that of the 16th century, reformed theologian John Calvin. One major audience adaptation challenge underpinning the theological writings of John Calvin would be his dismissive attitude towards the spiritual condition of the entire humanity – or in Calvin's own words "the entire posterity of Adam made damnable."[50] John Calvin formulated his doctrine of total human depravity upon spiritual rather than economic interests. That being said, the *total depravity*

44 J. J. Venter, "H. F. Verwoerd: Foundational Aspects of His Thought," 415–442.

45 J. J. Venter, "H. F. Verwoerd: Foundational Aspects of His Thought," 416.

46 Verwoerd's last academic publication was: Verwoerd, Hendrik Frensch. "Effects of Fatigue on the Distribution of Attention." *Journal of Applied Psychology* Vol. 12, No. 6 (1928).

47 *See, e.g. A, S. C. (1966, Mar 30).* "Verwoerd landslide today," *The Irish Times* (1921–Current File): "The Nationalist Party of Dr. Verwoerd in tomorrow's South African general election is virtually to wipe out the United Party opposition." "Hendrik Verwoerd, the Monster." *Daily Defender*, 1960: "Perhaps the attempted assassination of Dr. Hendrik Verwoerd, South Africa's Prime Minister, will bring the Union government to its senses ..." *See also*, H. Verwoerd, To The Editor Times of India D KUMAR, "Dr. Verwoerd" (March 15, 1961). *The Times of India* (1861–Current), where H. Verwoerd used "Dr. Verwoerd" to address himself in his letter to the newspaper editor.

48 Venter, "H. F. Verwoerd: Foundational Aspects of His Thought," 417.

49 Venter, "H. F. Verwoerd: Foundational Aspects of His Thought," 418.

50 John Calvin, "Every Thing Proceeding from the Corrupt Nature of Man Damnable." *Institutes of the Christian Religion*, trans. Henry Beveridge (Grand Rapids, MI: Wm. B. Eerdmans, 1989), at Chapter 3.

doctrine of Calvin and the "total segregation" doctrine of Verwoerd were considered radically controversial, thus both Calvin and Verwoerd faced the constraint *contra mundum*, or "speaking against all the others."[51]

John Calvin, who received his formal education in the field of rhetoric rather than theology, was likely to be acutely aware of this constraint. Calvin did not receive any formal education in theology. He attended University of Orleans from 1526 to 1529 as a student of law, and then enrolled at University of Bourges in 1529 to continue his study in humanistic law.[52] In contrast to his controversial, antinomial theology, John Calvin maintained a dry, analytical, and disinterested rhetorical style. Calvin's writings and public sermons have been described as "obtuse," "neutral on the matter" and with only a hint of "banal didacticism."[53]

In Calvin's own writings, he sought to dismiss the *contra mundum* constraint of his theology by positioning himself as acting upon the divine calling to deliver the plain, incontrovertible Truth. Calvin's truth in this sense is a God-term, not only in terms of its presumed goodness, but also in its presumed "extra-rhetorical" quality (as claims that cannot be refuted via "mere" rhetoric). "They cannot object that I am quibbling upon words," as Calvin proclaimed in his *Institution*, "[b]ut how eloquent so ever they may be, they will never prove by their eloquence that one and the same thing makes two."[54] It is also clear that Calvin's claim of being "extra-rhetorical" did not stem from mere naïveté about the role of rhetoric in relation to truth making. Calvin explicitly acknowledged, in a lengthy footnote to his *Institutions*, that his non-egoistic, matter-of-fact writing style is a deliberate rhetorical strategy:

> As the orator, when asked, What is the first precept in eloquence? answered, Delivery: What is the second? Delivery: What is the third? Delivery: so, if you ask me in regard to the precepts of the Christian Religion, I will answer, first, second, and third, Humility.[55]

Another contributing factor of John Calvin's analytical style is his epistemological realism and his apparent disdain for superstition and mysticism. In contrast to other major Protestant reformers in his time, Calvin went much further than to simply protest against (alleged) vices of the Catholic church, focusing his attention on the development of a systematic theological framework that is entirely distinct from Catholicism. Calvin accused the existent Christian institutions of "falling away into superstition," he argued that the restoration of Christian faith would only be possible through a theology grounded purely in reason and Scripture

51 Harro Höpfl, *The Christian Polity of John Calvin* (New York; Cambridge: Cambridge University Press, 1985), 8–9.
52 William J. Bouwsma, *John Calvin: A Sixteenth-century Portrait* (New York: Oxford University Press, 1989), 11–25.
53 William J. Bouwsma, *John Calvin: A Sixteenth-century Portrait*, pp.65–66.
54 John Calvin, *Institutes of the Christian Religion*, Chapter 11.
55 John Calvin, *Institute, Book Second,* Chapter 2 "Man now Deprived of Freedom of Will, and Miserably Enslaved" note 11.

alone. "No pretext can justify superstition." Calvin contended in Chapter 4 of his *Institution (Book one)*, "[t]his proved, first, from reason; and, secondly, from Scripture."[56] Calvin did not consider the Catholic theology as merely "flawed" knowledge, but rather the antithesis of knowledge and therefore something to be rejected as a whole. "Moreover," Calvin argued,

> while some lose themselves in superstitious observances, and others, of set purpose, wickedly revolt from God, and the result is that, in regard to the true knowledge of him, all are so degenerate, that in no part of the world can genuine godliness be found.

Thus, Calvin's rhetorical style effectively shares the spirit of *ens realissimum* as the Kantian rationalism that enchanted the rhetoric of Dr. Verwoerd.[57]

The most important dimension of the "extra-political" construction of the rhetorical persona of Dr. Verwoerd has to do with his strategic deployment of the messianic calling, or *kletos* frame. In biblical hermeneutics, *kletos* (κλητὸς, "being called") is a term exclusively associated with Paul the Apostle. In the opening lines of the Book of Romans (Romans 1:1 in the New Testament), Apostle Paul was introduced as follows: "Paul, a servant of Jesus Christ, **called** (κλητὸς) be an apostle, separated unto the gospel of God (Παῦλος δοῦλος Χριστοῦ Ἰησοῦ, κλητὸς ἀπόστολος, ἀφωρισμένος εἰς εὐαγγέλιον θεοῦ)."[58] The term *kletos* was used in the letters of Apostle Paul, as a device delineating a formal distinction between Paul the Apostle and other biblical prophets. By being "called" an apostle, Apostle Paul was tasked not with prophesying the future coming of the Messiah, but to bring the good news, or gospel, that the Messiah had arrived, and the conditions for redemption had already been completed via the sacrifice of Jesus.[59]

The concept of *kleto* became a major subject of research in Agamben's 2005 book *The Time that Remains: A Commentary on the Letter to the Romans.* [60] Agamben found that *kleto* was used in the letters of Apostle Paul as rhetorical device to construct a myth that divides the existing Jewish population into two diametrically opposite groups: separating Jews who have been redeemed via the sacrifice of Jesus as soteriologically distinct from the rest of the Jewish population. The rhetoric of *kleto,* according to Agamben, not only divided existing population into invented categories, it further perpetuated the division with a soteriological

56 Calvin, *The Institute, Book First,* "Chapter 4 – The Knowledge of God Stifled or Corrupted, Ignorantly or Maliciously."

57 As a single, unifying plane of reality that transcends time and space. *See* Immanuel Kant, *The Critique of Pure Reason*, Norman Kemp Smith (transl.) (New York: St. Martin's Press, 1965), A607/B635.

58 Romans 1:1 (KJV) Available: https://www.biblestudytools.com/kjv/romans/1-1.html, Attic Greek version Romans 1:1 (SBLG) Available: https://www.biblestudytools.com/sblg/romans/1-1.html

59 See generally, Book of Romans (KJV) Available: https://www.biblestudytools.com/kjv/romans/1-1.html,

60 Giorgio Agamben, *Il tempo che resta. Un commento alla Lettera ai Romani* (2000). Trans. Patricia Dailey as *The Time that Remains: A Commentary on the Letter to the Romans* (Stanford, CA: Stanford University Press, 2005).

narrative of predestined eternal salvation. Agamben contended that the political implication of Paul's messianic rhetoric is not trivial – *as kleto* was deployed as a discursive device for both the perpetual segregation and disenfranchisement of a population. In *The Time that Remains*, Agamben identified the *kleto* frame as a key discursive feature to the one-dimensional messianic political theology of modernity that asserts itself as the end-of-history (and therefore end of political potentialities).[61]

Similar use of the *kleto* is also widely observed in the rhetoric of Dr. Verwoerd, who often introduced himself as someone extra-political, with only the absolute good of his subjects as the goal. In his 1958 inaugural address role, he framed his Apartheid platform as simply that he was *being called* to perform his social-scientific expertise in bringing the absolute good to South Africa: "I am not using this occasion as a platform for putting forward ideas other than those which I hope will help to bring unity, prosperity, and happiness to South Africa."[62] Another good example of Verwoerd's use of the *kleto* frame can be found in his 1959 address "Celebration of the Reformed Church." In that speech, and in front of a consubstantiative audience, Dr. Verwoerd explicitly assumed his government to be the predestined realization of God's irresistible plan on earth:

> It is because our people are a Christian people that I convey to you these good wishes, not only in my personal capacity but also as the head of a government which fears God and which has been put there to rule a God-fearing people. ... Does the State recognize the Church and religion? And my reply is: Yes. It is the heritage of the forefathers which we hold dear. It has always been the case that Church and State, each in its own field and independently under the authority of God, could know and recognize the other.[63]

Coincidentally, a similar narrative of a predestined form of political arrangement was also expressed in the political-theological writings of John Calvin, in the final book of his *Institute* where he outlined his vision for a "pure" political order:

> If you fix your eyes not on one state merely, but look around the world, or at least direct your view to regions widely separated from each other, you will perceive that Divine Providence has not, without good cause, arranged that different countries should be governed by different forms of polity.[64]

Perhaps the most striking parallel feature between the rhetoric of Dr. Verwoerd and John Calvin is the use of the "double-predestination" argument in the construction of a non-falsifiable public exigency. Consider, for example, the opening lines of the April 14, 1961 parliamentary address by Dr. Verwoerd, the occasion where the Prime

61 *Ibid.*
62 H. F. Verwoerd, *Verwoerd Speaks: Speeches 1948–1966*, p.164
63 H. F. Verwoerd, *Verwoerd Speaks: Speeches 1948–1966*, 258–259
64 John Calvin, "Of Civil Government" in *Institutes of the Christian Religion*, tr. Henry Beveridge (sacred-texts.com, 1845): Chapter 20

Minister took part in the House debate and argued for the implementation of his "separate development" plan (which severed fiscal responsibilities of South African government to those newly established "native" reservation lands):

> As far as the United Party is concerned, its policy theoretically therefore includes a form of perpetual domination and discrimination by the Whites, even though I do not believe that will remain the position. They will lose against the powers that they are letting loose ... The inevitable result of such a democracy in a country with a mixed population, as in a country without a mixed population, must be majority rule. That is the only true democracy in a mixed fatherland.[65]

Notice the use of the end-time false dilemma of "perpetual dystopia" vs "inevitable utopia," plus the added emphasis of *the Apartheid* as the "only true democracy." This dichotomized framing not only assumed a manufactured "life-or-death" dilemma for policy options present-at-hand, but also rhetorically foreclosed future possibilities for viable alternatives. Here, Dr. Verwoerd framed his political belief not merely as a prophecy, but as a messianic gospel. This is what Agamben calls the "salvation of what is in *potentiality* by what is in *actuality*."[66] A messianic messenger not only foretells future inevitabilities of as a prophet would do, but also reveals the "good news," thus the gospel, that the one and only route to salvation has arrived.

A messianic gospel thus is not a narrative for the end time rather than for the times to come. At the core of Dr. Verwoerd's national revivalist message lies his doctrine of *double-predestination*: the so-called "separate development" is framed as being the singular predestined route towards "true democracy" in South Africa, whereas all alternative political potentialities are predestined to fail. His rhetorical effacement of political potentialities with his singular "extra-political" *actuality* can be understood as implying the absolute sovereignty of a higher political truth that cannot be resisted via human agency. Also consider, for example, the opening lines in the April 14, 1961 "Separate Development" Speech by Dr. Verwoerd in Parliament:

> The Honorable Member for Parktown has said that discrimination and domination are the soul of this whole debate and the situation in which we find ourselves. It is the soul. And the government is trying with its policy to escape from this dilemma.[67]

Dr. Verwoerd prefaced his address by invoking the messianic dual visions of a totally depraved soul ("discrimination and domination are the soul of this whole debate") of the body-politic one the one hand, and pointing to the "escape" from this corrupted "soul" on the other.

65 H. F. Verwoerd, *Verwoerd Speaks: Speeches 1948–1966*, 576

66 Giorgio Agamben, *Potentialities – Collected Essays in Philosophy*, Part III (Stanford, CA: Stanford University Press, 2010), 106–107.

67 H. F. Verwoerd, *Verwoerd Speaks: Speeches 1948–1966*, 651.

By framing Apartheid as the one and only route for the redemption of the "soul" of the South African nation, Dr. Verwoerd employed similar argumentative strategies as found in Calvin's writings concerning spiritual salvation. Whereas the eternal *salvation vs. damnation* spiritual worldview is broadly shared among Abrahamic religions, the teachings of Calvin delineated a totalizing soteriological framework that cuts across all multiplicities concerning the past, present, and future of human spiritual condition. Calvin assumed *total depravity* as the inescapable nature for entire humanity. The totality of human existence, as Calvin proclaimed in his *Institute*, from the *fall of man* to the end time, is locked in a state of sin that is fundamentally incompatible with God:

> Thus he thunders not against certain individuals, but against the whole posterity of Adam—not against the depraved manners of any single age, but the perpetual corruption of nature. His object in the passage is not merely to upbraid men in order that they may repent, but to teach that all are overwhelmed with inevitable calamity, and can be delivered from it only by the mercy of God. As this could not be proved without previously proving the overthrow and destruction of nature, he produced those passages to show that its ruin is complete.[68]

Calvin's radical presumption of total human depravity gave necessity for a route of salvation that is not contingent upon human agency. Thus God "thunders not against certain individuals," as Calvin wrote, "but against the whole posterity of Adam—not against the depraved manners of any single age, but the perpetual corruption of nature."[69] Calvin stipulated that the sacrifice of Jesus Christ alone was sufficient to atone for the sin of humanity in general, without the need for any human response. Thus, the sacrifice of Jesus Christ is framed in the Calvinist tradition as "non-rhetorical," as it dismisses the very notion of audience response as antithetical to atonement.

The condition for atonement under Calvinism is understood as a *new covenant* (which God unilaterally bestows upon man), and not a contract (an agreement between God and man). Following his radical anti-humanist logic of salvation, Calvin further stipulated that the New Covenant provides general, but not total, atonement for humanity. Only a limited number of individuals would be elected to eternal spiritual life in communion with God. Likewise, their election to salvation would be unconditional except through will and grace of God alone. As the whole spiritual deliberation process must be free of any human elements, Calvin also maintained that atonement and elections for deliverance were entirely predestined by God, irresistible by the act of man, and preserved in eternity. Likewise, those not elected were predestined for eternal damnation, forever foreclosed to even the *possibility* of receiving God's grace.[70] This also closes all possibilities for the future itself – as both salvation

68 John Calvin, "Every Thing Proceeding from the Corrupt Nature of Man Damnable," at Chapter 3.

69 Ibid.

70 Ibid.

and damnation are predestined and preserved in perpetuity with the New Covenant.[71]

Calvin further proclaimed, in his *Institute*, that: "*[d]epravation communicated not merely by imitation, but by propagation. This proved, 1. From the contrast drawn between Adam and Christ. Confirmation from passages of Scripture; 2 From the general declaration that we are the children of wrath.*"[72] There exists a similar genetic argument of the "original sin" in Verwoerd's total-segregation policy, where deprivation of resources were perpetually preserved "via propagation." Under the Apartheid total state, labels used define a given person's zone of total-confinement – as economic, social, political, and special lines that the person is categorically denied of legitimate ways to cross over – are transferred "via propagation," predetermined by the racial category of one's parents rather than acquired traits.

Lastly, both Calvin and Verwoerd tied their transcendent doctrines of *total depravity* and *double-destination* into their respective covenant theology that superseded the pre-existing covenant. Consider the following lines from the April 14, 1961 "Separate Development" speech:

> I say therefore that the United Party's policy is an iniquitous policy. Apart from all the arguments I have mentioned, it is based on the bias of permanent discrimination and permanent domination by the Whites, because the Hon. member himself said: "Who says that we do not want to discriminate? … Their policy of racial federation, as it has been explained to us this morning, implies deliberate permanent discrimination and permanent domination. Just as the Italians in France retain their vote in Italy, so the Bantu, who are living temporarily in our urban areas, must have a say in their homelands. They should be able to get it up to the highest level and we want to help them to attain that position. … That is why we adopt the policy that the Bantu, wherever he may live in various areas of his own, must be given political control and domination or dominion over his own areas and people.[73]

As shown above, Dr. Verwoerd re-appropriated well-recognized vocabularies of political liberation for his policy of racial totalitarianism – that is, racial segregation being the totalizing principle that regulates all aspects of public and private transactions. By employing existing constitutional God-terms concerning the "right to self-determination," Dr. Verwoerd effectively re-signified the pre-existing political covenant – the constitutional order – with entirely new substance without the risk of explicitly rejecting those God-terms. This is achieved via a "new covenant" rhetoric, where the messianic rhetor swaps the signification "political good and evil" vocabularies as recognized by the pre-existing constitutional ideal framework. Rather than inventing a whole new set of "good vs. evil" vocabulary and theological framework for its radical departure from the old political covenant, the messianic new covenant not only appropriates pre-existing signifiers of "political-

71 Höpfl, *The Christian Polity of John Calvin*.
72 Ibid.
73 H. F. Verwoerd, *Verwoerd Speaks: Speeches 1948–1966*, 578.

good" for itself, but also re-assigns those familiar aphorisms of "political-evil" as attributes of the old order.

The use of messianic language in political discourse has been extensively studied in the works of Italian political philosopher Giorgio Agamben. In his *Potentialities: Collected Essays in Philosophy* (1999), Agamben defined the concept of the *messianic* not as relating to any particular historical figure, but rather a rhetorical moment. It is a moment where the "experience of history" appropriates the "experience of language," as Agamben suggested, where the collective memory is "saved" by "being transformed into something that never was."[74] The messianic logic also assumes radically different temporality than historical revisionist narratives – it does not merely seek to reshape historical experience of the audience, but to claim the "end of their history."[75]

To better understand the messianic as a rhetorical moment, it is important to first consider the concept of the Messiah developed in Judaic tradition prior to Christian theology. There are two distinct messianic figures that emerged in rabbinic literature in the 1st century BC – "Messiah ben Joseph" (Hebrew: משיח בן־יוסף) and "Messiah ben David" (Hebrew: מָשִׁיחַ בֶּן־דָּוִד)[76]. Agamben argued that pre-Christian formulation of twin worldly messianic figures in Abrahamic religion also fed into the commonly held assumptions among believers on the role of political authority.[77]

In effect, Agamben argued, the political theology operating in pre-Christian Abrahamic religious communities assumed a similar binary ideal type for political messianic *ethos* – either as the *legislator* (Messiah ben Joseph) or the *redeemer* (Messiah ben David) of the political community. The twin *legislator* and *redeemer*, ideal types for worldly messianic figures, also shaped assumptions of political temporality – for the continuous dialectic cycles between periods of crisis and stability. The preceding *legislator* and subsequent *redeemer* serve as mutual-potentialities for each other's return: the state of stability is always under the potentiality of crisis, and the arrival of crisis requires the *legislator* messiah to save the community from collective doom; the struggle and self-sacrifice of the *legislator* messiah thereby gives potentiality for the arrival of the *redeemer* messiah to bring back peace and stability, and the cycle returns again to the potentiality of crisis.[78]

Agamben further maintained that the Christian re-invention of the messianic persona collapsed the former distinctions between Messiah b. Joseph and Messiah b. David. Instead, a singular messianic figure – Jesus Christ – concurrently embodies both *legislator* and *redeemer* role.[79] Agamben claims that Christianity's formal consolidation of messianic ideal type had profound impact on the political theology in the post-Christian West. The previous political temporal framework of continuous cycles

74 Giorgio Agamben, *Potentialities – Collected Essays in Philosophy* (Stanford, CA: Stanford University Press, 2010), 3. *Potentialities* is an edited selection of Agamben's essays, originally published in English translation by Daniel Heller-Roazen.

75 *See* Agamben, *Potentialities*, 31.

76 Joseph Jacobs and Moses Buttenwieser, "Messiah," *The Jewish Encyclopedia, Vol. VIII* (New York: Funk & Wagnalls Co., 1904), 505–512.

77 Agamben, *Potentialities – Collected Essays in Philosoph*, 106–107.

78 Agamben, *Potentialities – Collected Essays in Philosophy*, 173.

79 Agamben, *Potentialities – Collected Essays in Philosophy*, 174–175

between times of crisis and stability no longer hold. Instead, under Christian political theology, the legislative actions of the messianic leader are also acts of redemptions.

This integrated Christian messianic figure no longer represents the dialectical historical cycles of human struggles of creating more perfect political orders, to pave way for the potentiality of peace on earth. Instead, the legislative role of the Messiah became indistinguishable from his role as the redeemer. This, as argued in both the writings of Agamben as well as in earlier writings of Walters Benjamin, effectively transforms the political from a discourse of historical *potentiality* into a discourse of ahistorical *actuality*. [80] In other words, the cycling between stability and crisis is no longer assumed. An "end-of-history" linear political temporality instead takes hold, asserting that the final political ideal is already known and here-at-present. This effectively transforms politics, vis-à-vis actions of uncertainty, into depoliticized measures of certainty. Measure affirming the absolute ideal are assumed to be predestined to avail, whereas measures inconsistent such ideal are predestined to fail. The end-of-history ideal thereby replaces human potentiality as the ultimate end of human society, in ways that is deemed "too sacred to fail." Such assumption then gives into the rhetoric that all sacrifices are necessary in order to protect society from falling from the grace of its end-of-history ideal.[81]

One may rightfully question the historical accuracy of the messianic political theology as outlined in the aforementioned works of Agamben. However, in terms of effective rhetorical operation, it is reasonable to consider the messianic frames as schematized by Agamben and Benjamin are subjected to employment in strategic communicative transactions. Before proceeding into detailed rhetorical analysis, it is necessary to first re-examine the concept of the messianic as a rhetorical framework, and clarify the difference between prophetic and messianic *ethos*.

The *messianic* and the *prophetic* are two important character ideal types in Abrahamic religions. Both are broadly understood as a person being in contact with God, and tasked to communicate certain divine knowledge to the human world. Given the pervasive historical impact and social embeddedness of Abrahamic religions, these character ideal types have been appropriated into political and rhetorical studies, as metaphors for discursive characteristics that, in form and/or function, resemble the religious ideal types of the *Messiah* and *prophet*. [82] Indeed, given Dr. Verwoerd's carefully maintained "scientist" cult of personality, it may seem intuitive, as first glance, to associate his *ethos* with the recently published study *Scientists as Prophets* by Linda Walsh.[83] However, upon closer examination of the rhetorical patterns employed by Dr. Verwoerd in pages herein below, it is clear that his effective *ethos* should be considered a messianic rather than prophetic one.

80 Agamben, *Potentialities – Collected Essays in Philosophy*, 106–107.

81 Walters Benjamin, "On the Concept of History," *Gesammelten Schriften I: 2. Suhrkamp Verlag* (Frankfurt am Main, 1974), xviii:

82 Walters Benjamin, "On the Concept of History," ii. *See also*, Benjamin (1940) at VI. *See also, generally*, Linda Walsh, *Scientists as Prophets: A Rhetorical Genealogy* (UK: Oxford University Press, 2013).

83 Lynda Walsh, *Scientists as Prophets: A Rhetorical Genealogy* (New York: Oxford University Press: 2013)

The operational difference between messianic and prophetic rhetorical frames, albeit nuanced, is not a trivial one. The prophetic narrative operates on the frame of prediction – that is, the voice of a prophet seeks to transform unknown future possibilities into known potentialities. The messianic narrative, on the other hand, operates on the frame of *predestination* rather than *prediction*. The predestination frame not only foretells future inevitabilities, but reveals the "good news" that the one and only route to salvation has arrived, thereby collapsing all future possibilities into the present and perpetual *actuality*. In Walter Benjamin's words, that "the model of messianic time summarizes the entire history of humanity into a monstrous abbreviation."[84] A messianic narrative asserts itself as the total truth of the end time, rather than a prophecy for the times to come.

A brief conclusion

In most brief terms, the thesis of the rhetorical analysis presented in chapter can be summarized as follows: There are five interlocking frames supporting the rhetorical theology of Dr. Verwoerd: [1] *Total depravity* of the status quo for racial/ethnic relations. [2] *Unconditional* election for public taking/access denial via no reason other than one's assigned racial/ethnic category; [3] *Limited realization* of development benefits under Apartheid; [4] *Irresistible* racial segregation in all aspects of public and private life [5] *Perseverance* of the Apartheid system as the sole route towards "true democracy." Altogether, this can be summarized as the core framing doctrines supporting the *Apartheid* political theology of Dr. Verwoerd.

These five core doctrines seek to frame the political imaginary within the bounds of Apartheid logic. This framing seeks to manufacture a *mythos* that automatically assumes Apartheid is the sole imaginable response to all political exigencies in South Africa. Many dehumanizing measures of the Apartheid system would appear almost as "forces of nature," through rigid administrative institutionalization and ritual repetitions of public sacrifices. The relative effectiveness of the Dr. Verwoerd's political rhetoric, especially considering the radical authoritarian nature of his policies, has much to do with his carefully maintained messianic cult of personality, in conjunction with his flexible appropriation of prevailing economic ideals as non-falsifiable justifications for his policies.

The Apartheid rhetoric of Dr. Verwoerd epitomizes the *mythos* of public takings as a matter of predestination – something appears to be inevitable, "born-into," and irresistible via human agency. His rhetorical clearing of political imaginaries is accompanied by his hollowing of the material promises of economic development. Instead, "development" is used as a self-referencing God-term, which unconditionally justifies the application of Apartheid policies to society in general. By preaching Apartheid policies through the frame of predestination theology, Dr. Verwoerd seeks to transform otherwise patently exploitative political actions into something that appears "extra-political" or even "necessary." The objective developmental principles would, in turn, define the possibilities of a collective future like a force of nature, and assumes full

84 Walters Benjamin, "On the Concept of History," xviii.

sovereignty over collective imaginaries irrespective of individual good faith. Like the plaintiffs in *Kelo v. City of New London* and the Dongria Kondh tribe, being taken for "separate development" has nothing to do with individual virtue or vices, but by "inherent" labels, e.g. *original sin* entirely outside of their individual agency.

Manufactured racial categories, in the case of Apartheid South Africa, have been appropriated to signify the *original sin* of a class of population predestined to be sacrificed, in order to bring "unity, prosperity, and happiness for all."[85] Against this gospel of the predestined common good, however, is the limited realization of promised benefits to only a relatively small class of benefactors. Historical antagonistic class relations from colonial South African were preserved via the Apartheid civic rite. The Apartheid rhetoric of Dr. Verwoerd transformed colonial relations of economic exploitation into something that is "biological." Verwoerd's carefully cultivated messianic rhetorical persona helped to amplify the "ahistorical" and "apolitical" style of his policy arguments. Furthermore, his framing of "total segregation" as the predestined national eschatological path effectively concealed the exceptionally anti-constitutional and antinomial nature of Apartheid legislations. The material consequence of the Apartheid theology of Dr. Verwoerd, however, is the sweep removal of legal, political, and economic protections for all non-Europeans in South Africa. This transformed the majority population of South Africa into a "sacrificial class," locked in a physically separate, yet economically exploitative relation with minority European population. With the permanent physical separation and access denial for non-Europeans comes continuous transfer of economic resources, from the sacrificial majority to the minority benefactors.

85 H. F. Verwoerd, "Day of the Covenant Address at Blood River, December 16th, 1958" *Verwoerd Speaks*, p.206.

6 Conclusions and looking forward

The concept of human violence can be extremely broad, context driven, and self-contradictory. It is nonetheless sufficient to say that violent acts, when deployed as organized symbolic practices, necessarily involve transactions between actors, or groups of actors.[1] Violent transactions not only often entail the use of force and/or power, both threatened and actual, between social actors, but also involve the transfer of resources and rights from one group to the other. The practice of human ritual cannibalism, which was prevalent in prehistoric societies, not only involved consumption of human flesh for nutrimental gains, but also the taking of resources which the cannibalized victim possessed.[2] The rhetorical foundation of ritual sacrifice is not grounded in the act of taking *per se*, but the legitimation process of violent takings through ritual suspension of *nomos* (pre-existing formal and customary social protections). The rhetoric of ritual functions as an audience-adaptation framework, via symbolic processes of consubstantiality and liminality. The ritual framing of human sacrifice thereby effectively conceals the violent nature of the act of taking, and transforms an otherwise transgressive human transaction into an inescapable necessity, or even something for the "greater good."

Ritual takings in the post-World War II political worldview share a number overlapping justification frames. This book has so far identified five common frames, or doctrines, of ritual sacrifice which have been broadly observed in its case studies. These common frames may be explicitly stated or tacitly assumed, but they tend to broadly reflect the rhetorical and legal foundations for public ritual sacrifice under the hegemonic market-driven governmentality. They define the "appropriate and proper" occasions for suspending pre-existing rule of law and

1 See Thomas W Blum, "Social Perspectives of Violence" *Michigan Family Review*, Vol. 2, No. 1 (1996), pp. 9–23. *See also, generally*, Walter Burkert, Rene Girard, Jonathan Z. Smith and Robert Hamerton-Kelly, *Violent Origins: Ritual Killing and Cultural Formation* (Stanford, CA: Stanford University Press, 1987).

2 See generally, Timothy D. White, *Once were Cannibals. Evolution: A Scientific American Reader* (Chicago, IL: University of Chicago Press: 2001). See also, Sigmund Freud, *Totem and Taboo: Resemblances between the Psychic Lives of Savages and Neurotics* (New York: Random House, 1961), Chapter III.

rights protections, to regularize otherwise transgressive transfers of rights and possessions for the "greater good" of the economic order.

First common doctrine: total depravity against economic growth

The first common doctrine is the total depravity of an economically accursed condition. This common doctrine involves a two-fold anathema, formally delivered by the acting authority against the accursed party to be sacrificed. First is the identification of a certain pre-existing condition that is *always-already-depraved.* That is, certain general conditions (i.e. blighted inner-city neighborhoods) already bound by totalizing presumptions that these conditions would always, and without exception, totally deprave the collective economic outlook of the community. The second anathema is the explicit naming of the party the accursed condition is being inflicted upon (i.e. condemning the blighted city neighborhoods for regulatory seizure). In the case where the economically accursed condition is declared as "totally depraved" by institutions of authority, such declaration often triggers the mandatory seizure of valuable resources as necessary means to deliver the commons from economic doom.

The accursed condition could also manifest in a wide range of socio-economic forms. In *Kelo v. City of New London*, it is not the petitioners *per se*, the low-income neighborhoods they lived in that are accursed, and as such neighborhoods are automatically assumed to deprave the entire city from private developments. In the Vedanta case, it is not the indigenous tribe but their sacred living grounds that are accursed, as the tribe's "inefficient" utilization of the planned mining site "depraves" foreign investment and industrial growth. In the case of Apartheid South Africa, Dr. Verwoerd consistently employed the rhetoric that it is not "non-European races" themselves that are accursed, but rather the condition of a "mixed-race" South Africa. Furthermore, Dr. Verwoerd proclaimed that the "mixed-race" social condition is predestined to totally deprive South Africa of its economic development goals, and that ritual total segregation was framed as the mandatory and only appropriate response to his manufactured emergency.

Ritual sacrifice is deployed as the automatic and "appropriate" response to a certain pre-existing condition that is considered to be accursed by institutions of authority. Interestingly, it is observed that under the governmentality of late-liberalism, the accursed is often a certain pre-existing condition rather than the offering itself. This kind of "pre-existing condition" is assumed to be totally depraved; that is, a taboo that mandates ritual sacrifice to protect a certain totemic good that must be preserved. An accursed condition may exist in the literal form of the "pre-existing condition clause" in many for-profit health insurance contracts, for example. The rhetorical assumption is that it is not the patient him or herself that is the accursed. Rather, the curse is directed at certain conditions that are defined by the insurance company. It is assumed, typically without any material evidence, that the self-generated list of "pre-existing medical conditions" are taboos for the industry, as they total the abominations for the economic profitability of corporate stakeholders. Furthermore, the "economic profitability" is assumed to be so sacred that it does not seem proper to wait for material evidence to emerge in order to drop insurance coverage. Rather, the discovery of pre-existing conditions automatically triggers instant and negotiable denial from coverage.

Second common doctrine: unconditional election of sacrificial offerings

The second common doctrine frames the parameters of the offering being elected for ritual sacrifice. It also provides the *modus operandi* of their election. In all three case studies, the sacrificial victims were elected via entirely impersonal grounds (unconditional election). Furthermore, human sacrifices in these cases did not directly involve the *total oblation* (killing) of the victim. Instead, they demanded *modified* offerings in the form of economic resources and access to these resources.

In the *Kelo v. City of New London* case previously examined in Chapter 3, the petitioners had their otherwise well-maintained properties seized not due to any of their own wrongdoing, but simply being incidentally located in the condemned neighborhood. Similar, the "being in the wrong place at the wrong time" election process also applied to the indigenous tribe in the *Vedanta* case study from Chapter 4. In the case of Apartheid South Africa, the unconditional permanent surrender of resources and access was generally applied for no reason other than one's assigned genetic category. This seemingly arbitrary election of the sacrificial victim rhetorically conceals the human agent behind the violent transaction.

Ritual sacrifice involves formalized human transactions. The offering is the subject formally marked by institution of authority to be automatically taken and transferred from one party to another. This common doctrine is rather complex in its rhetorical operation. It would be more helpful to carefully and separately examine its "modified offering" and "unconditional election" components.

Recall the discussion in the introduction chapter on *oblative* (life-taking transactions) and *modified* (possession-taking transaction without the killing) forms of sacrificial transactions. Capital punishment and warfare are among the most historically enduring (and ritually complex) examples of this *oblative* form of human sacrifice. There are also instances of modified human sacrifice that involve the ritual transfer of human possessions without the taking of biological life itself. Eminent domain is a representative example of modified form of human sacrifice. It is important to note that *oblative* and *modified* forms of human sacrifice differ only in terms of their lethality as formally prescribed by their ritual framework. Both *oblative* and *modified* human sacrifice involve the ritual suspension of *nomos* (pre-existing formal and customary social protections) for the taking and transfer of resources of human value.

The two world wars of the 20th century marked the peak-intensity, both in terms of scope and destructiveness, of *oblative* human sacrifice. Erich Fromm observed that the psychological conditions driving 20th century warfare were comparable to that of ancient child sacrifice as practiced in Canaan at the time of Carthage (*c.*3rd century BC). The main conceptual difference between ancient and modern child sacrifices (war), Fromm claims, is merely in the name of the sacrificial cult, and the election process for sacrificial offerings. In short, same destructiveness, different idolatries:

> The fact that, in the case of child sacrifice, the father kills the child directly while, in the case of war, both sides have an arrangement to kill each other's children makes little difference. In the case of war, those who are responsible for it know what is going to happen, yet the power of the idols is greater than the power of love for their children.[3]

Terms such as "ideology" and "political imagination" simply do not to fully capture the rhetorical power of the nation-state as a transnational idolatry of destruction. Rhetorical theology, in this case, is a more appropriate frame to examine many of the regularized, tacit articulations of the politics of sacrifice. In Walter Burkert's study of social liminality, rituals are known for their role in regulating and normalizing traumatic human experiences via symbolically concealing the violence.[4] This is also congruent with René Girard's thesis on the socio-psychological dimension of religion: that "religion is, by definition, evasion – that is, avoidance of an unacceptable truth."[5] Even after World War II, the potential destructiveness of the nation-state idolatry did not subside, but further intensified. Elaborate and all-encompassing rites and infrastructure of nuclear deterrence and mutually assured destruction emerged in the Cold War era, transforming the human civilization itself as the always-ready offering for automated total annihilation.[6] The global nuclear deterrence regime persisted even after the end of the Cold War. The possession of nuclear weapon systems, and the ability to kills hundreds-of-millions of people within hours, are still recognized as ultimate signs of national prestige.[7]

Under the sacrificial regime of Cold War era nuclear deterrence, the election for its sacrificial offering is *unconditional, total* (as applied to the general population), and *oblative* (killing humans is the ritual's core objective), and *final* (as it cannot be repeated in the foreseeable future, either due to human extinction or long-term radioactive fallout). This doctrine of unconditional mutual homicide,

3 Erich S. Fromm, *The Anatomy of Human Destructiveness* (New York: Holt, Rinehart and Winston, Inc., 1973), 176.

4 Walter Burkert, "The Problem of Ritual Killing" in *Violent Origins: On Ritual Killing and Cultural Formation*, Walter Burkert, René Girard, Jonathan Z. Smith and Robert Hamerton-Kelly (Stanford, CA: Stanford University Press, 1987), 149–176.

5 René Girard, *Violent Origins: On Ritual Killing and Cultural Formation*, Walter Burkert, René Girard, Jonathan Z. Smith and Robert Hamerton-Kelly (Stanford, CA: Stanford University Press, 1987), 6.

6 See generally, Herman Kahn, *On Thermonuclear War* (Princeton, NJ: Princeton University Press, 1960).

7 160 million immediate death is a relatively conservative casualty estimation in an all-out nuclear war scenario, based on the model calculations by Herman Kahn, one of the chief architects of US nuclear deterrence policy. See, Herman Kahn, *On Thermonuclear War*, 40–96.

paradoxically, has been peculiarly comforting to those who believe it. It is not difficult to find reasonably sober and knowledgeable people professing full faith in the necessity of mutual homicide to protect peace and national security. "Nuclear weapons are the only peacekeeping weapons that the world has ever known." Said Kenneth Waltz, an preeminent expert of international relations, in his 2012 interview with *The Diplomat*, "[i]t would be strange for me to advocate for their abolition, as they have made wars all but impossible."[8]

Putting aside the apparent gap between Waltz's "made wars all but impossible" belief and empirical reality, there is an intrinsic contradiction within the "economy" of the *oblative* sacrificial rite of the nuclear state. This inner contradiction is best illustrated in the following table by Herman Khan, a major architect of the U.S. nuclear deterrence policy:

> Nuclear war-economy estimations by RAND Corporation war strategist Herman Kahn from 1960, titled "Tragic but Distinguishable Postwar States," where Dr. Kahn advocated for what he called a "winnable" nuclear war plan[9]

Table 6.1, poetically captioned "Will the survivors envy the dead?" presents the war-economy of limited nuclear conflict in various degrees of intensity. It is important to note that Herman Khan is a proponent of "winnable" nuclear war, or in his own words, calculated "strategically justified" use of nuclear weapons "of an acceptable price generally fall between 10 and 60 million deaths [up to one-third of the total US population]."[10] Note that the total population of the United States was 180 million when Mr. Khan made his calculations. Will the survivors envy the dead? Mr. Khan answered "yes." The *Economic Recuperation* column in the chart represents the estimated number of

Table 6.1 Will the survivors envy the dead?

DEAD	*ECONOMIC RECUPERATION*
2,000,000	1 year
5,000,000	2 years
10,000,000	5 years
20,000,000	10 years
40,000,000	20 years
80,000,000	50 years
160,000,000	100 years

8 Kenneth Waltz, "Kenneth Waltz on 'Why Iran Should Get the Bomb' " interview by Zachary Keck, *The Diplomat* (July 8, 2012) available: https://thediplomat.com/2012/07/kenneth-waltz-on-why-iran-should-get-the-bomb/

9 Herman Kahn, *On Thermonuclear War* (Princeton, NJ: Princeton University Press, 1960), 30.

10 Kahn, *On Thermonuclear War*, 29–30.

years required for survivors to escape "preindustrial living standards" following a limited nuclear exchange.[11]

In his policy treatise *On Thermonuclear War*, Herman Khan estimated that even in the aftermath of a "limited" nuclear strike with 10–60 million deaths, the average survivor would not expect to live beyond the age of 30 due to radioactive fallout.[12] Khan estimated widespread genetic defects and reduced life expectancy (less than 30 years) will persist in the U.S. for at least 25 generations following a so-called "survivable" nuclear exchange.[13] Many researchers have criticized Khan's estimations as unrealistically optimistic.[14] But even when assessing Khan's table at face value, the human and economic cost of a "winnable" nuclear war is uncomfortably high. Nonetheless, the current U.S. nuclear deterrence strategy still largely follows the economy of sacrifice as formulated by Herman Khan. This doctrine of sacrifice is only justifiable under the assumption that the survival of the state is more sacred than the survival of its economy and general population.[15]

The enduring nuclear deterrence regime epitomizes the lingering edifice of the cult of the Westphalian state. The state-centric orthodoxy maintains its institutional presence globally, it is being gradually displaced by an emergent market-centric governmentality. The rise of neoliberalism can be understood as a post-World War II *reformation* movement within the political theology of modernity. The economy of state-centric sacrifice run against the political economy of global marketization. Khan's "acceptable" sacrifice of 60-million dead and 50-year economic recuperation is simply too "costly" for the emergent transnational governmentality driven by trade and economic growth. The rite of the late-capitalist transnational governmentality displaces the *state* with economic growth as the new *telos* of the political. Human lives were no longer simply assumed as *means* to preserve the integrity of the idolized Westphalian state. Rather, both the state apparatus and its population have become a *means* to serve the *ends* of economic growth.

Within such a "grow-or-die" economic worldview, a person is simply more "profitable" living than dead. As growth in late capitalism is largely driven by overconsumption and structural debt, the distinction between economically productive and unproductive members of society is blurred. Under this kind of economic regime, value is generated not only from labor-productivity, but also from consumption and direct extraction (from commodified bodies). A chronically ill and disabled patient may have limited labor value potential, but can be extremely "profitable" for the pharmaceutical and healthcare industries. Within an increasingly privatized prison-industrial complex, even deviance and criminality can

11 Kahn *On Thermonuclear War*, 20–21.
12 Ibid., 50.
13 Ibid., 51–61.
14 R. P Turco, O. B. Toon, T. P. Ackerman, J. B. Pollack, Carl Sagan. "Nuclear Winter: Global Consequences of Multiple Nuclear Explosions." *Science*, Vol. 222, No. 4630, 1283–1292.
15 Peter C. W. Flory, "Nuclear Exchange: Does Washington Really Have (or Want) Nuclear Primacy?" *Foreign Affairs*, September/October 2006.

function as factors of value-extraction. A quote from the 2018 Goldman Sachs biotech research report, titled "The Genome Revolution," captures this dilemma poignantly: "is curing patients a sustainable business model?"[16]

At surface, given the high economic cost of oblative human sacrifice, ritual sacrifice in late capitalism may tend to appear less deadly than those "patriotic" ritual killings of two world wars. However, it is important to remember that this seemingly "life-affirming" consequence of neoliberalism is merely incidental to the working of its value-creation mechanism. It is nonetheless concerning to witness an emergent system in which a chronically ill or incarcerated individual could generate more corporate revenue than a healthy, productive individual could. As observed in the previous three case studies, rather than *total oblation, modified* offerings were elected to be sacrificed for the promise of economic growth. Negative power (or power of taking) was exercised not onto human life itself, but onto one's economic capacity and access to economic resources. Not only an individual is seen as a factor of labor production, but his everyday transactions and biometric data are all potential sources for revenue. Economic resources, personal transactions, biometrics, right-of-access and other socio, political and economic rights protections are the new *modified* human offerings always-ready-to-be-taken.

A notable exception to the aforementioned "more profitable alive than dead" rule is the military-industrial complex. War and conflict remains a multi-billion dollar industry in the 21st century. Conservative estimates of the global arms trade in 2015 fell around $100 billion USD.[17] Yet the "war economy" is constrained by the fact that conflict destabilizes economic growth. To best serve the interest of corporate stakeholders, arms dealers and defense contractors need to maintain a "profitable" level of violence without fundamentally destabilizing the global economy. Interestingly, economic data suggests that post-Cold War conflicts, from the First Gulf War to the Syrian Civil War, have been surprisingly "unthreatening" to global economic stability.

The increasing wealth gap in the capitalist world system and the economic disparity core in periphery regions lend themselves to an uncomfortable reality – that some lives are more "economically expandable" than others. Take the Syrian Civil War as an example. After seven years of continuous bloodshed, with multiple uses of weapons-of-mass-destruction (nerve agent attacks) and up to half-million dead, the war has made no observable impact on the world's major stock markets.[18] The sustained global conflict in a post-Cold War world is intrinsically contradictory and

16 Tae Kim, "Goldman Sachs Asks in Biotech Research Report: 'Is Curing Patients a Sustainable Business Model?' " *CNBC*, published 3:15 PM ET Wed, April 11, 2018 (accessed April 11, 2018), available: https://www.cnbc.com/2018/04/11/goldman-asks-is-curing-patients-a-sustainable-business-model.html

17 Stockholm International Peace Institute, "Financial value of the global arms trade," *SIPRI databases* (accessed March, 2018), available: https://www.sipri.org/databases/financial-value-global-arms-trade

18 Estimation by the Syrian Observatory for Human Rights (SOHR), available: www.syriahr.com/en/

volatile, despite its apparent "profitability." It is logical to suspect that the war economy in the late-capitalist world system may be the first to implode.[19]

Third common doctrine: limited realization of predestined economic deliverance

The third common doctrine serves to bridge the apparent gap between the promised blessing of neoliberal sacrifices and their actual fulfillment. In all three case studies, the "goodness" of the involved policy measures became an unfalsifiable doctrine of faith rather a materially justified fact. The universal benefit of economic growth was reframed by institutions of power as a matter of predestination, and are not subject to "second-guessing."[20] The doctrine of limited realization of the ideal thus became the rhetorical response by public authorities in the case studies to address constraints that arise from the unfulfilled promises of neoliberalism. Take, for instance, the *Kelo v. City of New London* (2005) case examined in Chapter 3, in which the city government justified its aggressive regulatory seizure of well-maintained private houses with the promise of bringing new jobs and businesses to the city. The actual employment data of New London reveals a very different reality. The unemployment rate of the city skyrocketed from 4.1 percent in 2006 to 8.9 percent in 2010.

To fully understand the disparity between neoliberal ideals and its material realization, let's first examine broader empirical observations on the growing gap between economic growth and net income over the third-wave marketization period (mid-1970s to 2010s).[21] There has been an increasing gap between gross domestic product (GDP, most common indicator for economic growth) and net national income (NNI) in the U.S. between 1970 and 2015.[22] Note that the NNI in practice is a significantly inflated representation of the sum-total wealth gains of all households in the United States. Not only that the NNI does not take into account the uneven wealth distribution among the American population, but does include business income and government expenditure.[23] Despite the inflated nature of the NNI, long-term

19 A 2016 study by the World Bank Group found that global conflicts have increased sharply since 2010. *See* Alexandre Marc, "Conflict and Violence in the 21st Century" (World Bank Group, 2016; accessed 12 April 2018), available: https://www.un.org/pga/70/wp-content/uploads/sites/10/2016/01/Conflict-and-violence-in-the-21st-century-Current-trends-as-observed-in-empirical-research-and-statistics-Mr.-Alexandre-Marc-Chief-Specialist-Fragility-Conflict-and-Violence-World-Bank-Group.pdf

20 Justice Stevens quote from *Kelo v. New London* supra Chapter 2, 93.

21 See World Bank Database: https://data.worldbank.org/indicator/NY.ADJ.NNTY.PC.CD?locations=US

22 *See* "GDP and NNI Gap in the US: 1970 to 2015" in Appendix A.

23 NNI = Consumption + Investments + Government Spending + Net Export + Net Foreign Factor Income – Indirect Taxes – Manufactured Capital Depreciation – Natural Resources Depletion.

trends nonetheless show that it has been increasingly lagging behind the GDP growth over the past 45 years. A similar income-GDP gap has been also observed in China over the same period.[24]

Another commonly used income indicator is the median household income.[25] It provides a more realistic estimation of the earning level of an average middle-income family in a given country.[26] When comparing the growth rates of GDP with the

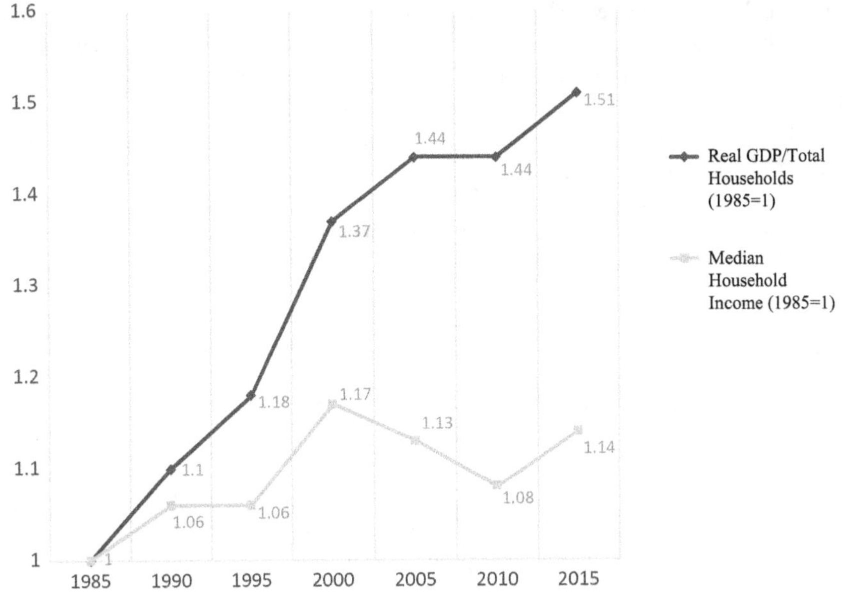

Figure 6.1 GDP/median household income gap in the U.S.: 1985–2015
Based on data from the U.S. Bureau of Economic Analysis, U.S. Bureau of the Census

24 *See* "GDP and NNI in the China: 1970 to 2015" in Appendix A.

25 The World Bank DataBank (https://data.worldbank.org) does not record statistics on household income. Estimation of median household income is based on data provided by the U.S. Census Bureau. *See*, Jessica L. Semega, Kayla R. Fontenot, and Melissa A. Kollar, "Income and Poverty in the United States: 2016," *U.S. Census Bureau*, Report Number: P60–259 (September 12, 2017), 2: "The Census Bureau presents annual estimates of median household income and poverty by state and other smaller geographic units based on data collected in the American Community Survey (ACS). Single-year estimates are available for geographic units with populations of 65,000 or more. Estimates of income and poverty for all geographic units, including census tracts and block groups, are available by pooling 5 years of ACS data."

26 Jessica L. Semega, Kayla R. Fontenot, and Melissa A. Kollar, "Income and Poverty in the United States: 2016," *U.S. Census Bureau*, Report Number: P60-259 (September 12, 2017), p.2: "All comparative statements have undergone statistical testing and are significant at the 90 percent confidence level unless otherwise noted. In this report, the

median household income in the U.S. from 1985 to 2015, the growing gap between the two became even more jarring (see timeline Figure 6.1).

Empirical observations shown above suggest a simple fact – that formal economic growth is increasingly outpacing real income on the ground. Did economic growth fail to materialize into tangible wealth? Yes and no. The economic growth in recent decades has resulted in real wealth for a small class of financial asset owners. From 1985 to 2016, average bonuses in the New York securities sector grew at a rate seven times higher than the federal minimum wage.[27] The following timeline chart compares the growth rates of the Dow Jones Industrial Average and average hourly earnings of U.S. employees between 2009 and 2018, compiled from FRED (Federal Reserve Economic Data). The timeline chart highlights two radically different economic realities between "Wall Street" and "Main Street" America following the 2009 financial crisis (see Figure 6.2).

Figure 6.2 Wall Street v. Main Street
Based on Federal Reserve economic data

variances of estimates were calculated using both the Successive Difference Replication (SDR) method and the Generalized Variance Function (GVF) approach."

27 Quentin Fottrell, "Bonuses in the New York securities industry have soared 890% over the last three decades," *Market Watch*, Published: May 23, 2017 6:09 p.m. (accessed 19 April 2018).

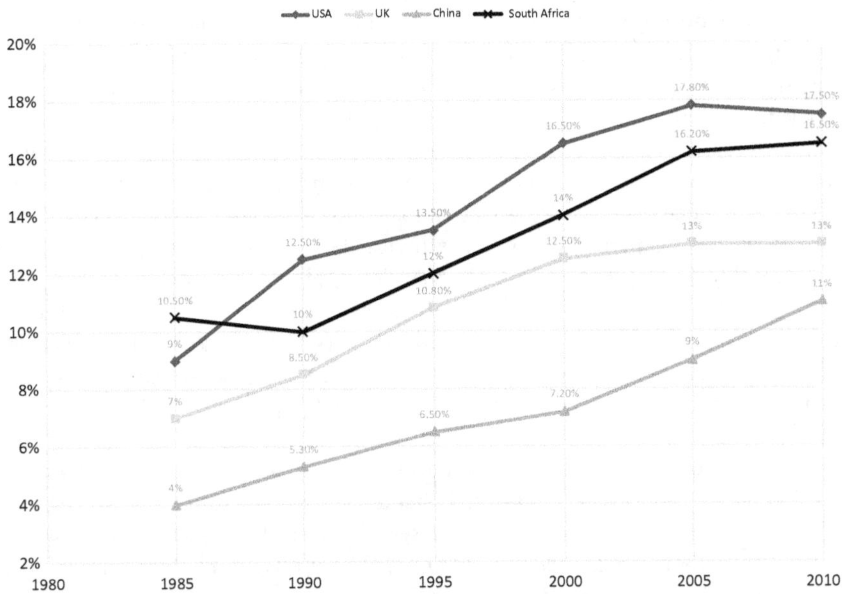

Figure 6.3 Share of top 1 percent in total income 1985–2010[28]

Not only did the "Wall Street" class recover far more quickly from the financial crisis than the "Main Street" class, there has been no observable "trickle down" effect. This limited realization of the blessings of economic growth is hardly unique to the U.S. Increasing wealth concentration among the top 1 percent is a global phenomenon. Since the 1980s, this trend has been widely observed in both developing and developed economies around the world. The timeline chart below visualizes the income distribution trends in United States, United Kingdom, China and South Africa from 1985 to 2010. It compares the changes in the share of the top 1 percent wealthiest population in the total national income of each country. These four economies are quite different both in terms of their organizing structures and stage of development. Nonetheless, the timeline chart shows a strikingly parallel trend in the increasing wealth share of the top 1 percent, or the "Wall Street" class (see Figure 6.3).

Other non-econometric human development has also remained stagnant or even worsened over the third-wave marketization period. The incarceration rate in the United States increased more than 400 percent from 1978 to 2010.[29] The prevalence and diagnosis rates of diabetes jumped more than

28 Source of data series: Thomas Piketty, piketty.pse.ens.fr/capital21c

29 E. Ann Carson, "Prisoners in 2016" *Bureau of Justice Statistics,* (US Department of Justice: NCJ 251149, 2018).

250 percent during the same period.[30] Globally, both the number and relative intensity of armed conflicts have increased sharply since 2010.[31] The amount of forcibly displaced populations worldwide also rose sixfold – from less than 10 million people in 2000 to 59.9 million people by the end of 2014.

A key rhetorical constraint for authorities in all three case studies is the disparity between the make-believe and lived reality in terms redeeming the material blessings of neoliberal sacrifice. *Mythos* legitimizes and reifies arguments that cannot be verified via lived experience. For metaphysical God-terms that transcend human empirical domain, *mythos* may be the only device available in human language to narrativize the immaterial.[32] However, economic growth is far from a God-term. It is a social-scientific and materially dependent concept, and is only verified via empirical observations of economic relations. Even the post-World War II generation of neoclassical economists, which included the likes of Milton Friedman and Eugene Fama, did not justify their free market ideals via faith alone. Any alleged positive causal relation between economic growth and human welfare must be falsifiable in order to be considered scientifically legitimate.

In practice, the sweeping material promises of growth-driven sacrifices do not fully realize except for a very limited class of financial asset owners, or the so-called "Top 1%" Empirical observations listed hereinabove largely confirm the uncomfortable (but transnationally proliferate) fact that material blessings of growth-driven sacrifices are ritually taken from the "Main Street" class and given to the "Wall Street" class. Only those very few who own the means of financial speculation are structurally "predestined" to receive the blessings of the global economic system.

When material justifications are wanting, mythical narratives may be employed to fill the gap of the political imaginary. The mythical narrative in this case does not provide an alternative justification to the material knowledge-gap. Rather, as Girard suggested, it functions as a means of evasion – "that is, avoidance of an unacceptable truth" as deemed by the dominant power structure.[33] Thus, in all three case studies examined so far, the public authority rhetorically transformed the empirically-grounded notion of "economic growth" into a self-justifying God-concept. This rhetorical transformation would not be possible without pre-existing, socially embedded idolization of "economic growth." Under the transnationally proliferated myth that economic growth is the predestined and singular route of the salvation for all political communities, the rhetoric of "limited

30 *See* National Diabetes Surveillance System (2016) published by the U.S Centers for Disease Control and Prevention, data available: https://www.cdc.gov/chronicdisease/resources/publications/aag/diabetes.htm

31 Alexandre Marc, "Conflict and Violence in the 21st Century", available: https://www.un.org/pga/70/wp-content/uploads/sites/10/2016/01/Conflict-and-violence-in-the-21st-century-Current-trends-as-observed-in-empirical-research-and-statistics-Mr.-Alexandre-Marc-Chief-Specialist-Fragility-Conflict-and-Violence-World-Bank-Group.pdf

32 See generally, Kenneth Burke, *The Rhetoric of Religion: Studies in Logology* (Boston, MA: Beacon Press, 1961).

33 Walter Burkert, Rene Girard, Jonathan Z. Smith and Robert G. Hamerton-Kelly, *Violent Origins: Ritual Killing and Cultural Formation*, 8.

realizations" of those promised blessings is sufficient to function as the singular legitimation basis of a wide range of ritual sacrifices. This is indeed case for all three ritual situations we have examined so far.

Fourth common doctrine: irresistible takings by institutions of public authority

This common doctrine seeks to establish the irresistibility of ritual takings. This doctrine responds to the constraint of rhetorical contestation. That is, to manage and constrain the capacity of those discontents of the sacrifice "to criticize or uphold an argument, to defend themselves or to accuse."[34] It defines the rhetorical boundaries contestability throughout the ritual taking process, and declares the infallibility of the acting authority to exercise its power of takings. In all three case studies, the irresistible takings doctrine is deployed via certain prescribed judicial, administrative and/or legislative processes.

Ritual takings are presented as automatically triggered via the formal invocation of public authority. In the case of public taking, the formal innovation (i.e. the condemnation notice) functions as a signifier of the "publicness" of the act-of-taking. The instant audience recognition of the invocation is possible because the governing authority and its subjects are bound in a state of constitutional consubstantiality. The constitutional framework organizes the subjects under a unified political *ecclesia* (community sharing a common-faith), in which the totemic field of habitus (or consubstantiality) is provided, which automatically implies certain role expectations and power-relations.[35] Upon audience identification of the formal invocation, an otherwise violent act-of-taking is instantly transformed into a regulated public ritual.

In all three rhetorical studies conducted in the previous chapters, the acting authorities seized the legitimation power of constitutional consubstantiality when they sought to expand the laws of public sacrifice. The pre-existing constitutional protections in these cases were all disrupted under the paradoxical rhetoric of "upholding the constitution." In the case of Apartheid South Africa, Dr. Verwoerd proved to be quite successful in his radical subversion of the constitutional principles while consistently maintaining a rhetoric of constitutional fidelity.

34 This is a quote from Aristotle's definition of rhetoric, see Aristotle, *Rhetoric*, trans. Aristotle in 23 Volumes, Vol. 22, translated by J. H. Freese. (Cambridge: Harvard University Press, 1926), Perseus Digital Library. http://data.perseus.org/citations/urn:cts:greekLit:tlg0086.tlg038.perseus-eng1:1.1 (accessed March 7, 2018), at 1.1: "Rhetoric is a counterpart of Dialectic; for both have to do with matters that are in a manner within the cognizance of all men and not confined to any special science. Hence all men in a manner have a share of both; for all, up to a certain point, endeavor to criticize or uphold an argument, to defend themselves or to accuse."

35 For additional info on the rhetorical concept of consubstantiality, *see* Kenneth Burke, *A Grammar of Motives* (Berkeley, CA: University of California Press, 1969), 29–30 and 110–112.

Subsidiary petition rituals are often put in place to make the "bitter pill" of public takings appear more equitable or even palatable. The *Kelo* and *Vedanta* cases in particular highlighted detailed workings of judicial petition mechanisms for regulatory seizures. In both cases the supreme courts sought to expand the scope of eminent domain through their *ethos* of infallibility. Under constitutional consubstantiality, the infallibility of the court as a last resort conceals the rhetorical agency behind the ritual takings. The politically driven sacrifices, via the matristic *ethos* of the court, were reaffirmed like forces of nature, both irresistible and non-negotiable.

Given the interdependent dynamics between constitutional doctrines and practicing believers of constitutionalism, the rhetorical strength of the court is dependent on the constitutional faith of the community. Even in a full-fledged liberal, constitutional society, the judiciary apparatus cannot entirely eliminate resistance against its rulings. In a situation where ritual sacrifice is both materially damaging and normatively transgressive, it tends to invite a higher degree of public resentment. For this reason, regulatory takings in *Kelo* and *Vedanta* encountered greater public frictions than ritual takings in the form of typical taxations. Often, subsidiary petition structures only allow the negotiation of compensation, but do not permit public takings themselves to be contested. These subsidiary rituals function as "pressure-release valves" to counterbalance the oppressive nature of the irresistible takings doctrine.

Apartheid legislations created separate (and much stricter) judicial process for reviewing petitions against forceful relocation of non-whites.[36] The lawsuit filed by the petitioners in *Kelo v. City of New London* only strengthened the city's claim for its regulatory condemnations. The seemingly successful petition by the indigenous tribe in the *Vedanta* case was proven to be a short-lived victory. After the *Vedanta* ruling by the Indian Supreme Court, the Odisha government re-submitted its bauxite mining proposal through the state-owned Orissa Mining Corporation (OMC). The Supreme Court allowed Odisha's government to form its own commission to review all in-state mining proposals.[37] In 2018, the Odisha government approved its own plan to mine bauxite from the controversial Niyamgiri deposit, and immediately sold its mining rights to Vedanta Resources.[38] Petition rituals thus function within the rhetorical field constitutional consubstantiality, to allow a more "sustainable" expansion of the laws of sacrifice. This in turn leads to the fifth common doctrine – the perseverance of the ritual.

36 See, *supra* Chapter 5, on Prevention of Illegal Squatting Act of 1951.

37 Meera Mohanty, "Odisha new Bauxite linkage policy to benefit Vedanta," *The Economic Times*, updated: February 12, 2018 (accessed April 11, 2018). Available: http://economictimes.indiatimes.com/articleshow/63018502.cms?utm_source=contentofinterest&utm_medium=text&utm_campaign=cppst

38 Subhashish Mohanty, "Capacity boost for Vedanta: Naveen nod to Lanjigarh refinery expansion," *The Telegraph India* (posted April 9, 2018, accessed April 12, 2018), available: https://www.telegraphindia.com/states/odisha/capacity-boost-for-vedanta-221986

Fifth common doctrine: perseverance of the ritual

The rhetorical inventive process by the acting authorities in all three case studies share the motivation of rendering exceptional sacrifices permanent. Ritual is, by definition, a symbolic act of preservation. Ritual preserves common values and norms of behavior via repetition and consubstantiality. Even destructive rituals, such as war and capital punishment, are formally conducted under the justification framework of preserving collective ideals. The normative structures of neoliberalism, too, reproduce its economic worldview via ritual inculcation of its core values and normative principles. Thus the post-World War II transnationally established norms of governance tend to gravitate towards a preference for the protection of private property, and free movements of goods, services, technology and financial assets. The transnational proliferation of neoliberal constitutionalism only accelerated since the end of the Cold War.

Neoliberalism, however, should not be understood as simply a particular set of ideas and teachings. Neoliberalism is also a historical moment. It is the historical unfolding of the qualitative and quantitative changes, fractures and fissures of capitalist global economy in the late 20th and 21st century. Even the most foundational liberal ideals, such as the individual's right to the quiet enjoyment of one's own property, are readily disposable for the sake of its economic articulations.

In all three rhetorical studies, the acting authorities employed the economic *logos* of neoliberalism to justify the sacrifice of the ideals are considered sacred under the neoliberal normative framework. The courts in *Kelo* and *Vedanta* commanded the sacrifice of private living spaces for the sake of private development. Dr. Verwoerd advocated policies that sacrificed the free flow of goods, services, technology and assets for the sake of "separate development." These are all considered exceptional ritual sacrifices in the sense that they significantly departed the pre-existing constitutional *nomos*. Furthermore, acting authorities in all three cases did not resort to the "state of emergency" argument. The "state of emergency" itself was formally permitted only momentary suspension of pre-existing legal protections. Yet the ritual sacrifices in the case studies were motivated not only by the act-of-taking present-at-hand, but also the perseverance of new sacrificial rituals to facilitate future takings.

The judicial, administrative and legislative organs involved in the case studies not only served as agents of sacrifice, but also legislation of new laws of sacrifice that can be applied in future cases. The rhetoric of the ritual projects its power not only over present disputes, but also over future possibilities. Dr. Verwoerd exploited a *de jure* representative constitutional republic structure to usurp substantive legislative power for the perpetuation of physical takings of economic resources from the non-white majority to the white minority population. The judiciary petition processes in *Kelo* and *Vedanta* cases, through their constitutional review authority, effectively transformed the exceptional transgressions of eminent domain laws into legal precedents that are applicable for future cases.

The SCOTUS ruling in *Kelo v. City of New London* not only confirmed the irresistibility of the particular regulatory property seizure by the New London city government, but also produced a new constitutional interpretation and legal precedent that permits future regulatory takings for private redevelopment in the entire U.S. The legally transgressive action of the New London city government, through the mystic *ethos* of the SCOTUS, is ritually merged into the pre-existing *nomos* of sacrifice as something "always-permitted" by the constitution. Ritual sacrifice in all three case studies not only preserved its ritual for future use, but also preserved their territorial separations, as well as the inequitable distribution of economic resources among their populations.

Advantages, constraints, and future directions

This project attempts to find innovative ways to bring interdisciplinarity and integrative analysis into rhetorical research. In terms of interdisciplinary research, this project introduces a diverse set of theoretical vocabularies from disciplines outside of rhetorical studies. An interdisciplinary approach is necessary for this project: the field of rhetoric is a disciplinary latecomer to the study of ritual practices. Even before the birth of modern scientific research, ritual has long been an essential element of theology and religious scholarship. Ritual has also been a relatively well-studied subject in a wide range of social-scientific inquiries, most notably in sociological, psychological, and historical-anthropological disciplinary areas. Meaningful theoretical advancement requires bringing "news" to the existing knowledge base of a subject area. When interpreting a concept which has already been broadly investigated, it is best for the rhetorician to build his or her "readings" upon a baseline of interdisciplinary common literacy. By grounding the rhetorical analysis upon a diverse and relevant set of interdisciplinary vocabularies, it allows the criticism task to proceed from a better informed and well-rounded point of departure. Introducing interdisciplinarity into rhetorical research thus opens up opportunities for innovative, and more nuanced readings of human symbolic practices. It also allows for the consideration of relevant theoretical perspectives that are overlooked within the traditional vocabulary of rhetorical study heuristically employed in the analysis.

That being said, there are practical limitations when it comes to introducing interdisciplinarity into rhetorical research. The most obvious risk would be interdisciplinary misappropriation, in which vocabularies and concepts from other academic fields are "misquoted" outside of their own disciplinary context. Taking quotations out of context is particularly damaging to the rigor of rhetorical analysis. As a rhetorician who is also trained in international relations (IR) studies, I can give this example. In IR theory, especially within a structural realist analytical framework, the idea of the "rational actor" is a formal concept that comes with its own disciplinary definition and analytical logic. The "rational actor" in IR nomenclature is completely divorced from the everyday meaning and usage of that phrase. If a disciplinary outsider, say a literary critic, were to directly toss the IR concept of "rational actor" into a work of literary criticism, yet did not use the concept in ways that conform to its actual role within the IR analytical framework, this kind of slapdash interdisciplinarity would not be very helpful. Constructive use of interdisciplinarity in rhetorical research requires the rhetorician to attain a corresponding level of interdisciplinary literacy.

The other focus of theoretical intervention in this project is to develop an integrative approach for rhetorical analysis and criticism. What does "integrative analysis" mean? It is an attempt to strike a balance between the need for scope and the need for resolution. Integrative rhetorical analysis seeks to accommodate close readings of a rhetorical moment, at the same time preserving the ability to relate that moment to global exigencies. Developing better integrative analytical tools is particularly important for researching ritual sacrifice in neoliberalism. Ritual is, by definition, a memory practice that is deeply territorial. It is impossible to reach a nuanced understanding of a particular ritual practice without close readings of its locally embedded historical, political, legal and cultural contexts. The discourse of neoliberalism, however, is a discourse of deterritorialization. Its implications are both hegemonic and global. Therefore, this project seeks to develop a suitable method for the study of the governing structures of neoliberalism's cut across the manifold of political, social, cultural, and economic boundaries.

However, scale and resolution are two diametrically opposite functions within a single frame of reference. When looking at a physical globe, the topography of the entire earth unfolds with a light spin at the fingertip. Yet it is impossible for one to discern, say, the urban topography of New York City from a spinning globe. The idea of an atlas proposes an elegant solution to this contradiction between resolution and scale. Instead of trying to display the entire world within a single frame of reference, the atlas divides the globe into individually mapped local frames. When I was a child, I would spend hours flipping through different atlases at the local library, entranced by the level of detail on each individual page. And yet because they were atlases, it was easy for me to immediately relate the local coordinates on each page back onto the global topography without feeling lost. This childhood fascination inspired me to work on developing a suitable integrative method for rhetorical research. To be clear, there are numerous unique advantages stemming from this "close reading" analytical impulse of rhetorical discipline. It is well-equipped to produce nuanced and detailed tracing of a symbolic practice at a level of resolution that is not offered in many other social-scientific disciplines. A collage of close tracings of individual rhetorical moments still can allow coordination of these moments in relation to the global discursive structures. For this project, the specific objective of integrative analysis is to give due consideration to the governing structures of neoliberalism that cut across political, social, cultural, and economic boundaries.

Of course, integrative analysis also has its share of limitations, despite the far greater potential advantages it could offer. The problem of translation between case studies presents an additional major obstacle for integrative rhetoric. The distillation of a set of global theses out of individual case studies must be conducted under the presumption that these studies piece together with coherence towards some kind of large global theme or motif. One could rightfully raise suspicion towards projects that try to bring together moments that took place in different time, locations, cultures, or political contexts. For rhetorical studies, this translation problem is even more apparent because symbolic practices are deeply embedded its operating language. Symbolic practices are inferior to human language; some nuance is always lost in translation. It is quite reasonable, and even necessary, to scrutinize the limitations of integrating rhetorics that are spoken in different languages. There are different vocabularies for human actions, yet it is possible to identify implications of human labor and transactions that cut across linguistic differences. It is through human doings that the physical environment and topography of our lifeworld has been terraformed, for better or worse. It would be unproductive and self-undermining to reject the possibility of acquiring substantive knowledge that transcends individually atomized linguistic subjectivity. Again, this issue of translatability remains on the theoretical frontier of rhetorical studies, especially in the area of transnational rhetoric. This is a much larger theoretical question than this work can fully address. But this issue, in turn, highlights possible routes for future theoretical and methodological interrogations in rhetorical studies.

The labor and resource intensity of integrative research could also pose major constraints. A rhetorical atlas integrates a wide range of well-focused case studies under a unified theme. It simply cannot be produced in the form of a journal-length article. Due to practical limitations in funding and time constraints, this project could only afford to accommodate three full-length case studies. A global atlas cannot be completed by three local mapping surveys. Therefore, it is more appropriate to consider this project as the beginning of a larger effort to compile a global rhetorical atlas on contemporary ritual sacrifice. Many more transnational case studies need to be conducted and comparatively analyzed. This practical constraint also highlights a definitive path for future research opportunities. The hope is to bring attention to the vast research opportunities that interdisciplinary and integrative approaches could bring to the field of rhetorical studies, especially in the area of transnational rhetoric.

Bibliography

Adorno, Theodor W. *Prisms*. London: Spearman, 1967.

Adorno, Theodor W. *Critical Models: Interventions and Catchwords*. New York: Columbia University Press, 1998.

Agamben, Giorgio. *Homo Sacer: Sovereign Power and Bare Life*. Stanford, CA: Stanford University Press, 1998.

Agamben, Giorgio. *The Time that Remains: A Commentary on the Letter to the Romans*. Stanford, CA: Stanford University Press, 2005.

Agamben, Giorgio. *Potentialities – Collected Essays in Philosophy, Part III*. Stanford, CA: Stanford University Press, 2010.

Agamben, Giorgio and Daniel Heller-Roazen. *Potentialities: Collected Essays in Philosophy*. Stanford, CA: Stanford University Press, 1999.

Aldhouse-Green, Miranda Jane. *Dying for the Gods: Human Sacrifice in Iron Age & Roman Europe*. Charleston, SC: Tempus Publishing, 2001.

Althusser, Louis. *Lenin and Philosophy and Other Essays*. New York: Monthly Review Press, 1971.

Amnesty International. "India: Generalisations, omissions, assumptions: The failings of Vedanta's Environmental Impact Assessments for its bauxite mine and alumina refinery in India's state of Orissa (Executive Summary)," London: Amnesty International UK, 2011.

Amnesty International, "Document – United Nations: General Assembly Makes Progress on the Human Rights to Water and Sanitation, But Only so Far as the USA Permits," November 26, 2013 IOR 40/005/2013.

Ando, Clifford. *The Matter of the Gods*. California: University of California Press, 2009.

Aparajita, Upali. *Culture and Development: Dongrias of Niyamgiri*. New Delhi: Inter-India Publications, 1994.

Aristotle, J. H.Freese. *Rhetoric*, 23 Volumes, Vol. 22. Cambridge: Harvard University Press, 1926.

Aristotle, W. Rhys Roberts, and Ingram Bywater. *Rhetoric*. 1st ed. New York: Modern Library, 1984.

Aristotle, Benjamin Jowett. *Politics*. Kitchener: Batoche Books, 1999.

Aristotle, W.Rhys Roberts. *Rhetoric*. MIT Internet Classics Archive, 2009, book I, part 2, http://classics.mit.edu/Aristotle/rhetoric.1.i.html

Atlenmüller, Hartwig. *Die Apotopaia und Die Götter Mitteläġyptens*. Munich: Ludwig-Maximilians University, 1965.

Ayres, James. *Domestic Interiors: The British Tradition, 1500–1850*. New Haven, CT: Yale University Press, 2003.

Backer, Larry Catá. "The Structural Characteristics of Global Law for the 21st Century: Fracture, Fluidity, Permeability, and Polycentricity." *Tilburg Law Review* Vol. 17 (2012): 177–199.

Baehr, Peter. "The 'Iron Cage' and the 'Shell as Hard as Steel': Parsons, Weber, and the Stahlhartes Gehäuse Metaphor in the Protestant Ethic and the Spirit of Capitalism." *History and Theory* Vol. 40, No. 2(2001): 153–169.

"Bantu Investment Corporation." *Parliament of South Africa.* Act No. 34 of 1959.

Barbalet, J. M. *Weber, Passion and Profits: 'The Protestant Ethic and the Spirit of Capitalism' in Context.* Cambridge; New York: Cambridge University Press, 2008.

Barthes, Roland, Annette Lavers. *Mythologies.* [1st American]. ed. New York: Noonday Press, 1972.

Bataille, Georges. *The Accursed Share: An Essay on General Economy.* New York: Zone Books, 1988.

Behringer, Wolfgang. "Climatic Change and Witch-Hunting: The Impact of the Little Ice Age on Mentalities." *Climatic Change*, Vol. 43, No. 1(1999): 335–351.

Benjamin, Walters. "On the Concept of History" (1940) *Gesammelten Schriften I: 2. Suhrkamp Verlag.* Frankfurt am Main, 1974.

Bianchi, Robert Steven. *The Mechanics of Ancient Egyptian Magical Practice.* Vol. 114American Oriental Society, 1994.

Bitzer, Lloyd F. "The Rhetorical Situation" *Philosophy and Rhetoric*, Vol. 1, No. 1 (Jan.,1968): 1–14.

Blum, Thomas W. "Social Perspectives of Violence," *Michigan Family Review*, Vol. 2, No. 1 (1996): 9–23.

Bourdieu, Pierre. *Outline of a Theory of Practice.* Vol. 16. Cambridge; New York: Cambridge University Press, 1977.

Bouwsma, William J. *John Calvin: A Sixteenth-century Portrait.* New York: Oxford University Press, 1989.

Bowers, Simon. "Vedanta stripped of safety awards in light of Indian site disaster." *The Guardian*, August 28, 2010.

Browlie, Ian. *Principles of Public International Law.* Oxford University Press, 2008.

Browne, Stephen H. "Rhetorical Criticism and the Challenges of Bilateral Argument." *Philosophy and Rhetoric* Vol. 40, No. 1(2007): 108–118.

Buchholz, Rogene A. "The Protestant Ethic as an Ideological Justification of Capitalism." *Journal of Business Ethics* Vol. 2, No. 1(1983): 51–60.

Burawoy, Michael. "Public Sociology vs. the Market." *Socio-Economic Review* Vol. 5, No. 2 (2007): 356–367.

Burke, A. "Mental Health Care during Apartheid in South Africa: An Illustration of How 'Science' Can be Abused," in Gozaydin en Madeira (ed) *Evil, Law and the State.* Oxford: Interdisciplinary Press, 2006.

Burke, Kenneth. *The Rhetoric of Religion: Studies in Logology.* Boston, MA: Beacon Press, 1961.

Burke, Kenneth. *A Grammar of Motives.* Berkeley, CA: University of California Press, 1969.

Burke, Kenneth. *Permanence and Change: An Anatomy of Purpose.* 3rd, with a new afterword. ed. Berkeley, CA: University of California Press, 1984.

Burkert, Walter, René Girard, Jonathan Z. Smith, and Robert Hamerton-Kelly. *Violent Origins: Ritual Killing and Cultural Formation.* Stanford, CA: Stanford University Press, 1987.

Buursma, Bruce. "Apartheid's Roots Nourished by Religion," *Chicago Tribune*, January 19, 1985).

Caldararo, Niccolo. "Human Sacrifice, Capital Punishment, Prisons & Justice: The Function and Failure of Punishment and Search for Alternatives." *Historical Social Research / Historische Sozialforschung* Vol. 41, No. 4(158) (2016): 322–346.

Calvin, Jean and Henry Beveridge. *Institutes of the Christian Religion.* Grand Rapids, MI: Wm. B. Eerdmans, 1989.

Canterbury, Dennis Compton. *Neoliberal Democratization and New Authoritarianism.* Aldershot: Ashgate Publishing, Ltd., 2005.

Cantillon, Richard, Henry Higgs, and William Stanley Jevons. *Essai Sur La Nature Du Commerce En Général.* London: Macmillan & Co., Ltd. for the Royal Economic Society, 1931.

Carey, James W. *James Carey: A Critical Reader.* Minnesota, MT: University of Minnesota Press, 1997.

Carson, Ann E. "Prisoners in 2016." *Bureau of Justice Statistics.* US Department of Justice: NCJ 251149, 2018.

The Central Empowered Committee (CEC) *Report in IA no. 1324 regarding the alumina refinery plant being set up by m/s Vedanta Alumina Limited at Lanjigarh in Kalahandi district, Orissa*, September 21, 2005.

Chagnon, Napoleon A. *Yanamamo: Case Studies in Cultural Anthropology.* Wadsworth Publishing, 2009.

Chamberlain, Kelianne. "Unjust Compensation: Allowing Revenue-based Compensation in Regulatory Takings." *Wyoming Law Review*, Vol. 14, No. 1 Article 8, 2014.

ChenQiyun 陈启云, "封建与大一统之间——关于中国传统政体的理论和史实," 学术月刊/*Xue shu yue kan* 2(2007).

Cherry, Roger Denni. *A Rhetoric of Doing Essays on Written Discourse: Pístis, Expression, and Belief.* Carbondale, IL: Southern Illinois University Press: 1992.

Cicero, M. Tillius, Andrew R. Dyck. *De Natura Deorum. Liber 1.* Cambridge: Cambridge University Press, 2003.

Cicero, Marcus Tullius and H. Rackham. *De Natura Deorum. Academica.* Rev. ed. Vol. 268. Cambridge, MA: Harvard University Press, 2014.

Cobley, Mark. "PGGM Joins Norway Fund in Vedanta Boycott." *Financial News*, July 7, 2010.

Cole, Catherine M. *Performing South Africa's Truth Commission: Stages of Transition.* Bloomington, IN: Indiana University Press, 2010.

Comaroff, Jean and Comaroff, John. "Privatizing the Millennium. New Protestant Ethics and the Spirits of Capitalism in Africa, and Elsewhere." *Africa Spectrum* (2000): 293–312.

Compton, Todd M. *Victim of the Muses: Poet as Scapegoat, Warrior and Hero in Greco-Roman and Indo-European Myth and History*, Hellenic Studies Series 11, Chapter 1. Washington, DC: Center for Hellenic Studies, 2006.

Coombes, Annie E. *History after Apartheid: Visual Culture and Public Memory in a Democratic South Africa.* Durham, NC: Duke University Press, 2003.

Council on Ethics, The Government Pension Fund of Norway. "Recommendation of 15 May 2007, To the Ministry of Finance," 2007.

Davies, Owen and Willem de Blécourt. *Beyond the Witch Trials: Witchcraft and Magic in Enlightenment Europe.* Manchester; New York: Manchester University Press, 2004.

Deleuze, Gilles and Félix Guattari. *A Thousand Plateaus: Capitalism and Schizophrenia.* Minneapolis, MN: University of Minnesota Press, 1987.

Demarest, Arthur Andrew. *Ancient Maya: The Rise and Fall of a Rainforest Civilization.* Vol. 3, No. 3. Cambridge; New York: Cambridge University Press, 2004.

DeMaris, Richard E. "Sacrifice, an Ancient Mediterranean Ritual." *Biblical Theology Bulletin* Vol. 43, No. 2(2013): 60–73.

Dmitriev, V. K. *Economic Essays on Value, Competition and Utility*. London; New York: Cambridge University Press, 1974.

Eagleton-Pierce, Matthew. *Neoliberalism: The Key Concepts*. Abingdon; New York: Routledge, 2016.

Eatwell, John, Murray Milgate, and Peter K. Newman. *The New Palgrave: Capital Theory*. 1st American ed. New York: Norton, 1990.

Ekroth, Gunnel. *The Sacrificial Rituals of Greek Hero-Cults in the Archaic to the Early Hellenistic Periods*. Vol. 12. Liège, Belgium: Presses universitaires de Liège, http://books.openedition.org/pulg/503 (accessed January 11, 2017), 2002.

Engels, Jeremy. *The Politics of Resentment: A Genealogy*. University Park, PA: The Pennsylvania State University Press, 2015.

European Union, Treaty on European Union, 2012/C 326/01, https://eur-lex.europa.eu/legal-content/EN/ALL/?uri=celex:12012M/TXT.

Fagan, Brian M. *The Little Ice Age: How Climate Made History 1300–1850*. New York: Basic Books, 2000.

Feinberg, Joel. *Harm to Others*. Oxford: Oxford University Press, 1984.

Flory, Peter C. W. "Nuclear Exchange: Does Washington Really Have (or Want) Nuclear Primacy?" *Foreign Affairs*, September/October2006.

Fottrell, Quentin. "Bonuses in the New York Securities Industry have Soared 890% Over the Last Three Decades." *MarketWatch*, May 23, 2017.

Foucault, Michel, M. Bertani, A. Fontana, D. Macey. *Il faut défendre la société Cours au Collège de France. 1975–1976*. Paris: Seuil/Gallimard, 1997.

Foucault, Michel. *Society Must Be Defended. Lectures at the Collège de France 1975–1976*. New York: Picador, 2003.

Freud, Sigmund, James Strachey, and Peter Gay. *Civilization and its Discontents*. New York: W.W. Norton, 1989.

Freud, Sigmund and A. A. Brill. *Totem and Taboo: Resemblances between the Psychic Lives of Savages and Neurotics*. New York: Random House, 1961.

Friedman, Thomas L. *The Lexus and the Olive Tree*. 1st ed. New York: Farrar, Straus & Giroux, 1999.

Fromm, Erich. *The Anatomy of Human Destructiveness*. New York: Holt, Rinehart and Winston, 1973.

GAO Ming 高明, *Zhongguo Guwenzi Xuetonglun* 中国古文字学通论. Beijing: Peking University Press, 1996.

Gide, Charles. "Has Co-Operation Introduced a New Principle into Economics?" *The Economic Journal* Vol. 8, No. 32(1898): 490–511.

Girard, René. *Deceit, Desire, and the Novel: Self and Other in Literary Structure*. Baltimore, MD: Johns Hopkins Press, 1965.

Girard, René. *Violence and the Sacred*. Baltimore, MD: Johns Hopkins University Press, 1977.

Girard, René. "Religion and Ritual" in *Violent Origins: Ritual Killing and Cultural Formation*, ed. Robert G. Hamerton-Kelly. Stanford, CA: Stanford University Press, 1987.

Glass, John B. "A Survey of Native Middle American Pictorial Manuscripts," article 22, *Guide to Ethnohistorical Sources Part 3; Handbook of Middle American Indians*. University of Texas Press, 1975.

Goodman, David and Paul Weinberg. *Fault Lines: Journeys into the New South Africa*. Berkeley, CA: University of California Press, 1999.

Government of India, Labour Bureau. *Report on Socio-Economic Conditions of Scheduled Tribes Labour at VAPI, VALSAD, NAVSARI AND SACHIN (GUJARAT)*. (2006–2007)

Grammaticas, Damian. "Tribe takes on global mining firm," *BBC News*, July 17, 2008.

Grandjean, Guy, Michael Tait, Surya Shankar Dash and John Vidal, "Tribal survival: the Dongria Kondh," *The Guardian*, May 28, 2009.

Greene, Ronald Walter. "Another Materialist Rhetoric." *Critical Studies in Mass Communication* Vol. 15, No. 1(1998): 21.

Grimaldi, William M. "A Note on the Pisteis in Aristotle's Rhetoric, 1354–1356." *The American Journal of Philology*, Vol. 78, No. 2 (1957): 188–192.

Grobbelaar, Pieter W. *This Was a Man*. South Africa: Human & Rousseau, 1967.

Grotius, Hugo, Francis Kelsey. *The Law of War and Peace*, originally published in 1625. Carnegie edition, 1925.

GUO Moruo 郭沫若(ed), *Jiaguwen Heji* 甲骨文合集. Beijing: 中华书局影印本, 1980–1983.

Harding, Roberta M. "Capital Punishment as Human Sacrifice: A Societal Ritual as Depicted in George Eliot's Adam Bede." *Buff. L. Rev.*, Vol. 48, No. 175 (2000): 1–72.

Harrington, Alexandra R. "Don't Mind the Gap: The Ride of Individual Complaint Mechanisms Within International Human Rights Treaties." *Duke Journal of Comparative and International Law* Vol. 22 (2012): 153–182.

Held, David. "From Postwar Stability to Political Crisis: The Polarization of Political Ideals," in *Models of Democracy*, 3rd ed. Stanford, CA: Stanford University Press, 2006.

"Hendrik Verwoerd, the Monster." *Daily Defender*, 1960.

Henry, George, Robert Scott Liddell. *A Greek-English Lexicon*, revised and augmented throughout by Sir Henry Stuart Jones, with the assistance of Roderick McKenzie. Oxford: Clarendon Press, 1940.

Hesiod, NormanOliver Brown. *Theogony*. Vol. 36. New York; Indianapolis, IN: Bobbs-Merrill Co, 1953.

Historical Society of the New York Courts. "Daniel Horsmanden: Judge and Chief Judge of the New York Supreme Court of Judicature, 1737–1777," http://www.nycourts.gov/history/legal-history-new-york/legal-history-eras-01/history-era-01-horsmanden.html.

Hobbes, Thomas. *Leviathan: Or, the Matter, Form, and Power of a Common-Wealth, Ecclesiastical and Civil*. South Australia: The University of Adelaide Library, Rare Books & Mss., 1651.

Hobsbawm, E. J. and T. O. Ranger. *The Invention of Tradition*. Cambridge; New York: Cambridge University Press, 1983.

Hoey, Edwin. "Terror in New York – 1741." *American Heritage*, June1974.

Höpfl, Harro. *The Christian Polity of John Calvin*. New York; Cambridge: Cambridge University Press, 1982.

Hopkins, Kathryn. "Indian tribe appeals for Avatar director's help to stop Vedanta," *The Guardian*, February 8, 2010.

Horsmanden, Daniel. *A Journal of the Proceedings in the Detention of the Conspiracy*. Gilder Lehrman Collection, 1744: GLC04205.01

Hubert, Henri and Marcel Mauss. *Sacrifice: Its Nature and Function*. Chicago, IL: University of Chicago Press, 1964.

"Immorality Amendment Act, 1950" Parliament of South Africa. Act No. 21 of 1950.

India. Ministry of Law and Justice and India. *The Constitution of India: As on 9th November, 2015*. New Delhi: Government of India, Ministry of Law and Justice (Legislative Department), 2016.

Innis, Harold Adams. *The Bias of Communication*. 2nd ed. Toronto: University of Toronto Press, 2008.

Institute of Archaeology, Chinese Academy of Social Sciences/ 中国社会科学院考古研究所. *Yinxu yu Shang wenhua – Yinxu kexue 80 zhounian jinian wenji*. Beijing: Kexue Chubanshe / 科学出版社, 2011.

Isaac, Barry L. "The Aztec 'Flowery War': A Geopolitical Explanation." *Journal of Anthropological Research* Vol. 39, No. 4(1983): 415–432.

Isendahl, Christian. The Ancient Maya, 6th Ed. Vol. 11*Society for Latin American Anthropology*, 2006.

Jacobs, Joseph and Moses Buttenwieser. "Messiah" in *The Jewish Encyclopedia, Vol. VIII.* New York: Funk & Wagnalls Co., 1904: 505–512.

Johnson, Davi. "Mapping the Meme: A Geographical Approach to Materialist Rhetorical Criticism." *Communication and Critical/Cultural Studies*, Vol. 4, No. 1(2007): 27–50.

Johnson, James Weldon. *Black Manhattan.* New York: A. A. Knopf, 1930.

Kahn, Herman. *On Thermonuclear War.* Princeton, NJ: Princeton University Press, 1960.

Kant, Immanuel and Norman Kemp Smith. *Critique of Pure Reason.* [Second Impression with corr.]. ed. New York: St. Martin's Press, 1965.

"Keesing's Contemporary Archives." *Keesing's Contemporary Archives 1937–1940.* London: Keesing's Limited, 1931.

"Kelo Et Al. v. City of New London Et Al." *Preview of United States Supreme Court Cases* No. 8(2005): 521.

Kennedy, Maev. "Witches' Marks: Public Asked to Seek Ancient Scratchings in Buildings," *The Guardian.*

Kerr, Justin. n.d. Maya Vase Database, FAMSI, 2008. http://research.famsi.org/kerrmaya.html

Kim, Tae. "Goldman Sachs Asks in Biotech Research Report: 'Is Curing Patients a Sustainable Business Model?'," *CNBC*, April 11, 2018https://www.cnbc.com/2018/04/11/goldman-asks-is-curing-patients-a-sustainable-business-model.html (accessed April 11, 2018).

Kirkup, Alex and Tony Evans. "The Myth of Western Opposition to Economic, Social, and Cultural Rights? A Reply to Whelan and Donnelly." *Human Rights Quarterly* Vol. 31 (2009): 221–238.

Krastev, Ivan. "Paradoxes of the New Authoritarianism." *Journal of Democracy* Vol. 22, No. 2(2011): 5–16.

Krishnamurti, Bhadriraju. *The Dravidian languages.* Cambridge: Cambridge University Press, 2003.

de Landa, Diego and William Gates. *Yucatan before and After the Conquest.* Vol. 20. New York: Dover Publications, 1978.

"Legislation: 1950s." *South African History Online* (accessed May 3, 2010).

Lentz, Harris M., III. *Heads of States and Governments: A Worldwide Encyclopedia of Over 2,300 Leaders, 1945 through 1992.* Jefferson, NC: McFarland & Company, 1994.

Lepore, Jill. *New York Burning: Liberty, Slavery, and Conspiracy in Eighteenth-Century Manhattan.* 1st ed. New York: Alfred A. Knopf, 2005.

Lianos, Theodore P. "The Rate of Surplus Value, the Organic Composition of Capital and the Rate of Profit in Greek Manufacturing." *Review of Radical Political Economics* Vol. 24, No. 1(1992): 136–145.

Locke, John. *Some Considerations of the Consequences of the Lowering of Interest, and Raising the Value of Money: In a Letter to a Member of Parliament.* London: Printed for Awnsham and John Churchill, 1692.

Machiavelli, Nicolo, W. K. Marriott. *The Prince.* Project Gutenberg, 2006.

Mackenzie, Donald. *Material Markets: How Economic Agents are Constructed.* Oxford: Oxford University Press, 2009.

Mamre, Mechon "Job." *English Bible According to the Masoretic Text and the JPS 1917 Edition*, http://www.mechon-mamre.org/e/et/et0.htm, 1917.

Marc, Alexandre. "Conflict and Violence in the 21st Century." World Bank Group, 2016.

Marcuse, Herbert. *Eros and Civilization: A Philosophical Inquiry into Freud.* Boston, MA: Beacon Press, 1966.

Marshall, Gordon. *In Search of the Spirit of Capitalism: An Essay on Max Weber's Protestant Ethic Thesis.* New York: Columbia University Press, 1982.

Mather, Cotton. *Memorable Providences Relating to Witchcrafts and Possessions: A Faithful Account of Many Wonderful and Surprising Things that have Befallen several Bewitched and Possesed Person in New-England, Particularly a Narrative of the Marvellous Trouble and Releef Experienced by a Pious Family in Boston, very Lately and Sadly Molested with Evil Spirits : Whereunto is Added a Discourse Delivered Unto a Congregation in Boston on the Occasion of that Illustrious Providence : As also a Discourse Delivered Unto the Same Congregation on the Occasion of an Horrible Self-Murder Committed in the Town : With an Appendix in Vindication of a Chapter in a Late Book of Remarkable Providences from the Calumnies of a Quaker at Pen-Silvania.* Vol. 1487, No. 38. Printed atBoston in N. England: By R.P., sold by Joseph Brunning, 1689.

Midelfort, H. C. E. *Witch Hunting in Southwestern Germany 1562–1684: The Social and Intellectual Foundations.* Stanford, CA: Stanford University Press, 1972.

Mikkonen, Teemu, Tere Vadén, and Niklas Vainio. "The Protestant Ethic Strikes Back: Open Source Developers and the Ethic of Capitalism." *First Monday* Vol. 12, No. 2 (2007).

Mill, John Stuart. *On Liberty.* London: Longmans, Green, and Company, 1865.

Miller, Mary Ellen and Karl A. Taube. *An Illustrated Dictionary of the Gods and Symbols of Ancient Mexico and the Maya.* 1st pbk. ed. New York: Thames and Hudson, 1997.

Minca, Claudio. "Giorgio Agamben and the New Biopolitical Nomos." *Geografiska Annaler. Series B, Human Geography*, Vol. 88, No. 4 (2006): 387–403.

Mirels, Herbert L. and James B. Garrett. "The Protestant Ethic as a Personality Variable." *Journal of Consulting and Clinical Psychology* Vol. 36, No. 1(1971): 40–44.

Mohanty, Meera. "Odisha New Bauxite Linkage Policy to Benefit Vedanta," *The Economic Times*, February 12, 2018, http://economictimes.indiatimes.com/articleshow/63018502.cms?utm_source=contentofinterest&utm_medium=text&utm_campaign=cppst (accessed April 11, 2018).

Mohanty, Subhashish. "Capacity Boost for Vedanta: Naveen nod to Lanjigarh refinery expansion," *The Telegraph India*, April 9, 2018, https://www.telegraphindia.com/states/odisha/capacity-boost-for-vedanta-221986 (accessed April 12, 2018).

Mora, George. *Geoffrey Scarre, "Witchcraft and Magic in Sixteenth- and Seventeenth- Century Europe" (Book Review).* Vol. 30. Brandon, VT: Clinical Psychology Pub. Co, 1994.

Munson, Eve Stryker and Catherine A. Warren. *James Carey: A Critical Reader.* Minneapolis, MN: University of Minnesota Press, 1997.

"National Diabetes Surveillance System" published by the U.S. Centers for Disease Control and Prevention, https://www.cdc.gov/chronicdisease/resources/publications/aag/diabetes.htm, 2016.

Naumann, Joe. "Apartheid Legislations." Minneapolis, MS: University of Missouri, 2017.

Nelson, Dean. "Indian Villagers Defeat British Billionaire Over Plans to Mine Sacred Mountain," *The Telegraph*, August 9, 2013.

O'Malley, Padraig. "1959. Extension of University Education Act No 45." Nelson Mandela Center of Memory and Dialogue (accessed May 3, 2010).

Overman, Steven J. *The Protestant Ethic and the Spirit of Sport: How Calvinism and Capitalism Shaped America's Games.* Macon, GA: Mercer University Press, 2011.

Parry, John T. *Evil, Law and the State: Perspectives on State Power and Violence.* Vol. 24. Kenilworth: Rodopi, 2006.

Patnaik, Antosh. "Dongria Kondhs Have Shown the Way," *The Hindu*, August 21, 2013.

Patton, Paul. “Concept and Politics in Derrida and Deleuze.” *Critical Horizons* Vol. 4, No. 2 (2010).

Pérez, Ventura. “New Perspectives on Human Sacrifice and Ritual Body Treatments in Ancient Maya Society.” *International Journal of Osteoarchaeology* Vol. 19, No. 4(2009): 566–568.

Peirce, Sarah. “Death, Revelry, and ‘Thysia’.” *Classical Antiquity*, Vol. 12, No. 2(1993): 219–266.

Perugini, Nicola and Neve Gordon. “Distinction and the Ethics of Violence: On the Legal Construction of Liminal Subjects and Spaces.” *Antipode* Vol. 49, No. 5(2017): 1385–1405.

Plato, John Burnet. *Platonis Opera.* New York; Oxonii: E Typographeo Clarendoniano, 1903.

Plato, Paul Shorey. *Republic.* Cambridge, MA: Harvard University Press; London: William Heinemann Ltd., 1969.

Plato, Lewis Cambell and Benjamin Jowett. *Plato's Republic.* Vol. 22. New York: Garland, 1987.

“Population Registration Act” *Parliament of South Africa.* Act No. 30 of 1950.

“Prohibition of Mixed Marriages Act” (Act No. 55 of 1949).

The Reformation Society. “Calvinism in Africa,” South Africa: Reformation Society, http://www.reformationsa.org/index.php/history/65-calvinismafrica?format=pdf, 2010.

Renaissance City Development Association, “Fort Trumbull Municipal Development” RCDA, 2014.

Reuters. “Norway Ejects Vedanta Resources from Oil Fund,” *The Indian Express*, November 8, 2007.

Ritner, Robert. *The Mechanics of Ancient Egyptian Magical Practice.* Chicago, IL: The Oriental Institute of Chicago, 1988.

Romano, James F. *The Origin of Aha (also called Bes).* New York: College Art Association, 1978.

Rosenfeld, Michel. “The Rule of Law and the Legitimacy of Constitutional Democracy.” *Southern California Law Review* 74, no. 5(2001): 1307.

Rosenmeyer, Thomas G. *Senecan Drama and Stoic Cosmology.* Berkeley, CA: University of California Press, 1989.

Rousseau, Jean-Jacques and Charles William Eliot. *On the Inequality among Mankind. Vol. XXXIV, Part 3.* New York: P.F. Collier & Son, 1909.

Rousseau, Jean-Jacques and Lester G. Crocker. *The Social Contract and Discourse on the Origin and Foundation of Inequality among Mankind.* Vol. W-1039. New York: Washington Square Press, 1967.

Rudolph, Michael. *Ritual Performances as Authenticating Practices.* Berlin: LIT Verlag Münster, 2008.

Sagan, Scott Douglas and Kenneth N. Waltz. *The Spread of Nuclear Weapons: An Enduring Debate.* 3rd ed. New York: W.W. Norton & Co, 2013.

Schultze, Quentin J. “Communication as Religion: In Memory of James W. Carey, 1935–2006.” *Journal of Media and Religion* Vol. 6, No. 1(2007): 1–15.

Semega, Jessica L., Kayla R. Fontenot and Melissa A. Kollar. “Income and Poverty in the United States: 2016.” *U.S. Census Bureau*, Report Number: P60–259, September 12, 2017.

Sen, Amartya. “Human Rights and Asian Values.” *The New Republic*, July 14–July 21 (1997).

Sharer, Robert J. and Loa P. Traxler. *The Ancient Maya*, 6th ed. Stanford, CA: Stanford University Press, 2006.

Shlapentokh, Dmitry. “The Ideological Framework of Early Post-Soviet Russia's Relationship with Turkey: The Case of Alexander Dugin's Eurasianism.” *Journal of Balkan and Near Eastern Studies* Vol. 18, No. 3(2016): 263–281.

Silkenat, James R., James E. Hickey, Petr Barenbo⊠m and SpringerLink (Online service). *The Legal Doctrines of the Rule of Law and the Legal State (Rechtsstaat)*, 1st ed. Vol. 38. Cham: Springer International Publishing, 2014.

Singer, Isidore and Cyrus Adler. *The Jewish Encyclopedia: A Descriptive Record of the History, Religion, Literature, and Customs of the Jewish People from the Earliest Times to the Present Day*. London; New York: Funk & Wagnalls Company, 1901.

Singh, Kavaljit. "Norwegian Medicine for Vedanta," in *Why Investment Matters: The Political Economy of International Investments*. FERN, The Corner House, CRBM and Madhyam Books, 2007.

Sloterdijk, Peter and Wieland Hoban. *In the World Interior of Capital: For a Philosophical Theory of Globalization*. Cambridge: Polity Press, 2013.

Smith, Adam and William Playfair. *An Inquiry into the Nature and Causes of the Wealth of Nations*. Hartford: O. D. Cooke, 1811.

Smith, Peter. "Apologetics," in *A Concise Encyclopedia of the Bahá'í Faith*. Oxford: Oneworld Publications, 2000: 39–40.

South African History Online. "Hendrik Frensch Verwoerd Collection." Archive 7 (accessed January 4, 2018).

Steedman, Ian and Judith Tomkins. "On Measuring the Deviation of Prices from Values." *Cambridge Journal of Economics* Vol. 22, No. 3(1998): 379–385.

Stierle, Karlheinz "Ist die Geisteswissenschaft eine Wissenschaft?" *Magazin Forschung 2/2007*. Germany: Kontaktstelle für Wissens-und Technologietransfer, 2007: 37–39.

Stiglitz, Joseph E. *Globalization and its Discontents*. New York: W.W. Norton, 2003.

SUN, Zhe孙喆, *Tianming wangchao*天命王朝. Beijing: 中国青年出版社, 2008.

Surror, Hasan. "Avatar Actors Join Protest in Support of Orissa Tribals," *The Hindu*, July 29, 2010.

Survival International. "Complaint to the UK National Contact Point under the Specific Instance Procedure of the OECD Guidelines for Multinational Enterprises." December 19, 2008.

Swatos, William H. Jr and Lutz Kaelber. *The Protestant Ethic Turns 100: Essays on the Centenary of the Weber Thesis*. Boulder: Paradigm Publishers, 2005.

Tiesler, Vera and Andrea Cucina. *New Perspectives on Human Sacrifice and Ritual Body Treatments in Ancient Maya Society*. 1. Aufl. ed. DE: Springer-Verlag, 2007.

Torre, Joseph. *Apologetics: A Justification of Christian Belief John Frame*. P&R Publishing: 2015.

Turco, R. P.; Toon, O. B.; Ackerman, T. P.; Pollack, J. B.; Sagan, Carl. "Nuclear Winter: Global Consequences of Multiple Nuclear Explosions." *Science*, Vol. 222, No. 4630 (1984): 1283–1292.

Tylor, Edward B. *Primitive Culture: Researches into the Development of Mythology, Philosophy, Religion, Language, Art, and Custom*. 7th ed. New York: Brentano's, 1924.

UK Department for Business, Innovation & Skills. "UK National Contact Point for the Organisation for Economic Co-operation and Development (OECD) guidelines for multinational enterprises," 2010.

UK National Contact Point for the OECD Guidelines for Multinational Enterprises. "Final Statement by the UK National Contact Point for the OECD Guidelines for Multinational Enterprises," September 25, 2009.

UK National Contact Point for the OECD Guidelines for Multinational Enterprises. "Follow up to Final Statement by the UK National Contact Point for the OECD Guidelines for Multinational Enterprises," March 12, 2010.

United Nations. *Statute of the International Court of Justice*. April 18, 1946. Art. 38.1(c) http://www.refworld.org/docid/3deb4b9c0.html.

UN Business & Human Rights Resource Centre. "UN 'Protect, Respect and Remedy' Framework Guiding Principles," http://www.business-humanrights.org/SpecialRepPortal/Home/Protect-Respect-Remedy-Framework/GuidingPrinciples, 2011.

UN General Assembly. *Universal Declaration of Human Rights*, December 10, 1948, 217 A (II), http://www.un.org/en/documents/udhr/index.shtml.

Union of South Africa. Coloured Persons Communal Reserves Act, Act No 3 of 1961. South Africa: Government Printer, 1961.

United Nations, Security Council. *The rule of law and transitional justice in conflict and post-conflict societies: Report of the Secretary-General*, S/2004/616. August 23, 2004.

Venter, J. J. "H. F. Verwoerd: Foundational Aspects of His Thought." *Koers* Vol. 64, No. 4 (1999): 415–442.

Vermander, Benoit. *Ritual Performances as Authenticating Practices, Cultural Representations of Taiwan's Aborigines in Times of Political Changes* Vol. 57, 2012.

Verwoerd, H. F. "A Method for the Experimental Production of Emotions." *The American Journal of Psychology* Vol. 37, No. 3 (July, 1926): 357–371.

Verwoerd, Hendrik Frensch. "Effects of Fatigue on the Distribution of Attention." *Journal of Applied Psychology* Vol. 12, No. 6 (1928).

Verwoerd, H. To The Editor Times of India D KUMAR, "Dr. Verwoerd" (March 15, 1961). *The Times of India (1861–Current)*.

Verwoerd, *Verwoerd Speaks: Speeches 1948–1966*. Edited by A. N. Pelzer. Johannesburg: APB Publishers, 1966.

"Verwoerd Landslide Today." *The Irish Times (1921–Current File)*, 1966.

Waddell, Austine. *Tibetan Buddhism: With Its Mystic Cults, Symbolism and Mythology, and in Its Relation to Indian Buddhism*. London: W.H. Allen & Co., 1895.

Walsh, Lynda. *Scientists as Prophets: A Rhetorical Genealogy*. New York: Oxford University Press, 2013.

Wander, Philip. "The Ideological Turn in Modern Criticism." *Central States Speech Journal* Vol. 34, No. 1(1983): 1–18.

Wang, Keren. "Human Sacrifice during Shang Dynasty," May 27, 2015, https://sites.psu.edu/kerenw/?p=102 (accessed March 13, 2017).

Wang, Keren. "A Brief Note on Human Sacrifice in Classical Mayan Culture," *Rhetorics and Rituals*, June 2, 2015, https://sites.psu.edu/kerenw/?p=142 (accessed March 13, 2017).

Wang, Ping and Kubin, Wolfgang 甲骨文与殷商人祭 / *Oracle Bone Inscriptions and Human Sacrifice During the Yinshang Period / Jia gu wen yu Yin Shang ren ji*, Chinese, 1st ed. Zhengzhou, China: 大象出版社, 2007.

Weber, Max. *Economy and Society: An Outline of Interpretive Sociology*. Vol. 1. Stanford, CA: University of California Press, 1978.

Weber, Max. *General Economic History*, originally published in 1924. Transaction Publishers: 1981.

Weber, Max. *The Sociology of Religion*. Boston: Beacon Press, 1993.

Weber, Max. *The Protestant Ethic and the" Spirit" of Capitalism and Other Writings*, originally published in 1905. London: Penguin, 2002.

Weber, Max. *The Theory of Social and Economic Organization*, originally published in 1915. New York: Simon and Schuster, 2009.

Weber, Max and Edward Shils. *Max Weber, on the Methodology of the Social Sciences*. 1st ed. Illinois: The Free Press of Glencoe, 1949.

WEN Yao文耀. "殷墟与商文化殷墟科学发掘80周年纪念文集." 考古 No. 3 (2012): 96.

White, Timothy D. *Once were Cannibals. Evolution: A Scientific American Reader*. Chicago, IL: University of Chicago Press, 2001.

Wichelns, Herbert A. "The Literary Criticism of Oratory." *Annual Bibliography of English Language and Literature*, 1925.

Wikramanayake, G. H. "A Note on the Písteis in Aristotle's Rhetoric." *The American Journal of Philology* Vol. 82, No. 2(1961): 193–196.

Wilford, John Noble. "At Ur, Ritual Deaths that were Anything but Serene: Science Desk." *New York Times*, October 26, 2009, Late (East Coast) www.nytimes.com/2009/10/27/science/27ur.html

Wilson, Kirt H. "The Racial Contexts of Public Address: Interpreting Violence during the Reconstruction Era." *The Handbook of Rhetoric and Public Address.* New Jersey: John Wiley & Sons, Inc., 2010.

Wolf, Loammi. "David Beresford Pratt: die Mens Agter die Sluipmoordpoging." *LitNet Akademies*, Vol. 9, No. 3 (1998): 102–107.

Wrage, Ernest J. "Public Address: A Study in Social and Intellectual History." *Quarterly Journal of Speech* Vol. 33, No. 4(1947): 451–457.

Wright, David P. *The Disposal of Impurity: Elimination Rites in the Bible and in Hittite and Mesopotamian Literature.* Vol. 101, No. 101. Atlanta: Scholars Press, 1987.

Ximénez, Francisco, Fernando de Alva Ixtlilxóchitl, and Marshall N. Peterson. *The Highland Maya in Fact and Legend: Francisco Ximénez, Fernando Alva De Ixtlilxóchitl, and Other Commentators on Indian Origins & Deeds.* Lancaster, CA: Labyrinthos, 1999.

YANG, Baocheng / 楊寶成, *Yin xu wen hua yan jiu* / 殷墟文化研究. Taipei: Taiwan gu ji chu ban she, 2004.

Young, Katharine. "The Minimum Core of Economic and Social Rights: A Concept in Search of Content." *The Yale Journal of International Law*, Vol. 33 (2008): 113–175.

ZHOU, Gong, *1105 BC.* 周禮 *Zhou Li.* Chinese Text Project (Chinese: 中國哲學書電子化計劃), 2008, https://ctext.org

Appendix

Additional charts

GDP and NNI Gap in the US: 1970 - 2015 (in trillions 2018 US$)

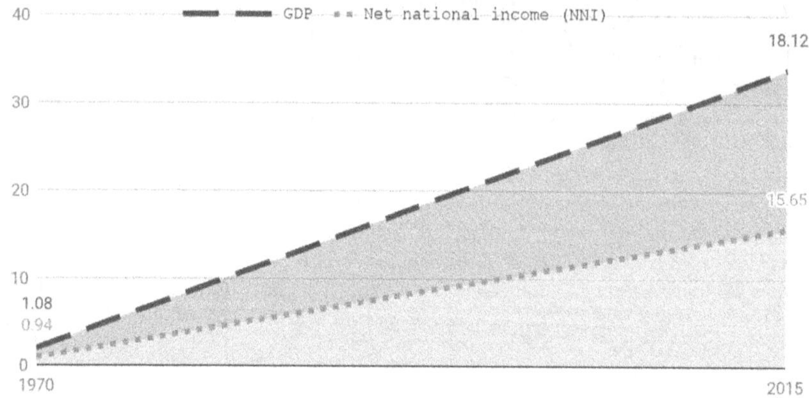

Source: World Bank Data

GDP and NNI in China: 1970 - 2015 (in trillions 2018 US$)

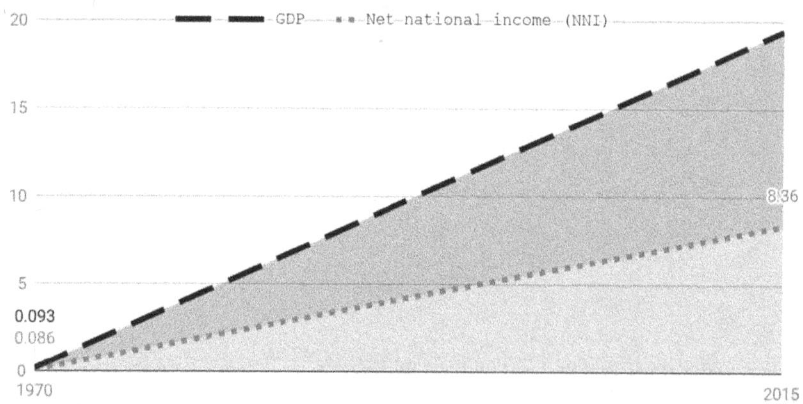

Source: World Bank Data

Index

For Product Safety Concerns and Information please contact our EU
representative GPSR@taylorandfrancis.com
Taylor & Francis Verlag GmbH, Kaufingerstraße 24, 80331 München, Germany

www.ingramcontent.com/pod-product-compliance
Lightning Source LLC
LaVergne TN
LVHW021037011026
849160LV00009BA/675
* 9 7 8 0 3 6 7 7 2 7 8 2 6 *